Minnesota Valley
National Wildlife Refuge and
Wetland Management District
Comprehensive Conservation Plan Approval
U.S. Fish and Wildlife Service, Region 3

Submitted by:

Richard D. Schultz   9/13/04

Richard D. Schultz   Date
Project Leader

Concur:

James T. Leach   9-14-04

James T. Leach
Refuge Supervisor (RFS 3)   Date

Nita M. Fuller   9.14.2004

Nita M. Fuller   Date
Regional Chief
National Wildlife Refuge System

Approve:

Charles M. Wooley
Acting Regional Director

Charlie Wooley   9/15/04

for

Robyn Thorson   Date
Regional Director

U.S. Fish & Wildlife Service

Minnesota Valley
*National Wildlife Refuge and
Wetland Management District*

Comprehensive
Conservation Plan and
Environmental Assessment

Comprehensive Conservation Plans provide long-term guidance for management decisions; set forth goals, objectives and strategies needed to accomplish refuge purposes; and, identify the Fish and Wildlife Service's best estimate of future needs. These plans detail program planning levels that are sometimes substantially above current budget allocations and, as such, are primarily for Service strategic planning and program prioritization purposes. The plans do not constitute a commitment for staffing increases, operational and maintenance increases, or funding for future land acquisition.

Acknowledgments

Minnesota Valley National Wildlife Refuge is rooted in enthusiasm and concern for natural resources. Looking to the future of the Refuge and Wetland Management District has given us an opportunity to look back at those roots, and we are deeply grateful for all of the people who have cared so much about the Refuge, the habitat of the Minnesota River Valley and the wildlife inhabiting the Valley.

Because it will serve as a guide to Refuge and District management for the next 15 years, public input into the comprehensive conservation plan is vital. We would like to thank all of the people who have contributed their time, expertise and ideas to this planning process. All of your ideas are valuable and will contribute to the success of the plan.

We are especially grateful to Scott Sharkey for the use of his superb photographs in this comprehensive conservation plan. We thank members of the Friends of the Minnesota Valley for their help and their unflagging dedication to the environment. And, finally, we are grateful to everyone who contributes time and energy as a Refuge volunteer. You are truly the backbone of conservation.

Contents

List of Tables

List of Figures

Chapter 1: Introduction and Background

Photograph by Scott Sharkey

Introduction

In the midst of 2.5 million people, down the road from the largest shopping mall in the nation, Minnesota Valley National Wildlife Refuge is a small vestige of Minnesota wildness. Bald Eagles nest here, Woodcock preen, and Black-crowned Night Herons stand poised on the edge of ponds, still as statues, waiting for the glint of an unlucky fish. Waterfowl nest here, and Tundra Swans rest up from a long migration. River otters play, beavers build their meticulous and highly effective dams, and foxes den within a few miles of the Twin Cities of Minneapolis and St. Paul, Minnesota.

It is a truly unique place. Of the more than 500 national wildlife refuges managed by the U.S. Fish and Wildlife Service (Service), Minnesota Valley National Wildlife Refuge (Refuge) is one of only four urban refuges. Long Meadow Lake, the northern most unit of the Refuge, is just 10 miles south of downtown Minneapolis.

Established in 1976, the Refuge was borne out of citizen concern for the diverse and abundant fish, wildlife, and plant communities of the Lower Minnesota River Valley. Today it consists of eight units along a 34-mile stretch of the Minnesota River located between historic Fort Snelling and the City of Jordan (Figure 1). The Savage Fen Unit is also located in the valley but is not immediately adjacent to the river. Nearly 12,500 acres of the authorized 14,000 acres are currently owned in fee or managed as part of the Refuge. Some areas are not owned by the Service but are administered through management agreements. Although the Refuge is the single largest landowner along this portion of the river, the valley itself contains a patchwork of ownerships including private landowners, non-profit organizations, corporations, cities, counties, and lands administered by Minnesota Department of Natural Resources (MnDNR). This mosaic of ownerships offers great opportunities for partnerships but also requires a great deal of coordination and cooperation among all land managers.

Minnesota Valley National Wildlife Refuge provides the Service a great opportunity to showcase a variety of activities that occur within the National Wildlife Refuge System. From strong citizen support to a variety of wildlife-dependent recreational programs to an active habitat restoration and management program, this Refuge has a wonderful story to tell. These features, plus the opportunity to significantly expand the Refuge land base over the next 15 years, offers a very bright future for both the Service and the citizens who support this effort.

The Round Lake Unit (Figure 2), a 152-acre tract containing a large permanent wetland located in the City of Arden Hills, is also administered as a remote part of the Refuge.

Figure 1: Minnesota Valley National Wildlife Refuge

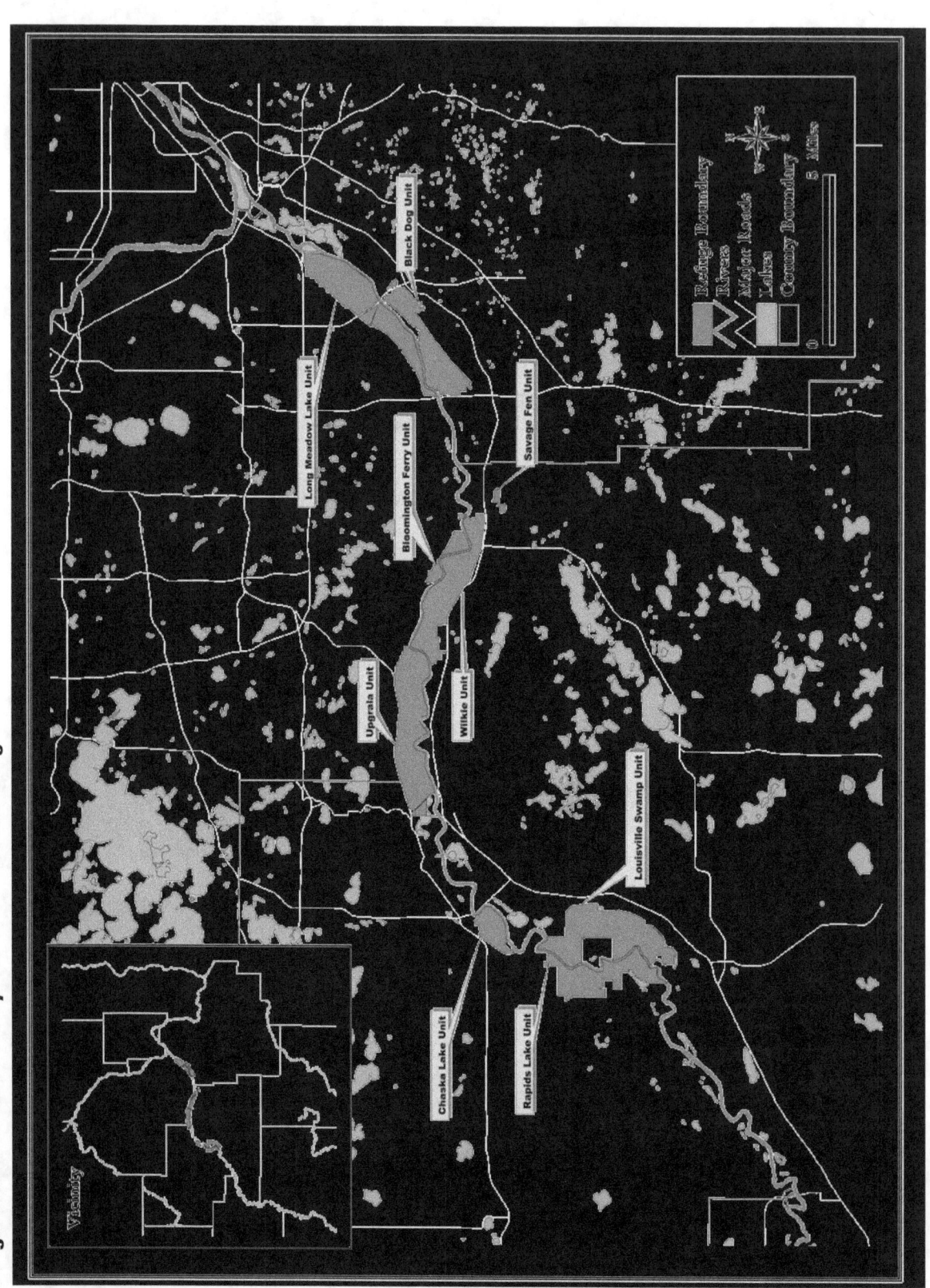

Figure 2: Round Lake Unit

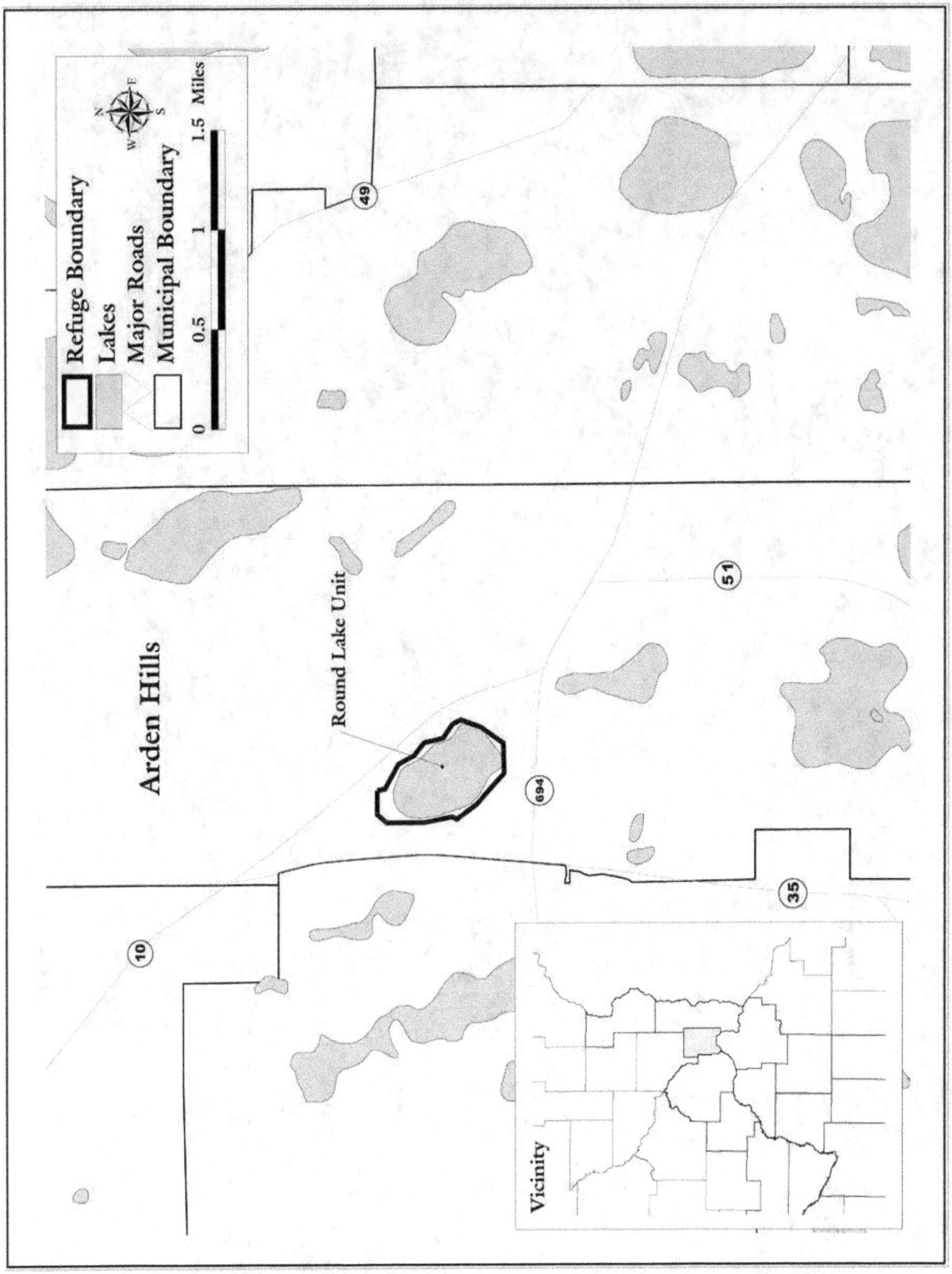

Figure 3: Minnesota Valley National Wildlife Refuge and Wetland Management District

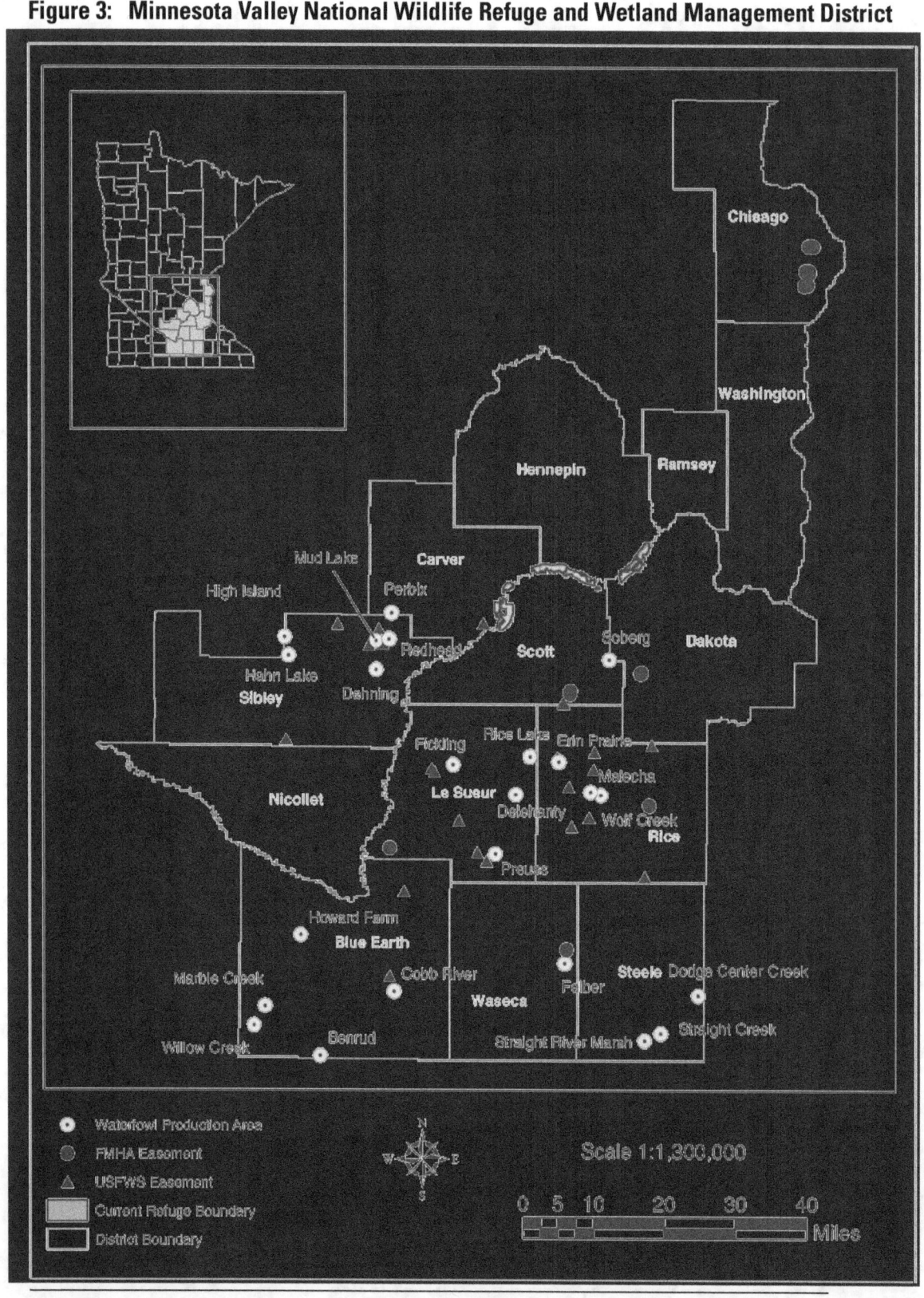

Minnesota Valley National Wildlife Refuge and Wetland Management District

Unless stated otherwise, the use of the term "Refuge" in this document refers to all Refuge units including Round Lake and the Savage Fen.

The Refuge is also responsible for a 14-county region known as the Minnesota Valley Wetland Management District (District). It currently consists of more than 5,000 acres of waterfowl production areas and conservation easements (Figure 3). District activities, plus a very active Partners for Fish and Wildlife program, are seamlessly applied within the watershed to complement the Refuge as well as other important natural areas associated with the Minnesota River and the Cannon River watersheds.

A state-of-the-art Visitor and Wildlife Interpretive Center was completed in 1990 and serves as the gateway to the Refuge at its Bloomington location, near the Mall of America. Its exhibits, environmental education classrooms, and 125-seat auditorium help make the Refuge a place where students and citizens of all ages have the opportunity to learn, enjoy, respect, and develop an appreciation for wildlife in their natural habitats. An estimated 300,000 visitors annually visit the Refuge and its associated waterfowl production areas for a variety of reasons, including hunting, fishing, wildlife observation and interpretive programs. Minnesota Valley is truly a place where modern technology and development coexist with some of nature's most primitive and timeless rhythms of life.

The U.S. Fish and Wildlife Service

The Refuge and District are administered by the U.S. Fish and Wildlife Service (Service), the primary federal agency responsible for conserving, protecting, and enhancing the nation's fish and wildlife populations and their habitats. The Service oversees the enforcement of federal wildlife laws, management and protection of migratory bird populations, restoration of nationally significant fisheries, administration of the Endangered Species Act, and the restoration of wildlife habitat such as wetlands. The Service also manages the National Wildlife Refuge System.

The National Wildlife Refuge System

Refuge and District lands are part of the National Wildlife Refuge System, which was founded in 1903 when President Theodore Roosevelt designated Pelican Island in Florida as a sanctuary for brown pelicans. Today, the System is a network of over 500 refuges covering more than 93 million acres of public lands and waters. Most of these lands (82 percent) are in Alaska, with approximately 16 million acres located in the lower 48 states and several island territories. The National Wildlife Refuge System is the world's largest

collection of lands specifically managed for fish and wildlife. Overall, it provides habitat for more than 5,000 species of birds, mammals, fish, and insects. As a result of international treaties for migratory bird conservation as well as other legislation, such as the Migratory Bird Conservation Act of 1929, many refuges have been established to protect migratory waterfowl and their migratory flyways from their northern nesting grounds to southern wintering areas.

Refuges also play a vital role in preserving endangered and threatened species. Among the most notable are Aransas National Wildlife Refuge in Texas, which provides winter habitat for the whooping crane. Likewise, the Florida Panther Refuge protects one of the nation's most endangered predators.

Refuges also provide unique opportunities for people. When it is compatible with wildlife and habitat conservation, they are places where people can enjoy wildlife-dependent recreation such as hunting, fishing, wildlife observation, photography, environmental education, and environmental interpretation. Many refuges have visitor centers, wildlife trails, automobile tours, and environmental education programs. Nationwide, approximately 30 million people visited national wildlife refuges in 1997.

The National Wildlife Refuge System Improvement Act of 1997 established several important mandates aimed at making the management of national wildlife refuges more cohesive. The preparation of Comprehensive Conservation Plans is one of those mandates. The legislation directs the Secretary of the Interior to ensure that the mission of the National Wildlife Refuge System and purposes of the individual refuges are carried out. It also requires the Secretary to maintain the biological integrity, diversity, and environmental health of the National Wildlife Refuge System.

Goals of the National Wildlife Refuge System:
- Fulfill our statutory duty to achieve refuge purpose(s) and further the System mission.

- Conserve, restore where appropriate, and enhance all species of fish, wildlife, and plants that are endangered or threatened with becoming endangered.

- Perpetuate migratory bird, interjurisdictional fish, and marine mammal populations.

- Conserve a diversity of fish, wildlife, and plants.

- Conserve and restore, where appropriate, representative ecosystems of the United States, including ecological processes characteristic of those ecosystems.

- Foster understanding and instill appreciation of fish, wildlife, and plants, and their conservation, by providing the public with safe, high-quality, and compatible wildlife-dependent public use. Such use includes hunting, fishing, wildlife observation and photography, and environmental education and interpretation.

The Mississippi Headwaters/Tallgrass Prairie Ecosystem

The Refuge and District are located in the Mississippi Headwaters/Tallgrass Prairie Ecosystem as currently defined by the U.S. Fish and Wildlife Service. This ecosystem is primarily located in Minnesota and North Dakota with small sections extending into Wisconsin and Iowa. This ecosystem occupies a major portion of the Prairie Pothole Region of North America. The Prairie Pothole Region produces 20 percent of the continental waterfowl populations annually.

Historically, this portion of North America was subject to periodic glaciation and consequently, glacial meltwaters were instrumental in forming the five major river systems located or partly located within this ecosystem. These river systems are the Mississippi River, St. Croix River, Red River, Missouri River, and the Minnesota River. Likewise, glacial moraines and other deposits resulted in a myriad of lakes and wetlands that are common throughout this area. Significant variation in the topography and soils of the area attest to its dynamic glacial history.

The three major ecological communities within this ecosystem are the tallgrass prairie, the northern boreal forest, and the eastern deciduous forest. Vegetation common to the tallgrass prairie includes big bluestem, little bluestem, Indian grass, sideoats grama, and switch grass. Native prairie also supports numerous ecologically important forbs such as prairie cone flower, purple prairie clover, and blazing star. The northern boreal forest is primarily comprised of a variety of coniferous species such as jack pine, balsam fir, and spruce. Common tree species in the eastern deciduous forest include maple, basswood, red oak, white oak, and ash. Current land uses range from tourism and timber industries in the northern forests to intensive agriculture in the historic tallgrass prairie. Of the three major ecological communities, the tallgrass prairie is by far the most threatened with more than 99 percent of it having been converted for agricultural purposes.

Due to its ecological and vegetative diversity, this ecosystem supports at least 121 species of neotropical migrants and other migratory birds. It provides breeding and migration habitat for significant populations of waterfowl plus a variety of other waterbirds. The ecosystem supports several species of candidate and federally-listed threatened and endangered species including the Bald Eagle, Piping Plover, Higgins eye pearly mussel, Karner blue butterfly, prairie bush clover, Leedy's roseroot, dwarf trout lily, and the western prairie fringed orchid. The increasingly rare paddlefish and lake sturgeon are also found in portions of this ecosystem.

Refuge Purpose

The Refuge was established by Congress in 1976 through the Minnesota Valley National Wildlife Refuge Act *(Public Law 94-466; October 8, 1976)*. In general, its purposes are to (1) provide habitat for a large number of migratory waterfowl, fish, and other wildlife

Photograph by Scott Sharkey

species; (2) to provide environmental education, wildlife recreational opportunities, and interpretive programs for hundreds of thousands of Twin Cities residents; (3) to protect important natural resource areas from degradation; and to (4) protect the valley's unique social, educational, and environmental assets.

The Act authorized the purchase of 9,500 acres for the Refuge. It also acknowledged the presence of the Minnesota Valley State Trail and the establishment of a wildlife recreation area, both to be administered by MnDNR. The specific lands, waters, and interests of the Refuge and the adjacent recreation area were to be identified through the development of a cooperatively prepared conservation plan. That plan was completed in 1984 and has served as the basis for Refuge development and management since that time. In 1984, the Act was amended to include an additional 2,000 acres in the Refuge. This amendment plus the addition of the Mittelstad tract (Rapids Lake Unit) in 1995 has now increased the authorized Refuge size to approximately 14,000 acres.

Of particular note is Section 9 of the Act entitled "Continued Public Services." This section acknowledges the Refuge's urban presence and does not allow the prohibition of *vital public services*. Vital public services are defined in the Act as the continuation of commercial navigation of the Minnesota River; the construction, improvement, and replacement of highways and bridges; or any other activity that the Secretary of Interior determines to be necessary. Consequently, several of these projects that directly affected Refuge lands have occurred since establishment. Where these projects occurred, Refuge staff have worked to minimize the impact of these projects through mitigation.

Wetland Management District Purpose

Minnesota Valley Wetland Management District was established in 1988 when the Midwest Region of the Service implemented its broad-based Partners for Wildlife program. Between 1988 and 1994, several Farmers Home Administration easements within this 14-county district were assigned to Minnesota Valley National Wildlife Refuge for management purposes. The Farmers Home Administration easements were obtained by the Service through the Consolidated Farm and Rural Development Act 7 (U.S.C. 2002) for "conservation purposes...." In addition, numerous high quality wetlands were restored on private lands as part of this effort. The first waterfowl production area, Soberg WPA, was purchased in 1994. Since 1988, over 5,000 acres of fee and easement lands have been acquired as part of the District.

The Wetlands Loan Act of 1961 initiated the Small Wetlands Acquisition Program in Minnesota. Lands are acquired under the authority of the Migratory Bird Hunting and Conservation Stamp Act, and since 1958, under Public Law 85-585 as "Waterfowl Production Areas". The purpose of lands acquired under the Migratory Bird Hunting Conservation Stamp Act is "...as Waterfowl Production Areas" subject to "...all the provisions of such act (the Migratory Bird Conservation Act of 1929,16 U.S.C. 715d) ...except the inviolate sanctuary provisions...," and "...for any other management purpose, for migratory birds."

The primary purpose of Minnesota Valley Wetland Management District, or District, is to administer a complex of wetlands, grasslands, and limited amount of forests that provide good habitat for waterfowl, grasslands nesting birds, and associated species. Secondary objectives of the District include providing wildlife-dependent recreation, wildlife interpretation, and environmental education to area citizens. In addition, the restoration of wildlife habitats on fee, easement, and private lands contributes to the restoration and protection of the Minnesota River watershed as well as the Cannon River in the Mississippi River drainage basin.

Refuge and District Vision

The Refuge and the District will add richness to the social, cultural, economic, and ecological communities by holding in public trust, a portion of the natural heritage of the Minnesota River Basin and the Cannon River Watershed for the continuing benefit of the American people. Within its area of influence, the Refuge and District will make significant contributions toward:

- Establishing an unbroken corridor of floodplain and hillside forest, wetlands, oak savanna, and native prairie along the Minnesota River beginning at historic Fort Snelling and proceeding up river to its origin at Big Stone Lake;

- Managing diverse and abundant native fish and wildlife populations that use healthy and productive native plant communities of the Minnesota River and its watershed plus the Cannon River and its watershed;

- Providing Minnesota citizens the opportunity to revitalize their spirits through high quality wildlife-dependent recreation such as hunting, fishing, wildlife observation, wildlife photography, environmental education, and interpretation;

- Supporting a community-based effort where citizens, businesses, private conservation organizations, and local, state, and federal agencies combine their efforts to restore and protect the Minnesota and Cannon rivers and their watersheds for future generations.

Purpose and Need for Plan

This Comprehensive Conservation Plan (CCP) articulates the management direction for the Refuge and the District for the next 15 years. Through the development of goals, objectives, and strategies, this CCP describes how the Refuge and District also contribute to the overall mission of the National Wildlife Refuge System. Several legislative mandates within the National Wildlife Refuge System Improvement Act of 1997 have guided the development of this plan. These mandates include:

- Wildlife has first priority in the management of refuges.

- Wildlife-dependent recreation activities, namely hunting, fishing, wildlife observation, wildlife photography, environmental education and interpretation are priority public uses of refuges. We will facilitate these activities when they do not interfere with our ability to fulfill the Refuge's purpose or the mission of the Refuge System.

- Other uses of the Refuge will only be allowed when determined appropriate and compatible with Refuge purposes and mission of the Refuge System.

The plan will guide the management of Minnesota Valley National Wildlife Refuge and the Minnesota Valley Wetland Management District by:

- Providing a clear statement of direction for the future management of the Refuge and the District.

- Making a strong connection between Refuge activities and those activities that occur off-Refuge in the District.

- Providing Refuge and District neighbors, users, and the general public with an understanding of the Service's land acquisition and management actions on and around the Refuge.

- Ensuring the Refuge and District management actions and programs are consistent with the mandates of the National Wildlife Refuge System.

- Ensuring that Refuge and District management is consistent with federal, state, and county plans.

- Establishing long-term continuity in Refuge and District management.

- Providing a basis for the development of budget requests on the Refuge's and District's operational, maintenance, and capital improvement needs.

In addition to the above, this CCP will identify specific projects that will mitigate impacts upon the Refuge from the construction and operation of runway 17/35 being built by the Minneapolis-St. Paul International Airport. This issue will be discussed in greater detail in Chapter 4 and Appendix L of the CCP.

Friends of the Minnesota Valley

Minnesota Valley National Wildlife Refuge owes it existence to a group of citizens who were concerned about protecting the important fish, wildlife, and plant resources of the Lower Minnesota River Valley in the early 1970s. Through hard work and determination, they enlisted the support of more than 40 private groups and many citizens for conserving these important resources through the establishment of a national wildlife refuge. Subsequent to their efforts, Minnesota Senator Walter Mondale introduced a bill to establish the Refuge on July 11, 1975. On October 8, 1976, Congress passed the Minnesota Valley National Wildlife Refuge Act.

The Friends of the Minnesota Valley incorporated as a non-profit organization on June 21, 1982. Its mission is to support conservation and management of the natural and cultural resources of the Lower Minnesota River Watershed, and to promote environmental awareness. The organization has a membership of approximately 500 and is governed
by a Board of Directors. Since 1982, The Friends of the Minnesota Valley has been very supportive of Refuge acquisition and development and due to its efforts, the Refuge has been able to acquire nearly 11,500 acres and to complete its visitor and wildlife interpretive center in 1990.

In 1991, the Friends employed part-time staff to begin implementing the Heritage Registry program. This program is designed to encourage Refuge neighbors and other private landowners in the Minnesota River Valley to adopt land management practices that benefit fish, wildlife and plant communities. The Friends of the Minnesota Valley has enrolled more than 125 private landowners in this program, including several corporations.

Due to very similar goals and objectives, the Friends of the Minnesota Valley merged with the Minnesota Valley Interpretive Association (MVIA) in 1998. Up until that time, MVIA was a cooperating association and was largely responsible for administering the Blufftop Bookshop, which is located in the Refuge visitor center. The Friends currently serves as the cooperating association for this sales outlet. The Friends of the Minnesota Valley employs full-time staff who are responsible for a variety of programs beyond the Heritage Registry. Of particular note is the Leadership in Stewardship campaign, which seeks to promote a healthy Lower Minnesota River Valley through an informed and involved citizenry.

History and Establishment

The Lower Minnesota River Valley was long recognized as an important natural resource. Individuals as well as local, regional, state, and federal agencies supported specific legislation to protect and enhance the natural, recreational, and cultural resources of the valley. A major milestone of their efforts was the passage of the Minnesota Valley National Wildlife Refuge Act of 1976 (PL 94-466). This Act established the original 9,500-acre Refuge, which was later expanded to 14,000 acres, and acknowledged an adjacent 8,000-acre wildlife recreation area. In addition, the Act acknowledged that the Minnesota Valley State Trail would provide an integral link between the Refuge and wildlife recreation area along the lower 36 miles of the Minnesota River.

Among other items, the Act called for the completion of a comprehensive plan for the Minnesota Valley National Wildlife Refuge, Recreation Area and State Trail. This plan was completed in 1984 as a cooperative effort between the MnDNR and the Service. Since its completion, this plan has provided guidance for the acquisition and management of Minnesota Valley National Wildlife Refuge as well as the management and development of the State Trail and Recreation Area.

The Round Lake Unit of Minnesota Valley National Wildlife Refuge was transferred as U.S. Army surplus property to the U.S. Fish and Wildlife Service in October, 1973. This 152-acre tract was administered by Sherburne National Wildlife Refuge until 1979, when management was assumed by Minnesota Valley.

The first portion of the Savage Fen Unit (26 acres) was added to the Refuge in 1987. It came about as a settlement between the U.S. Army Corps of Engineers (COE) and Fabcon, Inc., which had filled a portion of the wetland. Other lands have since been added to this unit either through donations or actions initiated by the COE. The Service first accepted management of these lands with the understanding that MnDNR would consider them for exchange for habitats more closely aligned with the mission of the Refuge.

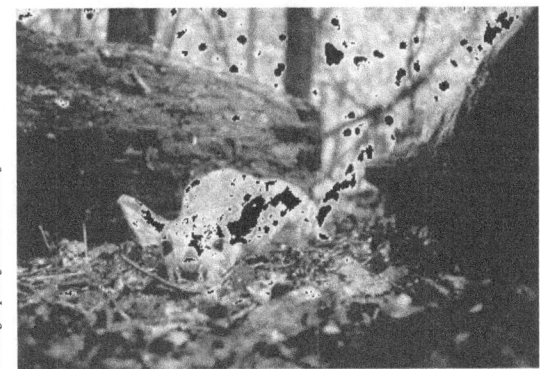

Photograph by Scott Sharkey

The 114-acre Soberg Waterfowl Production Area, which is located in Scott and Dakota counties, was purchased in 1994 and became the first Waterfowl Production Area to be administered by the District. Since that time, 23 Waterfowl Production Areas totaling 4,105 acres have been acquired within the 14-county District. In addition, more than 1,000 acres of wetland conservation easements have been acquired. The Refuge also administers several conservation easements obtained from the Farmers Home Administration.

Lands Managed Under Leases or Agreements

The 1,400-acre Black Dog Lake Unit stretches along the south bank of the river from Interstate Highway 35 on the west and Highway 77 on the east. In 1982, the Service entered into a 50-year lease with Northern States Power to manage the area as part of the Refuge. A portion of the Black Dog Preserve is managed as a Scientific and Natural Area, a program run by the Minnesota Department of Natural Resources that preserves certain lands for their unique habitats. In 1997, the Service entered into a Memorandum of Understanding with the City of Bloomington to manage the 735-acre Bloomington Bluffs Open space. The Agreement calls for the area to be kept in a natural state while still allowing for recreational use by the public. In addition, several small parcels of land adjacent to the west side of the Rapids Lake Unit are managed under a Memorandum of Agreement with the State of Minnesota.

Legal Context

In addition to the Refuge's establishing legislation and the National Wildlife Refuge System Improvement Act of 1997, several Federal laws, executive orders, and regulations govern administration of the Refuge. Appendix F contains a partial list of the legal mandates that guided the preparation of this plan and those that pertain to Refuge management activities.

Chapter 2: The Planning Process

Photograph by Scott Sharkey

This CCP has been written with input and assistance from citizens, conservation organizations, and employees of local and state agencies. The participation of these stakeholders is vital and all of the ideas have been valuable in setting the future direction of the Refuge and the District. Refuge staff and the U.S. Fish and Wildlife Service as a whole are very grateful to everyone who has contributed time, expertise and ideas throughout this process. We remain impressed by the passion and commitment expressed by many for the lands administered by the Refuge.

The CCP planning process began in October 1998 when a team comprised of Refuge staff, a regional planner, an employee of the Twin Cities Ecological Services Field Office, a representative from the Minnesota Department of Natural Resources, and the Executive Director of the Friends of the Minnesota Valley were assembled. During the months of November 1998 to March 1999, the planning team reviewed the original Comprehensive Plan and associated documents. In addition, this group identified a number of issues and concerns that would likely affect the future of the Refuge and the District. A list of required CCP elements such as maps, photos, and GIS data layers was developed. Concurrently, federal and state mandates plus applicable local ordinances, regulations, and plans were reviewed for application to this planning effort. Ultimately, the team agreed to a process for obtaining public input and for completion of the Refuge and District CCP.

Public input was obtained using several methods including open houses, issue-based focus groups, public use surveys, and personal contacts.

Open Houses

Seven open houses were conducted during the spring and summer of 1999. The primary purpose of the open houses was to obtain public input into the future direction of the Refuge and its District. These events also gave Refuge staff the opportunity to revitalize old friendships and develop some new ones. These citizens, non-profit organizations, and cooperating agencies were notified of the events via news releases, posters displayed in the various communities, the Refuge Calendar of Events, and direct mailings. Those unable to attend the open houses were encouraged to submit written comments using a pre-printed comment card or through regular correspondence. Many people who attended open houses gave the comment cards to friends, family, and colleagues. A total of 241 people attended the open houses and submitted 110 comment cards. We also received 21 letters in the mail.

- On March 31, 1999, an open house at the Refuge visitor center was held for non-profit organizations and local agencies. Its purpose was to share knowledge, identify existing or planned projects that may affect the Refuge and its District, establish face-to-face contacts, and to ask for feedback regarding the planning process.

- On April 27, 1999, a public open house was held at the Refuge visitor center in Bloomington, Minnesota.

- On May 6, 1999, a public open house was held at the Student Union, Mankato State University, Mankato, Minnesota.

- On May 11, 1999, a public open house was held at Carver Village Hall, Carver, Minnesota.

- On May 19, 1999, a public open house was held at the City Hall, Burnsville, Minnesota.

- On May 25, 1999, a public open house was held at the Don Ney Environmental Learning Center, Henderson, Minnesota.

- On August 24, 1999, a public open house was held at Bethel College and Seminary, Arden Hills, Minnesota. The primary purpose of this event was to obtain public input into the future management of the Round Lake Unit.

Issue-based Work Groups

Based in part on the input received from the open houses, the Refuge planning team decided to form issue-based work groups to discuss issues and obtain specific recommendations for the CCP. Members of these work groups were chosen by the planning team and were selected based on their interest, knowledge, and desire to participate in this process. Individuals from a variety of backgrounds served on these work groups, including technical experts plus county commissioners, avid hunters and anglers, volunteer rangers, bird watchers, environmental educators, city recreation directors, MnDNR employees, and Refuge staff. Each focus group was moderated by trained facilitators from the MnDNR or the Service's Regional Office. A brief description of their charge is summarized in the following paragraphs.

Refuge Recreational Uses: This 21-member group reviewed existing Refuge and District recreational activities in light of the six priority wildlife-dependent uses identified in the National Wildlife Refuge System Improvement Act of 1997.

Threats and Conflicts: External threats and potential conflicts such as incompatible development and contaminants were addressed by this 21-member group.

Refuge Management and Biology: Ongoing habitat management activities plus associated biological monitoring programs were the primary topics of discussion for this 22-member focus group.

Refuge Expansion and Watershed Activities: This 20-member focus group concentrated on habitat restoration or protection opportunities beyond existing Refuge boundaries and out into the District.

Environmental Education and Interpretation: This 18-member group reviewed current environmental education and interpretive activities.

The Refuge hosted the initial meetings for the five focus groups on October 5, 1999, and October 19, 1999, at the Refuge visitor center. Between October and December 1999, each focus group convened from three to four times for two-hour meetings. Among other items, they provided feedback on the Refuge's mission, vision, and goals. In addition, each focus group developed several recommendations to help the Refuge and its District achieve their purposes over the next 15 years.

Meetings and Other Public Forums

In addition to open houses and focus groups, Refuge staff made presentations and solicited comments about the CCP from various clubs and organizations over the nearly 3-year planning process. In February 2000, the Refuge manager and a MnDNR representative spoke to more than 200 mountain bike enthusiasts at the Bloomington REI store concerning the issue of trail usage. Throughout the Spring of 2000 Refuge staff gave presentations to various clubs such as the Society of Professional Engineers regarding issues related to recreation and biology.

Public Use Survey

Minnesota River Valley Area Survey

In cooperation with the Refuge, Friends of the Minnesota Valley, and several other public and corporate sponsors, the MnDNR conducted a survey of public attitudes toward the Minnesota River Valley including recreational use, conservation and associated issues. This survey was distributed to 1,500 river-area residents during July and August 2001. The river was divided into five segments from Fort Snelling upstream to Le Sueur, thus surveys were mailed to residents of both rural and urban areas.

Survey results were made available in May 2002. The planning team has reviewed our recommended objectives and strategies in light of the public attitudes revealed by the survey. The following are a few results that we found to be of interest:

- 73 percent of respondents strongly to moderately agreed, or were neutral, when asked if the government should buy land along the river for fish and wildlife habitat or public recreation.

- 74 percent of respondents strongly to moderately agreed there should be more effort to preserve fish and wildlife habitat in the area.

- Less that 3 percent of respondents thought that the level of effort to protect wildlife habitat was too aggressive.

- The most popular types of recreation activity in the area include nature/wildlife observation, hiking/walking, sightseeing, and visiting historic or cultural sites (35 percent to 55 percent of respondents participate).

- 59 percent to 69 percent of respondents strongly to moderately agree that opportunities for recreation, wildlife viewing, and learning about nature and history should be expanded in the area.

Preparation and Publishing of CCP

The Refuge and District CCP and Environmental Assessment (EA) were primarily written by Refuge staff with a great deal of assistance, review, and support from the Regional Office. It was published in two phases and in accordance with the National Environmental Policy Act. The Final EA (Appendix A) presents a range of alternatives for future management and identifies the preferred alternative. A public review period of at least 45 days followed release of the draft plan. Alternative C, Balanced Public Use and Habitat Management, was ultimately selected and is the basis of this CCP.

Summary of Issues, Concerns and Opportunities

An array of issues, concerns, and opportunities were addressed during the planning process. Numerous discussions among citizens, focus group participants, resource specialists, and Refuge planning staff brought to light several recurring themes.

Refuge Recreational Uses

Minnesota Valley National Wildlife Refuge provides a variety of wildlife-dependent recreational uses including hunting, fishing, wildlife observation, wildlife photography, environmental education and interpretation. To facilitate these uses, a system of parking lots, trails, and interpretive structures have been developed over the years. In addition, the Refuge has worked cooperatively with the MnDNR to establish and maintain the Minnesota Valley State Trail. Upon completion, the State Trail will transect several Refuge units as it meanders through the Minnesota River Valley between Fort Snelling State Park and the City of LeSueur.

Overall, many participants identified a need for greater public understanding and appreciation of the Refuge and District lands and the recreational opportunities they offer. This need can be addressed by several ways including enhanced communications through appropriate brochures, web sites, signage, visitor center exhibitry, and high quality recreational programming. A number of recreational issues became apparent during the planning process and deserve further discussion. Specific recreational concerns, issues, and opportunities are summarized as follows:

Elimination of Confusing Rules and Regulations
Due in part to the land ownership patterns within the Minnesota River Valley, there is a great deal of public confusion about what type of recreation is appropriate on Refuge lands and where this recreation is allowed. This perplexity is compounded by several issues including inconsistent use regulations among public land management agencies, lack of appropriate signs and brochures, a limited law enforcement presence, and the yet to be completed Minnesota Valley State Trail. It was recognized that the first steps toward addressing this very important issue are enhanced interagency coordination and a commitment by all public land managers to address this issue.

Completion of Minnesota Valley State Trail

As indicated previously, the Minnesota Valley State Trail has not been completed as originally planned. Although the MnDNR is making progress toward this end, several significant trail sections through Refuge lands await completion. To some degree, the absence of this multiple-use trail has lead to some inappropriate uses of Refuge lands. For example, a myriad of informal and unmaintained trails have been established in several locations within the valley between Old Cedar Avenue and the Bloomington Ferry Bridge. Likewise, the absence of bridges and trail crossings over streams and creeks has contributed to the development of numerous braided trails by those seeking access across these obstructions. Without an established and maintained trail, it has been difficult to restrict public use along this corridor and limit damage to adjacent fragile natural habitats.

There are several reasons why the Minnesota Valley State Trail has not been completed including limited funding, unwilling sellers of keys tracts, and perhaps lack of public support. Its completion has also been recently complicated by a local debate over the proposed trail surface. More specifically, many mountain bike enthusiasts have expressed opposition to a hard surfaced and/or paved trail. Hardened trail surfaces were called for in the original Comprehensive Plan to provide access for elderly or disabled individuals.

We hope that preparation of this CCP will prompt a renewed effort by citizens, public agencies, private conservation organizations, and recreational users of the valley to place a high priority on the completion of the Minnesota Valley State Trail. Upon its completion, there is great potential for recreational users of this trail to develop an enhanced appreciation for the cultural and natural resource values of the Refuge as well as the greater Minnesota River Valley.

Continuance of High Quality Hunting and Fishing Opportunities

Although not endorsed by everyone, there was strong support among stake holders to continue hunting and fishing programs on Refuge and District lands. Consistent with requests to maintain these activities, the need to offer high quality recreational experiences to Refuge users was frequently expressed throughout the planning process. For example, public waterfowl hunting as it now occurs on Rice Lake is characterized by over-crowding and a great deal of competition between hunters. Likewise, this area is notable for hunting violations that occur each year including the killing of tundra swans, late shooting, and the use of lead shot. In this particular case, some people suggested improving the quality of this experience by initiating an adult hunter education program and limiting the number of hunters allowed to hunt Rice Lake at any one time.

Mountain Biking and Refuge Visitor Conflicts

A very vocal and organized mountain biking group expressed the desire to continue using much of the Minnesota River Valley for mountain biking. The rugged terrain and undeveloped landscape of the valley has attracted a growing number of bikers who use the new heavy-framed bikes designed to traverse rough and uneven terrain. With the exception of one semi-official trail established on City of Bloomington property, no mountain bike trails have been designated or developed in this area. As a result, some mountain bike enthusiasts took it upon themselves to establish a continuous trail between the Bloomington Ferry Bridge and Lyndale Avenue. Much of this single tract trail crosses both Refuge and private lands without authorization.

Several comments were received about the use of mountain bikes on Refuge lands and conflicts with other Refuge visitors. For example, bird watchers and nature photographers have encountered aggressive mountain bikers on Refuge trails. In many cases, these pedestrians were forced off hiking trails by these bikers. On a related issue, some people noted the excessive and unchecked erosion that currently exists in the Bloomington Bluffs area of the Refuge northeast of Lyndale Avenue. This natural resource degradation is due, in part, to improperly designed trails and off-trail usage by some mountain bikers.

Consistent with the Refuge System Improvement Act of 1997, bicycling beyond established roads or trails is not an appropriate use of a national wildlife refuge. In addition, the establishment of a single-track trail specifically for mountain biking purposes is also inappropriate, especially on Minnesota Valley National Wildlife Refuge. Consequently, the Refuge will address this issue through the completion of the CCP.

USFWS File Photograph

Horseback Riding Issues

Horseback riding is currently limited on the Refuge to those portions transected by the Minnesota Valley State Trail and a small, unofficial trail around Fisher Lake on the Wilkie Unit.
In light of the popularity of this activity, a number of equestrians attended the open houses to express their desire to maintain and possibly expand riding opportunities on Refuge lands. Most of the requests came from people who live upstream from Shakopee and who currently use portions of the State Trail for this pastime. Several individuals suggested that any new lands added to the Refuge allow for horseback riding.

As with mountain biking, unrestricted horseback riding is not an appropriate use of the Refuge. This CCP also addresses this issue by limiting horseback riding to the State Trail where it transects Refuge lands.

Environmental Education and Interpretation

Several comments were received in support of the Refuge's existing environmental education and interpretive programs. Some people suggested program modifications or improvements through enhanced partnerships and cooperation with other agencies, non-profit organizations, industry and neighboring landowners. It was also suggested that new sources of volunteers could be developed to improve educational and interpretive programs as well as other Refuge activities. More importantly, many people suggested that a renewed effort to strengthen partnerships with schools throughout the area would greatly benefit the Refuge.

In 1992, a concept plan for the Refuge's environmental education and interpretive programs was developed along the theme of "How Should We Live Together?" This plan examined the need to convey the Refuge's unique identity and create a thought provoking interpretive experience for Refuge visitors. Among other items, this plan sought to link the various units of the Refuge with the visitor center through consistent messages.

Several recommendations were included in this plan, some of which have since been implemented. Prior to incorporating any major changes to Refuge environmental and interpretive programs, it is very important that this concept plan be reviewed, modified, and/or updated. Topics that should be addressed through this review include environmental education curricula and programming and their relevance to Minnesota public school graduation standards, interpretive and special events, preservation of Refuge's cultural and historical features, and replacement of visitor center exhibitry and onsite informational kiosks.

Refuge Biology and Habitat Management

A thorough understanding of the biological communities and their processes is fundamental to sound fish and wildlife habitat management. Many stakeholders understand this concept and consequently, several expressed a strong desire to enhance the capability of the Refuge biological program. Among other items, participants recommended a comprehensive inventory of the flora and fauna, especially rare remnant native plant and animal communities existing on Refuge and District lands.

The group acknowledged the importance of continuing Refuge and District habitat management programs such as prescribed burning and marsh management, consistent with well prepared habitat management plans. Future efforts should include plans for target species such as neotropical migrants and the control of exotic plant and animal species. It was also recommended that scientifically-based monitoring programs be designed and implemented to document changes in plant and animal communities in response to habitat management.

Refuge Land Acquisition and Watershed Activities

Many stakeholders understood that the health and vitality of many natural resource areas, including Minnesota Valley National Wildlife Refuge, is very dependent upon the overall health of its watershed. In light of this, the Refuge was encouraged to continue its work within the watershed of the Minnesota River in cooperation with many others. In particular, the Partners for Fish and Wildlife Program and the acquisition of Waterfowl Production Areas and easements were believed to be very beneficial for a host of species and resource concerns.

Concurrent with the need to work within the watershed, many stakeholders suggested expanding the Refuge upstream by acquiring lands from willing sellers that would provide good quality wildlife habitat. Many suggested that adjacent hillside forest and bluff land should be acquired along with floodplain parcels to ensure long-term biological values of the Minnesota River Valley.

External Threats and Conflicts

Due to its urban location, the Refuge is subject to numerous threats and conflicts to its lands and natural resources. As the Twin Cities population increases, so does the demand to use any available open space for dissipation of noise, installation of utilities, and drainage of storm waters.

An ongoing issue of significant concern is the impact that existing storm water sewer discharges have upon the health of Refuge wetlands. In particular, the pollution entering Long Meadow Lake from the City of Bloomington storm water sewers is cause for great concern. As of this writing, Refuge staff have not been successful in finding agreement with the City to address this problem. In the future, however, Refuge staff, with the assistance of other conservation organizations, will attempt to work with the cities along the Minnesota River to avoid or eliminate storm water pollution before it enters Refuge lands.

Other potential conflicts include incompatible land use and development, toxic spills, and general degradation of the river and its watershed. Several stakeholders expressed their concern throughout the planning process about these threats and conveyed their views about how they should be addressed. Although the Service, as an agency, only plays a minor role in all of these issues, it was believed that the Refuge needs to continue to cooperate and communicate with developers and city/county planners to avoid or minimize any potential threats.

Mosquito Control

Since 1988, the Refuge has prohibited treatment of its lands for mosquitoes except in the case of a health emergency. The policy was implemented after the Defenders of Wildlife and other environmental organizations filed a suit against the Service for allowing control of mosquitoes on Refuge lands. An out-of-court settlement was reached after the Service agreed to conduct an environmental review of its program. Following the completion of an environmental assessment and because of potential negative environmental effects, the Service adopted a policy that allows treatment on the refuge to occur only in the event of a human health emergency. Since the policy was adopted, there has not been a human health emergency associated with mosquitoes on the Refuge.

Maintenance of Refuge and District Infrastructure

The Refuge and its facilities are considered some of the finest in the area and most stakeholders believed that they needed to be maintained at a high standard. As acknowledged by many, the maintenance of the Refuge's infrastructure is one of the largest challenges facing an urban national wildlife refuge. A large amount of capital improvements including a state-of-the-art visitor center, 17 entrance signs, 12 parking lots, nine information kiosks, six historic structures, six bridges, 10 water control structures, two maintenance complexes, and miles of hiking trails all translate into significant maintenance needs. These facilities, combined with a relatively high level of vandalism, arson, dumping, and boundary encroachment, place excessive demands upon the Refuge's maintenance staff and its limited budget. Added to these responsibilities are nearly 5,000 acres of fee and easement lands scattered throughout the District.

Many stakeholders were surprised to learn of the small size of the maintenance staff and the Refuge's limited budget in light of all its maintenance needs. Others expressed a strong opinion that current Refuge staffing and budget levels are not sufficient to maintain these facilities. They further suggested that the Refuge, the Service, and its support within the community will erode if the current maintenance backlog is left unaddressed.

Comments from the Public on the Draft CCP

Verbal and written comments received from the public concerning the Draft CCP contributed to several modifications in this document. The Service received 32 letters and e-mail comments during the review period. The comments covered a variety of topics and detail, and not all thoughts could result in direct changes to the CCP. For example, several writers simply endorsed the future direction of Refuge management or a specific program presented in the plan. In a few cases, reviewers offered technical changes in wording and we were able to easily incorporate those ideas. However, a few issues, including proposals for outdoor amphitheaters, required further discussion in the plan. We will examine those issues in Chapter 4.

Chapter 3: Refuge Environment

Introduction

All lands administered by Minnesota Valley National Wildlife Refuge are located in east central Minnesota. This portion of the State is characterized by the confluences of the Minnesota and the St. Croix rivers with the Mississippi River. The Cannon River and the Vermillion River, both smaller tributaries of the Mississippi, are also located in east central Minnesota.

These river systems lend a great deal of historic significance to this part of Minnesota. Today, it is the most populous portion of the State with more than 2.5 million citizens living within the seven-county Twin Cities metropolitan area. Its continued growth places additional development pressure on any remaining open space and natural resources. Consequently, many natural resource agencies and non-profit conservation organizations are doing what they can to save the most important natural resource sites in this area from development.

Photograph by Scott Sharkey

Geography, Topography, and Hydrology

Refuge River Units

The river units of the Refuge lie along a 34-mile stretch of the lower portion of the Minnesota River between historic Fort Snelling and the City of Jordan. Approximately 90 percent of the Refuge is located within the 100-year floodplain. The surrounding bluffs have slopes of 12-25 percent and at their crest average 100 feet elevation above the river valley. A natural levee along the river channel in several portions of the river has created many natural wetlands and shallow lakes in the floodplain. These wetlands are very productive and of considerable importance to waterfowl and waterbirds. A significant portion of these riverine wetlands are recharged from emerging groundwater seeps and springs along the toe of the bluff. Small feeder creeks and streams are also common in the floodplain on or near several Refuge units. Consequently, the water quality of these wetlands is high where the natural flows and recharge areas have not been altered by development.

The Minnesota River is the largest tributary of the Upper Mississippi River. From its source near Big Stone Lake in western Minnesota, the Minnesota flows southeast for 224 miles to Mankato, then northeast for 106 miles to its confluence with the Mississippi River at Fort Snelling. It transects the Minneapolis-St. Paul metropolitan area in a northeast direction and contains lands typical of an urban to rural continuum. The river itself meanders very slowly through the valley and averages a grade of 0.8 foot per mile from Mankato to Carver. Its gradient is nearly level from Carver to its confluence with the Mississippi River.

The watershed of the Minnesota River is approximately 16,900 square miles, of which 2,000 square miles are located in South Dakota and Iowa. Most of the area was historic tallgrass prairie with high densities of prairie potholes. Since development, modern day agriculture has converted over 99 percent and 90 percent of its historic grasslands and wetlands, respectively, to cropland.

Due in part to this dramatic change in land use, the Minnesota River is subject to frequent flooding that has precluded most development within its floodplain. Although water quality seems to be improving, the Minnesota River remains the most silt-laden and polluted tributary of the Upper Mississippi River. Other sources of pollution that may affect the Minnesota River and its associated resources include leachates from landfills, storm water runoff, and untreated municipal waste. Situated in the lower portion of the Minnesota River, the Refuge and its physical, biological, cultural, and historical features are greatly affected by the river's distinct personality.

Over 50 different soils have been identified in the Refuge and most are comprised of alluvial, marsh, and peat land soil types. Hayden, Estherville, and Peaty Muck are soil series typical of upland forests, dry prairies, and marshes, respectively.

Savage Fen

The 400-acre Savage Fen complex is located within the City of Savage at the toe of the north-facing Minnesota River bluff. As suggested by its name, this area contains a fen that was created in part, by the discharge of ground waters onto the floodplain of the river. Uncommon and unique plant communities evolved under these fen conditions. The Savage Fen is comprised of very poorly drained peat and muck soils ranging from 18 inches to 3 feet in depth. These areas are typically underlain by mineral soils. Over the years, urban development has encroached upon and destroyed portions of the Savage Fen. The Refuge currently owns 200 acres of this fen while the remaining lands are either owned by MnDNR or by private landowners.

Round Lake

The 152-acre Round Lake Unit is within the City of Arden Hills in Ramsey County. It is adjacent to the now dismantled Twin Cities Army Ammunition Plant and is bounded on the west by industrial development and on the south and east by private homes. This unit lies within an area known as the Anoka Sand Plain, which was historically characterized by oak savanna and sand prairie. Its topography is highly variable and its upland soils are a dark sandy loam that support a heterogeneous mixture of grassland, trees and shrubs. Hydric soils dominate the 120-acre permanent wetland.

The deep sediments of the wetland have elevated concentrations of heavy metals including zinc, chromium, and cadmium. The origin of these contaminants was the Ammunition Plant, which during World War II allowed industrial pollutants to enter area surface waters and consequently, some of these contaminants found their way into Round Lake.

Ongoing investigations by the U.S. Army in cooperation with Service staff and several other agencies are intended to determine the threat, if any, that these contaminants have on the biological communities of this area.

Wetland Management District

The District consists of 14 counties that overlay a major portion of east central Minnesota. The northeastern portion of this District (Chisago and Washington counties) is adjacent to the St. Croix River and is characterized by rolling terrain interspersed with wetlands, lakes, and small creeks. Both of these counties are experiencing phenomenal population increases. Hennepin and Ramsey counties are where Minneapolis and St. Paul are located, respectively, and for the most part there is only limited opportunity to undertake habitat restoration and protection activities. Historically, however, these counties contained an array of lakes, wetlands, and streams that offered excellent fish and wildlife habitats. Any remaining wildlife habitats have been largely influenced by these cities and their infrastructure.

Photograph by Scott Sharkey

The central counties of the District, namely Carver, Scott, and Dakota, lie primarily within the Minnesota River watershed and contain a variety of lakes, wetlands, and remnant habitats that attest to its glaciated past. However, much of the open space and agricultural lands in these counties are rapidly being converted to suburban developments or rural residential. The western and southern counties of the District are Sibley, Nicollet, Le Sueur, Rice, Blue Earth, Waseca, and Steele. Most of these counties are rural in nature and lie within the immediate watersheds of the Minnesota River or the Cannon River. Topography in these counties is also quite variable due to their glacial history and the presence of the river systems.

A wide variety of soils occur throughout the District. In general, soil productivity increases from north to south within the District where sandy soils of northern Ramsey County transition into highly productive silt-loams of Blue Earth County. Most of the lands and easements administered by the Refuge in the District are comprised of a high percentage of hydric soils that are marginal for cropland use.

Climate

The climate in east central Minnesota is classified as a subhumid continental type characterized by significant variations between summer and winter temperatures. The region has four distinct seasons with moderate spring and fall weather. Summer is comfortable because lakes and trees serve as natural air conditioners. In contrast, Minneapolis is the second coldest city in the United States with an average daily temperature of 35 F (1.8 C). The region receives on average 34 inches of precipitation each year and most of this occurs as rainfall between May and September. Annual snowfall averages approximately 45 inches.

Natural History

Eleven thousand years ago, during the Pleistocene Epoch, an inland sea named Glacial Lake Agassiz was formed from the meltwaters of the retreating eastern edge of the Des Moines Lobe of the Lurentide Ice Sheet. Lake Agassiz was 700 feet deep and covered over 100,000 square miles in Minnesota, North Dakota, and Manitoba. Torrential meltwater drainage from Lake Agassiz created the River Warren, which varied from 1 to 7 miles in width and from 75 to 200 feet in depth. In most of the lower river valley, the river action carved out a very wide and deep channel. As the Ice Age diminished and a northern outlet to Hudson Bay developed, the levels of both Lake Agassiz and the River Warren receded. The resulting underfit stream meandered through the extremely wide floodplain bordered by broad terraces of rock, sand, and gravel. The higher terraces have been rounded-off and dissected by later erosion. These terraces form the bluffs of what is now known as the Minnesota River Valley. Today, the Minnesota River Valley is a corridor of floodplain, forest, and wetlands that extends across some of Minnesota's most productive and intensively cultivated agricultural lands. The valley is classified as a northern floodplain forest ecosystem and flows through the Big Woods, Mississippi Sand Plains, and Southern Oak Barrens landscape regions of the State.

Archeological and Cultural Values

Archeological evidence shows that people have lived in the vicinity of the Lower Minnesota River Valley and south of the valley for almost 12,000 years. The first people, known as Paleo Indians, arrived shortly after the glaciers left the area. They are considered to have been nomadic family groups subsisting on the large mammals of that period and left behind little evidence of their occupancy. Even if these people used the valley, the catastrophic floods of the ancient glacial River Warren and accumulating siltation in the Minnesota River floodplain would have destroyed and deeply buried archeological remains. Although no Paleo Indian sites have been discovered in the vicinity, their distinctive projectile points have been found. Paleo Indian sites could be expected on the bluff tops along the Minnesota River as well as away from the river.

The people of the 5,000-year Archaic period that followed continued in the hunting-gathering tradition. However, the large mammals had died off and the evidence for these people shows larger groups with some seasonal settlement and a wider array of lithic tools exploiting a more diversified environment. Bison appear to have been an important part of their subsistence. This period includes the hot and dry altithermal (4700-3000 B.C.) when most surface water disappeared. Archaic period sites would likely be found in the trickle remnant of the Minnesota, Cannon, and other rivers, and in the bottom of formerly and subsequently large wetland basins.

Sites of the Woodland period are numerous and are found within the Refuge and the District as well as many more on other lands in the area. This period is characterized by pottery, ritual human burials, the bow-and-arrow, and semi-permanent settlements. The population increased and diversified. The people followed a diverse subsistence pattern based on a seasonal round of various habitat resource harvesting and storage, and included gardens. Some evidence for warfare exists. Sites are usually but not always associated with water, and are otherwise found in a variety of landforms including river floodplains. These woodland cultures existed until the arrival of Europeans in the middle of the 17th century.

The Minnesota River Valley has been a major route for exploration, trade, and commerce throughout its history. Pierre LeSueur first explored the Minnesota River in the 1680s and 1690s. Likewise, the Dakota Indians used the river to transport beaver, deer, and bison hides through the fur trading era of the 1700s and 1800s. Fort Snelling was constructed in 1820 to regulate Indian trade and to guard the region from British intrusion.

Fur posts, missions, and Dakota villages were common throughout the Lower Minnesota River Valley in the 1830s. River and keel boat traffic increased which gave life to increased commerce and the promise of new lands. The signing of the treaty of Traverse Des Sioux in 1851 opened the Minnesota Territory to European settlement and over the next 20 years, paths and oxcart trails became roads and ferries were replaced by bridges. During the 1870s riverboats were replaced with railroads as seemingly endless grasslands succumbed to the mow board plow. Lands that were inhabited by Native Americans and roaming herds of bison and elk went through a very significant change in less than one generation. By the turn of the century, the Minnesota River Basin had become one of the most productive agricultural regions in North America.

In the early 1900s, a myriad of wet meadows and shallow wetlands within the Minnesota River watershed were converted into cropland. Initially, shallow ditches were constructed to drain these areas into nearby creeks and lakes. As horse-drawn plows and planters were replaced by tractors capable of handling increasingly larger machinery, deeper and wider ditches were constructed and many of the natural creeks and streams were straightened and significantly altered. Ultimately, most of this drainage ended up in the Minnesota River.

At the same time, Twin Cities residents began to use portions of the Minnesota River Valley for recreation. Country homes were constructed on its bluffs and many joined privately-owned gun clubs that offered good waterfowl hunting. As the interest in these natural resources began to grow, so did the desire to conserve the Minnesota River. The recreational significance of the valley was first formally recognized in 1934 by Governor Floyd B. Olson when he proposed a 42,000-acre park between Fort Snelling and the City of Shakopee. Likewise, Theodore Wirth proposed a similar park in 1935, as did the State of Minnesota in 1939. Unfortunately, none of these dreams materialized, in part because of the onset of World War II.

After World War II, the Cargill Corporation purchased shipyards at Savage for a grain elevator and barge loading facility for shipment of grain downstream to St. Louis and New Orleans. To facilitate this, portions of the river were straightened and a 9-foot channel was dredged between Shakopee and its confluence with the Mississippi River.

Interest in the Minnesota River as an important natural resource resurfaced in the 1960s when the State of Minnesota established Fort Snelling State Park in 1961. The Minnesota River was one of four rivers in the state designated by the Legislature as a state canoe and boating route in 1963. Subsequently, the Legislature authorized the Minnesota Valley State Trail in 1969 which extends from Fort Snelling to LeSueur. During this period, local units of government also began preserving the natural resources of the valley. For example, the Hennepin County Park Reserve District acquired the James J. Wilkie Park Reserve located near Shakopee and Savage. Likewise, Bloomington acquired portions of the valley for park purposes. Some of these lands eventually became part of the Refuge.

The 1970s brought increased environmentalism and significant change to the Valley. In reaction to the proposed expansion of the Burnsville landfill, which is located in the floodplain, a non-profit citizen's organization known as the Burnsville Environmental Council proposed the creation of a national wildlife refuge and recreation area. With the support of the Bloomington Natural Resource Commission in 1973, an ad hoc Lower Minnesota Valley Citizen's Committee was established to promote the refuge and recreation area concept. Their dreams were realized in 1976 with the passage of the Minnesota Valley National Wildlife Refuge Act (Public Law 94-466).

Social and Economic Context

The seven-county Twin Cities Metropolitan Area is a vibrant community that serves as a major hub for agriculture, transportation, industry, finance, trade, and technology. Several renowned universities, including the University of Minnesota, make significant contributions to education, science, and medical research. The well-known Guthrie Theater and the world-class Minneapolis Institute of Art reflect area residents' interest in the arts. The world famous Mall of America in Bloomington is located directly upstream from Refuge lands. Year-round outdoor recreation is very important to the citizens of the area and many enjoy activities such as boating, fishing, swimming, skating, skiing, and snowmobiling. These residents are concerned about the quality of their environment as reflected by the presence of more than 30 environmental education and interpretive centers. Over the past decade, this vibrant economy has seen unprecedented growth which has lead to significant suburban sprawl. New or modernized infrastructure that support this growth includes roads, bridges, utilities, and airports. To a large degree, all of this places added developmental pressure on any remaining open space in this portion of Minnesota.

Natural Resources

Plant Communities

The Refuge and the District are located within the transition zone between the Eastern Broadleaf Forest and the Prairie Parkland ecoregions as defined by Bailey, et al. Plant communities within this transition contain a mixture of hardwood forest, oak savanna, and mesic prairie. The many lakes, wetlands, streams, and springs of these ecoregions exhibit diverse emergent and submergent aquatic vegetation. The specific community types and their quality are dependent upon a number of factors including climate, soils, historical vegetation, previous disturbance, and habitat restoration and management activities.

The Minnesota County Biological Survey, a program of the MnDNR, has mapped rare biological features on the Refuge and most of the Wetland District. The goal of the Survey is to identify significant natural areas and to collect and interpret data on the distribution and ecology of rare plants, rare animals, and native plant communities.

On a refined scale, Refuge and District vegetation have been mapped using the Minnesota Land Cover Classification System as developed by the MnDNR in partnership with The Nature Conservancy. This five-tier system integrates cultural features, non-native vegetation, natural and semi-natural vegetation into a comprehensive land cover classification system. To the degree possible, we will use the terminology and definitions of this system to describe site-specific plant communities.

Wetlands

Refuge units contain a variety of wetlands ranging from shallow wet meadows and calcareous fens to permanently flooded mixed emergent marshes. The river units are dominated by the latter where water is continuously present. Nearly all of these wetlands are spring fed and most of these large riverine basins are surrounded by mature cottonwood, willow, silver maple, and box elder. Water control structures have been installed on several basins and water levels are managed to control rough fish and greatly improve the productivity of the aquatic communities. Many species of waterfowl, marsh, and waterbirds are attracted to the resulting hemi marsh conditions in search of food and cover. Purple loosestrife occurs in some of these wetlands and is a major concern as an invasive, exotic plant.

Calcareous fens are also present on a few units, most notably on the Savage Fen. These wetlands are typically located at the toe of the Minnesota River bluff and occur on shallow or deep peaty soils in areas of calcareous groundwater discharge. The high concentrations of dissolved salts plus discharge water low in oxygen promotes the occurrence of rare plant species in the community. The long-term viability of fens is very much dependent upon land uses. Any significant reduction in the amount of upstream permeable soils and related groundwater discharge can threaten this rare plant community.

Round Lake is a 120-acre permanent wetland surrounded by cottonwood, maple, and box elder. The shallow lake is an open body of water and aquatic emergents are limited to a narrow fringe of cattail, slender bulrush, and water lily. Two storm water sewers enter Round Lake and have the potential to impact its water quality. A previously installed water control structure provides water level management capabilities. Due to a number of factors, including the potential exposure of heavy metals, water levels for Round Lake have been maintained at a constant level over the past 15 years.

The Waterfowl Production Areas and easements located within the District are characterized by temporary, seasonally flooded, and semipermanent emergent and cattail marshes. These wetlands overlay hydric soils and most have been restored on land formerly used for agriculture. The productivity of these wetlands is generally high due to periodic drought and recharging. The value of these areas to birds, mammals, reptiles, amphibians, and invertebrates increases as the diversity of wetland types increases within any geographic area.

Forests

Floodplain forests historically dominated much of the floodplain along the Minnesota River and its tributaries. Today, this plant community remains on several of the Refuge river units and a few Waterfowl Production Areas. Typical tree species found in these seasonally flooded areas include silver maple, cottonwood, American elm, green ash, boxelder, and occasionally, bur oak. The understory of these forests is generally open and in places the groundcover consists of wood nettle. In the past several years, former Refuge croplands that were historical floodplain forest have been replanted with species typical of this community.

Oak forests dominated by northern pin and white oaks are the most common upland forest community on the Refuge. These stands occur on nutrient-poor hillsides and well-drained sandy soils along the Minnesota River Valley. The shrub layer in these communities is frequently dense where American hazel, dogwood, and blackberries are commonly found. The control of European buckthorn, a prolific exotic in some of these plant communities, is a very significant challenge.

Oak Savannas

Oak savanna, a mixture of prairie and oak stands, is critically imperiled throughout the Midwest. Many of the oak forests described above were historic oak savanna prior to European settlement and the subsequent control of fires. Natural regeneration of this plant community is rare due to the inability of oak to reproduce under forest canopies. Since 1994, several oak savanna restoration sites have been identified on the Refuge. Restoration has been initiated on these sites through a rigorous combination of mechanical treatment and prescribed burning. Initial results are encouraging as evidenced by the return of a diverse understory of native grasses and forbs.

Grasslands

Remnant native prairie is some of the most diverse and important plant communities that exist in the Midwest. These rare and unique grasslands on Refuge units include both mesic and dry prairie and they are frequently interspersed with woodland areas, especially those forested sites protected from periodic fires. Mesic prairie is dominated by tall grasses including big bluestem and Indiangrass. Medium-height grasses such as little bluestem and side oats grama dominate dry prairies. Both mesic and dry prairies found on the Refuge contain shrubs such as leadplant and wild rose. Pasque flower and purple prairie clover are commonly found in both plant communities.

Native grassland restoration has occurred on upland sites of Refuge units, Waterfowl Production Areas, easements, and associated private lands for many years. Former croplands are typically planted to native grass mixtures consisting of big bluestem, little bluestem, switch grass, side oats grama, and Canada wild rye. A mixture of forbs is also planted to enhance the biological diversity of many of these sites.

Fish and Wildlife Communities

The habitats described above support an array of wildlife species that are common to east central Minnesota. A rich diversity of birds, mammals, fish, reptiles, and amphibians inhabit lands administered by Minnesota Valley National Wildlife Refuge.

Birds

The Refuge and its associated District attracts over 260 species each year to its diverse habitats. Of these, over 120 are known to nest in the area. Common waterfowl of the area include Canada Goose, Mallard, Wood Duck, Blue-winged Teal, Gadwall, and American

Wigeon. Waterfowl concentrate on Refuge and District wetlands during spring and fall.

Marsh and waterbirds frequently observed in the valley and surrounding areas include Great Egrets, Double-crested Cormorant, Great Blue Heron, Green Heron, and Black-crowned Night- Heron. A heron rookery consisting of an estimated 750 nest sites exists on the Wilkie Unit. The most prolific species of this colony are Great Blue Herons and Great Egrets. Exposed mud flats on Refuge riverbanks and Water-fowl Production Area wetlands attract shorebirds including Greater and Lesser Yellowlegs and Spotted Sandpiper. Both Common Snipe and American Wood-cock are commonly found on these lands as well.

Neo-tropical migrants attracted to forested habitats include thrushes, vireos and warblers. Year-round residents include Downy, Hairy, Pileated and Red-bellied Woodpecker; Wild Turkey; and Ring-necked Pheasant. Birds of prey inhabiting Refuge lands include Red-tailed Hawk, American Kestrel, Sharp-shinned Hawk and Cooper's Hawk.

Photograph by Scott Sharkey

Mammals
At least 50 mammals occur on Refuge lands as year-round residents and the most visible of these, of course, is the whitetail deer. During the 1970s and 1980s, deer populations exceeding 100 per square mile within the urban portions of the Refuge significantly damaged the area's vegetation. Populations have since been de-creased to a more sustainable level of 20-25 deer per mile using a combination of con-trolled hunts and sharpshooting. The removal of an average of 45 deer each year on Refuge lands is necessary to keep the populations at this level.

Mammals attracted to aquatic habitats include mink, muskrat, raccoon and beaver. As with most refuges, relatively high populations of beaver tend to complicate water man-agement activities. River otter, once nearly eliminated in this area, are now occasionally seen utilizing Refuge wetlands and river banks.

Small mammals typical of this area include short-tail shrew, white-footed mouse, thir-teen-lined ground squirrel, and plains pocket gopher. Eastern chipmunks plus eastern gray, eastern fox, and red squirrels are commonly founded in forested habitats. Both big and little brown bats use the Refuge and its associated lands. Red fox are the most common carnivores of the area followed by coyote and gray fox.

Fish
The Minnesota River is inhabited by an array of fish including game species such as northern pike, large mouth bass, walleye, bluegill, and crappie. Other species include shovel nose sturgeon, catfish, and red horse. Like most other fresh water systems in the United States, high populations of carp inhabit the Minnesota River. Due to regular

spring flooding, many of the Refuge wetlands contain a diversity of fish that originate in the river. For some species, these wetlands offer spawning and nursery habitat.

<u>Reptiles and Amphibians</u>
Thirty species of reptiles and amphibians have been reported on the Refuge but little is known about their populations or their limiting factors. Many of these, such as the snapping and painted turtles, are associated with marsh and open waters while others, such as the common garter snake and the hognosed snake, occur in oak savanna and prairie. The chorus of spring peepers is common throughout the Minnesota River Valley during spring.

Cultural Resources

Several hundred archaeological and cultural sites exist in the Lower Minnesota River Valley and many are located on Refuge lands. These sites include prehistoric burial mounds and village sites, early 19th century trading posts and ferry crossings, and early 20th century bridges and farmsteads. As an important part of this CCP process, the Service contracted for a cultural resources study of Minnesota Valley National Wildlife Refuge and associated areas. The product of this study is a report entitled *"Cultural Resources Management Plan for Cultural Resources within the Minnesota Valley National Wildlife Refuge"* prepared by Anthony Godfrey, Ph.D. of U.S. West Research, Inc. in Salt Lake City, Utah. This plan builds upon the previous work that has been accomplished in this area plus offers significant documentation and guidance concerning the management of these resources.

In light of the large number of archaeological and cultural sites on or near Refuge lands, considerable care will be exercised to avoid any potential impact. If needed, site-specific archaeological surveys will be completed before any significance ground disturbance occurs. Likewise, any effort to upgrade or stabilize historical structures will be done in such as fashion to maintain their historical character.

Migratory Bird Conservation Initiatives

Several migratory bird conservation plans have recently been published that can be used to help guide management decisions for the Refuge and District. Over the last decade, bird conservation planning efforts have evolved from a largely local, site-based focus to a more regional, landscape-oriented perspective. Several trans-national migratory bird conservation initiatives have emerged to help guide the planning and implementation process. The regional plans relevant to the Minnesota Valley Refuge and District are:

(1) The Upper Mississippi River/Great Lakes Joint Venture Implementation Plan of the North American Waterfowl Management Plan;
(2) The Partners in Flight Prairie Hardwood Transition [land] Bird Conservation Plan;
(3) The Upper Mississippi Valley/Great Lakes Regional Shorebird Conservation Plan; and
(4) The Upper Mississippi Valley/Great Lakes Regional Waterbird Conservation Plan.

All four conservation plans will be integrated under the umbrella of the North American Bird Conservation Initiative in the NABCI Prairie Potholes, Eastern Tallgrass Prairie and Prairie Hardwood Transition Bird Conservation Regions (BCR 11, 22 and 23).

Each of the bird conservation initiatives has a process for designating priority species, modeled to a large extent on the Partners in Flight method of calculating scores based on independent assessments of global relative abundance, breeding and wintering distribution, vulnerability to threats, area importance, and population trend. These scores are often used by agencies in developing lists of priority bird species. The Service based its 2002 list of nongame Birds of Conservation Concern primarily on the Partners in Flight, shorebird, and waterbird status assessment scores.

Fish, Wildlife and Plant Species of Management Concern

Table 1 summarizes information on the status and current habitat use of important fish, wildlife, and plant species found on lands administered by the Refuge. Individual species, or species groups, were chosen because they are listed as Regional Resource Conservation Priorities or State-listed threatened or endangered species. Other species are listed due to their importance for economic or recreational reasons or for their status as a nuisance or invasive species.

Table 1: Wildlife and Plant Species of Concern to the Minnesota Valley NWR and Wetland Management District

Species (* = managing habitat for these species)	Refuge Status	Monitored on Refuge by Staff or by MnDNR?	Regional/State Status (R3: Conservation Priority R3, E: Federal Endangered, T: Federal Threatened, SE: State Endangered, ST: State Threatened, SSC: State Species of Concern)	Potential Benefit by Habitat Habitat used for Production (P) or Migration (M)				
				Wetlands	Floodplain Forest	Upland Forest	Oak Savanna	Grasslands
White-tailed Deer*	Recreation/economic Common/abundant	Yes		P	P	P		
Eastern Spotted Skunk	Uncommon	Yes	ST		P			P
Prairie Vole	Rare	No	SSC		P			P
Least Weasel	Rare	No	SSC	P	P			P
Northern myotis	Rare	No	SSC		P			P
Plains Pocket Mouse	Uncommon	No	SSC				P	P
Eastern pipistrelle	Rare	No	SSC		P			P
Common Loon	Occasional	Yes	R3	M				
Horned Grebe	Rare	Yes	ST	M				
American White Pelican*	Common seasonally	Yes	SSC	M				
Double-crested Cormorant	Common/increasing	Yes	R3 (nuisance)	M,P				
Franklin's Gull	Rare	Yes	SSC	M				M
Black Tern*	Uncommon	Yes	R3	M,P				
Common Tern	Rare	Yes	R3, ST	M				
Forster's Tern	Uncommon	Yes	R3, SSC	M,P				
Great Blue Heron*	Common/increasing	Yes		M,P	P			
Great Egret*	Common/increasing	Yes		M,P	P			

Table 1: Wildlife and Plant Species of Concern to the Minnesota Valley NWR and Wetland Management District

Species (* = managing habitat for these species)	Refuge Status	Monitored on Refuge by Staff or by MnDNR?	Regional/State Status (R3: Conservation Priority R3, E: Federal Endangered, T: Federal Threatened, SE: State Endangered, ST: State Threatened, SSC: State Species of Concern)	Potential Benefit by Habitat Habitat used for Production (P) or Migration (M)				
				Wetlands	Floodplain Forest	Upland Forest	Oak Savanna	Grasslands
Black-Crowned Night Heron*	Uncommon	Yes	R3	M,P	P			
American Bittern	Occasional	Yes	R3	M,P				M
Least Bittern	Uncommon	Yes	R3	M,P				
Common Moorhen	Rare	Yes	R3, SSC	M,P				
King Rail	Rare	No	R3, SE	M				
Trumpeter Swan*	Uncommon	Yes	R3, ST	M,P				
Snow Goose	Occasional	Yes	R3 (nuisance)	M				
Canada Goose (Migrants)	Recreation/economic Common	Yes	R3	M				
Canada Goose (Residents)*	Recreation/economic Common/nuisance	Yes	R3 (nuisance)	M,P				P
Blue-winged Teal*	Recreation/economic Common	Yes	R3	M,P				P
Canvasback*	Recreation/economic Uncommon seasonally	Yes	R3	M				
Lesser Scaup*	Recreation/economic Common seasonally	Yes	R3	M				
Mallard*	Recreation/economic Common	Yes	R3	M,P				P
Northern Pintail*	Recreation/economic Common seasonally	Yes	R3	M				
Wood Duck*	Recreation/economic Common	Yes	R3	M,P	P	P	P	

Table 1: Wildlife and Plant Species of Concern to the Minnesota Valley NWR and Wetland Management District

Species (* = managing habitat for these species)	Refuge Status	Monitored on Refuge by Staff or by MnDNR?	Regional/ State Status R3: Conservation Priority R3 E: Federal Endangered T: Federal Threatened SE: State Endangered ST: State Threatened SSC: State Species of Concern	Potential Benefit by Habitat Habitat used for Production (P) or Migration (M)				
				Wetlands	Floodplain Forest	Upland Forest	Oak Savanna	Grasslands
American Woodcock	Recreation/economic Uncommon	No	R3	M	M		M,P	M,P
Marbled Godwit	Rare	No	R3, SSC	M				M,P
Hudsonian Godwit	Rare	No	R3	M				M
Upland Sandpiper*	Rare	No	R3					M,P
Buff-breasted Sandpiper	Rare	No	R3	M				M
Short-billed Dowitcher	Occasional	No	R3	M				
Stilt Sandpiper	Occasional	No	R3	M				
Greater Yellowlegs	Uncommon	No	R3	M				
Wilson's Phalarope	Rare	No	R3, ST	M				
Bald Eagle*	Threatened/recovering	Yes	T, SSC, R3	M	M,P		M,P	
Northern Goshawk	Rare	No	R3	M	M	M		
Northern Harrier*	Occasional	No	R3	M,P				M,P
Peregrine Falcon*	Uncommon	No	ST, R3	M				M
Red-shouldered Hawk*	Rare	No	R3, SSC		M,P	M,P		
Short-eared Owl	Rare	No	SSC, R3	M				M,P
Long-eared Owl	Occasional	No	R3	M		M	M	M

Table 1: Wildlife and Plant Species of Concern to the Minnesota Valley NWR and Wetland Management District

Species (* = managing habitat for these species)	Refuge Status	Monitored on Refuge by Staff or by MnDNR?	Regional/ State Status R3: Conservation Priority R3 E: Federal Endangered T: Federal Threatened SE: State Endangered ST: State Threatened SSC: State Species of Concern	Potential Benefit by Habitat Habitat used for Production (P) or Migration (M)				
				Wetlands	Floodplain Forest	Upland Forest	Oak Savanna	Grasslands
Black-billed Cuckoo	Occasional	No	R3, R3		M,P	M,P	M,P	
Whip-poor-will	Rare	No	R3		M	M,P	M,P	
Red-headed Woodpecker*	Uncommon	No	R3		M,P	M,P	M,P	
Northern Flicker	Common	No	R3		M,P	M,P	M	M
Olive-sided Flycatcher	Occasional	No	R3	M	M	M	M	
Loggerhead Shrike*	Rare	No	R3, ST				M,P	M,P
Bell's Vireo	Rare	No	R3	M,P			M,P	M,P
Sedge Wren*	Uncommon	No	R3	M,P				M,P
Wood Thrush	Occasional	No	R3	M	M	M,P		
Louisiana Waterthrush	Rare	No	R3, SSC	M	M,P			
Golden-winged Warbler	Rare	No	R3		M	M	M,P	
Cerulean Warbler	Rare	No	R3, SSC		M,P	M,P		
Blue-winged Warbler	Rare	No	R3		M,P	M,P		
Connecticut Warbler	Rare	No	R3		M	M		
Canada Warbler	Occasional	No	R3		M	M		
Cape May Warbler	Occasional	No	R3		M	M		
Hooded Warbler	Very Rare	No	SSC		M,P			
Prothonotary Warbler	Occasional	No	R3	M	M,P			

Table 1: Wildlife and Plant Species of Concern to the Minnesota Valley NWR and Wetland Management District

Species (* = managing habitat for these species)	Refuge Status	Monitored on Refuge by Staff or by MnDNR?	Regional/ State Status R3: Conservation Priority R3 E: Federal Endangered T: Federal Threatened SE: State Endangered ST: State Threatened SSC: State Species of Concern	Potential Benefit by Habitat Habitat used for Production (P) or Migration (M)				
				Wetlands	Floodplain Forest	Upland Forest	Oak Savanna	Grasslands
Black-throated Blue Warbler	Rare	No	R3	M	M	M		
Field Sparrow	Uncommon	No	R3				M,P	M,P
Grasshopper Sparrow*	Occasional	No	R3				M,P	M,P
Henslow's Sparrow	Rare	No	R3, SE				M,P	M,P
Le Conte's Sparrow	Occasional	No	R3				M	M
Nelson's Sharp-tailed Sparrow	Rare	No	R3, SSC				M	M
Dickcissel*	Occasional	No	R3				M,P	M,P
Bobolink*	Uncommon	No	R3				M,P	M,P
Rusty Blackbird	Uncommon	No	R3	M	M			M
Orchard Oriole	Occasional	No	R3				M, P	M, P
Western Meadowlark	Uncommon	No	R3				P	M,P
Eastern Meadowlark*	Uncommon	No	R3				P	M,P
Blandings Turtle	Rare	No	ST	P	P		P	
Northern Cricket Frog*	Rare	Yes	SE	P	P			
Smooth Softshell	Common	No	SSC	P				
Snapping Turtle	Common	No	SSC	P	P			
Wood Turtle*	Rare or Absent	No	ST	P	P			
Five-lined Skink	Rare	No	SSC	P	P	P	P	

Table 1: Wildlife and Plant Species of Concern to the Minnesota Valley NWR and Wetland Management District

Species (* = managing habitat for these species)	Refuge Status	Monitored on Refuge by Staff or by MnDNR?	Regional/ State Status R3: Conservation Priority R3 E: Federal Endangered T: Federal Threatened SE: State Endangered ST: State Threatened SSC: State Species of Concern	Potential Benefit by Habitat Habitat used for Production (P) or Migration (M)				
				Wetlands	Floodplain Forest	Upland Forest	Oak Savanna	Grasslands
Gopher (Bull) Snake	Common	No	SSC				P	P
Racer	Uncommon	No	SSC			P	P	P
Western Hognose Snake	Common	No	SSC				P	P
Brook Trout	Uncommon	No	R3					
Least Darter	Uncommon	No	SSC					
Paddlefish	Rare	No	R3, SSC					
Pugnose Shiner	Rare	No	SSC	P				
Higgins Eye Pearly Mussel	Absent (Historic)	No	E					
Arogos Skipper (Butterfly)	Rare	Yes	SSC				P	P
Leonardus Skipper	Rare	Yes	SSC				P	P
Powesheik Skipper	Rare	Yes	SSC				P	P
Regal Fritillary	Rare	Yes	SSC				P	P
Karner Blue	Rare or Absent	No	T					
Dwarf Trout Lily	Rare	No	E, SE		P	P		
Prairie Bush Clover	Rare or Absent	No	T, ST					P

Chapter 4: Refuge and District Management

Current Refuge and District Programs: Where We Are Today

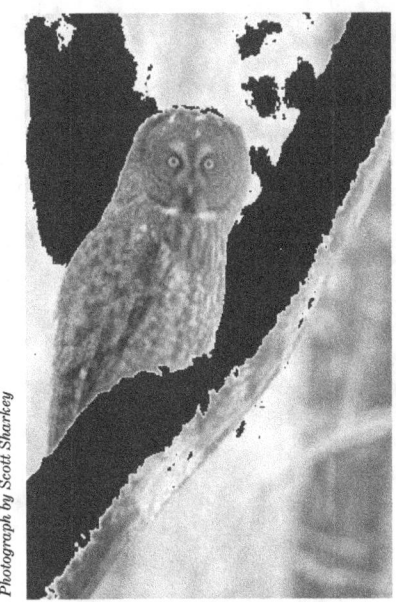

Photograph by Scott Sharkey

Consistent with its authorizing legislation, Minnesota Valley National Wildlife Refuge conducts a wide array of wildlife conservation activities within the Lower Minnesota River Valley and its District. The Master Plan for the Refuge, which was completed in 1984, called for the establishment of grasslands and food plots (corn and soybeans) on Refuge floodplain to enhance the area for waterfowl nesting and migration. Following some unsuccessful attempts to meet these objectives, the Refuge reassessed its habitat restoration and management programs and, with the input of other conservationists, developed its Landscape Plan in 1993. This plan basically set forth the philosophy of restoring Refuge plant communities to native species. It also identified the importance of using natural processes such as prescribed fire and water management to maintain the diversity and productivity of these communities. This philosophy remains today and will be integral within this Comprehensive Conservation Plan. In brief, the Refuge's habitat restoration and management program can be summarized by the phrase "native species and natural processes."

The Refuge's urban setting also offers unique opportunities to interact with diverse and supportive audiences. For example, Refuge staff have the privilege of providing environmental education programs to inner-city schools as well as those located in suburban or rural locations. Likewise, hunting, fishing, and wildlife observation, photography, and interpretive opportunities are provided on Refuge and District lands.

Habitat Restoration

Since its establishment, nearly 12,000 acres have been acquired or placed under management agreement within the Refuge. Initially, some of the former agriculture lands (less than 100 acres) were converted to floodplain grasslands for waterfowl nesting purposes. Introduced species such as Reed's canary grass and others were planted to a variety of native grasses. However, during 1992-93 all cropping ceased on remaining Refuge agricultural fields (less than 200 acres). No deliberate attempts were made to re-establish a preferred plant community on these areas. Consequently, early succession species such as cottonwood, willow, and box elder emerged as well as thistle and ragweed.

In recent years, the Refuge has emphasized the restoration of all lands to native plant communities. For example, bur oak, silver maple, and green ash have been planted to complement natural succession and to increase diversity in the floodplain. Likewise, a diverse mixture of native grasses and forbs have been reestablished on upland sites that historically contained grasslands. Wetland restoration activities have included the plugging of drainage ditches, the mechanical removal of woody vegetation from wet meadows and fens, and the installation of outlet ditches and water control structures on larger wetlands.

Habitat restoration activities on waterfowl production areas and easements also follow this same philosophy. Native grasses are restored on upland areas and wetlands are restored to historic levels when possible. Due to logistical concerns, water control structures are generally not installed on wetlands located on Waterfowl Production Areas or easement lands.

Habitat Management on the Refuge

The primary objective of the habitat management program at the Refuge is to maintain diverse, productive, and sustainable native plant communities. Through periodic treatments, these lands maintain their value to Refuge wildlife and help meet their production, feeding, and migration requirements.

To assist in the management of these habitats, the Refuge in cooperation with the MnDNR and others has completed cover-type GIS mapping for all units of the Refuge. These units are mapped using the Minnesota Land Cover Classification System, which integrates cultural features such as residences and roads, non-native vegetation, and natural and semi-natural vegetation into a comprehensive system (Figures 4-8).

Deep Water Habitats

Horseshoe Lake on the Rapids Lake Unit is one of two deep water habitats on the Refuge. Historically, this lake was an oxbow of the Minnesota River, but it has since become disconnected from the main channel. The depth of this lake is currently unknown, as is the composition of its fishery. The Refuge shares ownership with private parties on Long Lake, the other deep water habitat on the Rapids Lake Unit. A 1998 fishery survey showed that 18 species of fish occupied the lake, along with many large snapping turtles. The most numerous species were black crappie, gizzard shad, black and brown bullhead, and carp. Aquatic exchange with these lakes and the Minnesota River does occur nearly every year during spring flooding. The open water pools serve as a loafing area for waterfowl, marsh birds, and occasional seasonal habitat for shorebirds. The trees surrounding the lakes provide good perch sites for a number of species including herons, bitterns, and raptors such as the Bald Eagle and Red-tailed Hawk.

Small Streams

Several small streams exist on the Refuge and some of these historically supported native brook trout populations. The origins of the larger streams, such as Sand Creek, are in the watershed above the river valley. Some streams originate from springs within the bluff and bluff/floodplain transition zone of the Minnesota River. To date, no active habitat management has been undertaken on these streams.

Wetlands

The Refuge contains a variety of wetlands including fens, wet meadows, and large riverine marshes. Water control structures and outlet ditches have been installed on several of the riverine marshes. Over the years, three moist soil management units and one green tree reservoir have also been established within the floodplain of the Minnesota River. Most of these wetlands provide good quality production, brood rearing,

Figure 4: Existing Habitat (2002), Long Meadow Lake and Black Dog Units

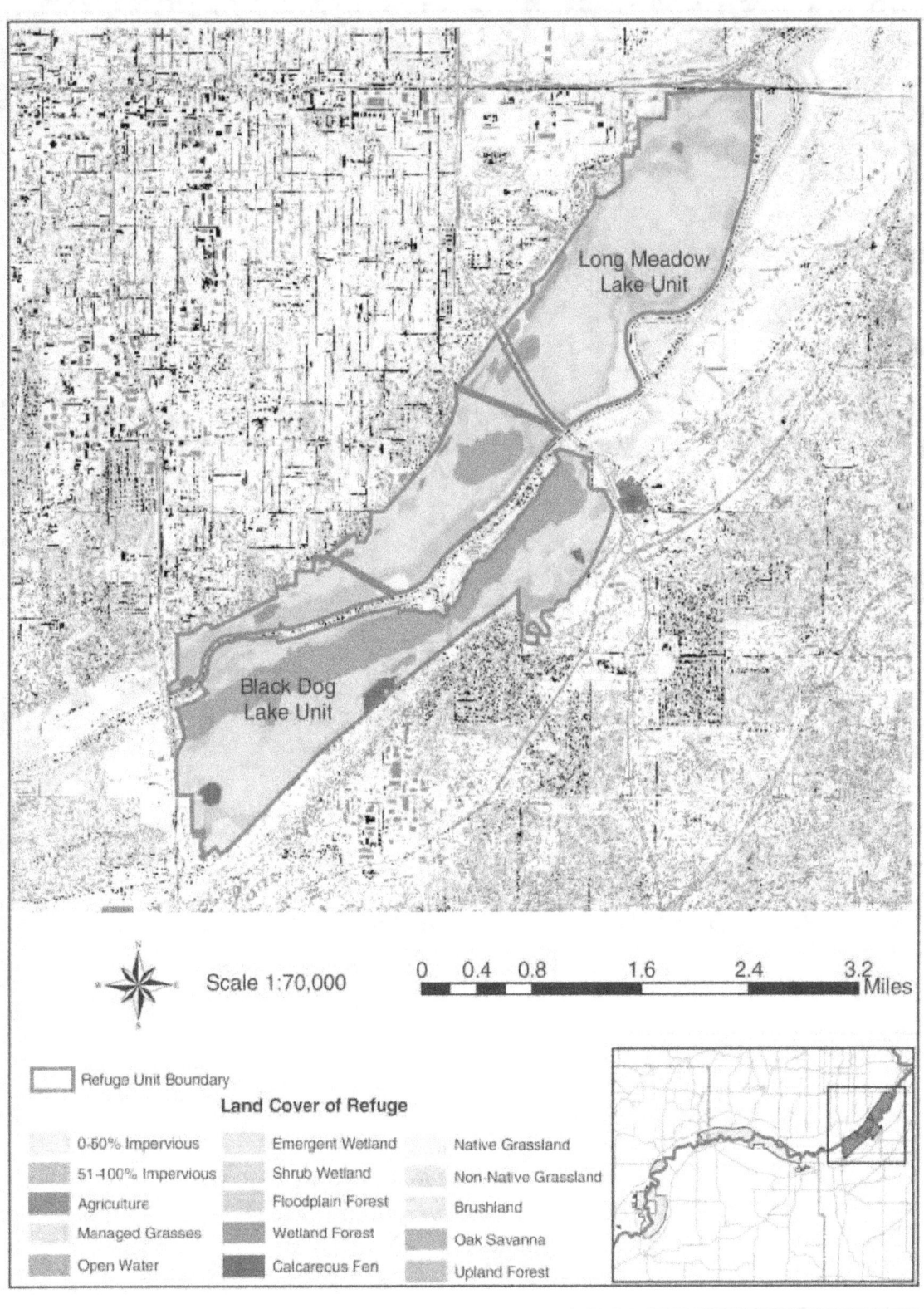

Long Meadow
Lake Unit

Black Dog
Lake Unit

Scale 1:70,000

0   0.4   0.8   1.6   2.4   3.2
                                                Miles

☐ Refuge Unit Boundary

Land Cover of Refuge

0-50% Impervious	Emergent Wetland	Native Grassland
51-100% Impervious	Shrub Wetland	Non-Native Grassland
Agriculture	Floodplain Forest	Brushland
Managed Grasses	Wetland Forest	Oak Savanna
Open Water	Calcarecus Fen	Upland Forest

Figure 5: Existing Habitat (2002), Upgrala, Wilkie and Bloomington Ferry Units

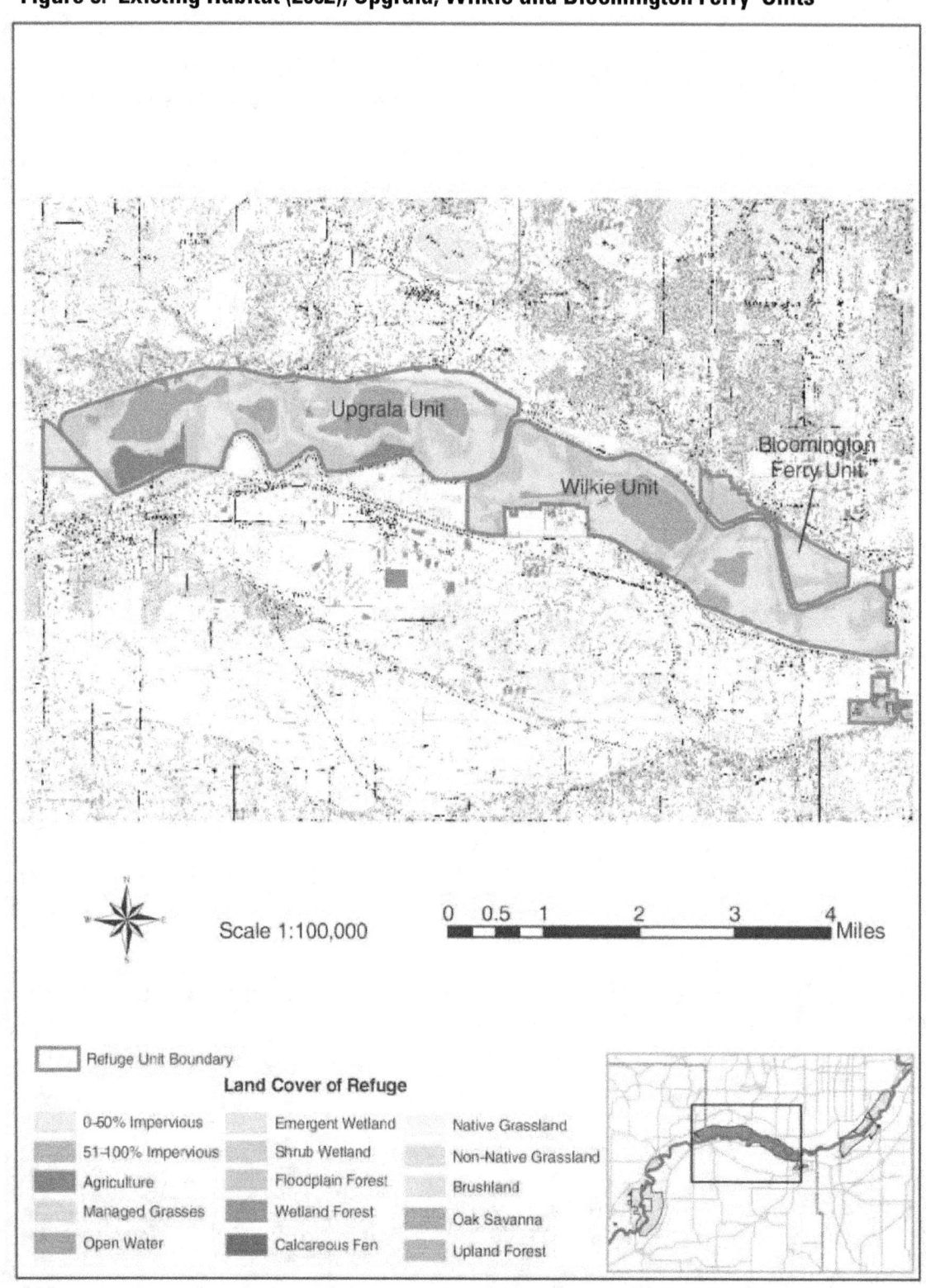

Figure 6: Existing Habitat (2002), Savage Fen Unit

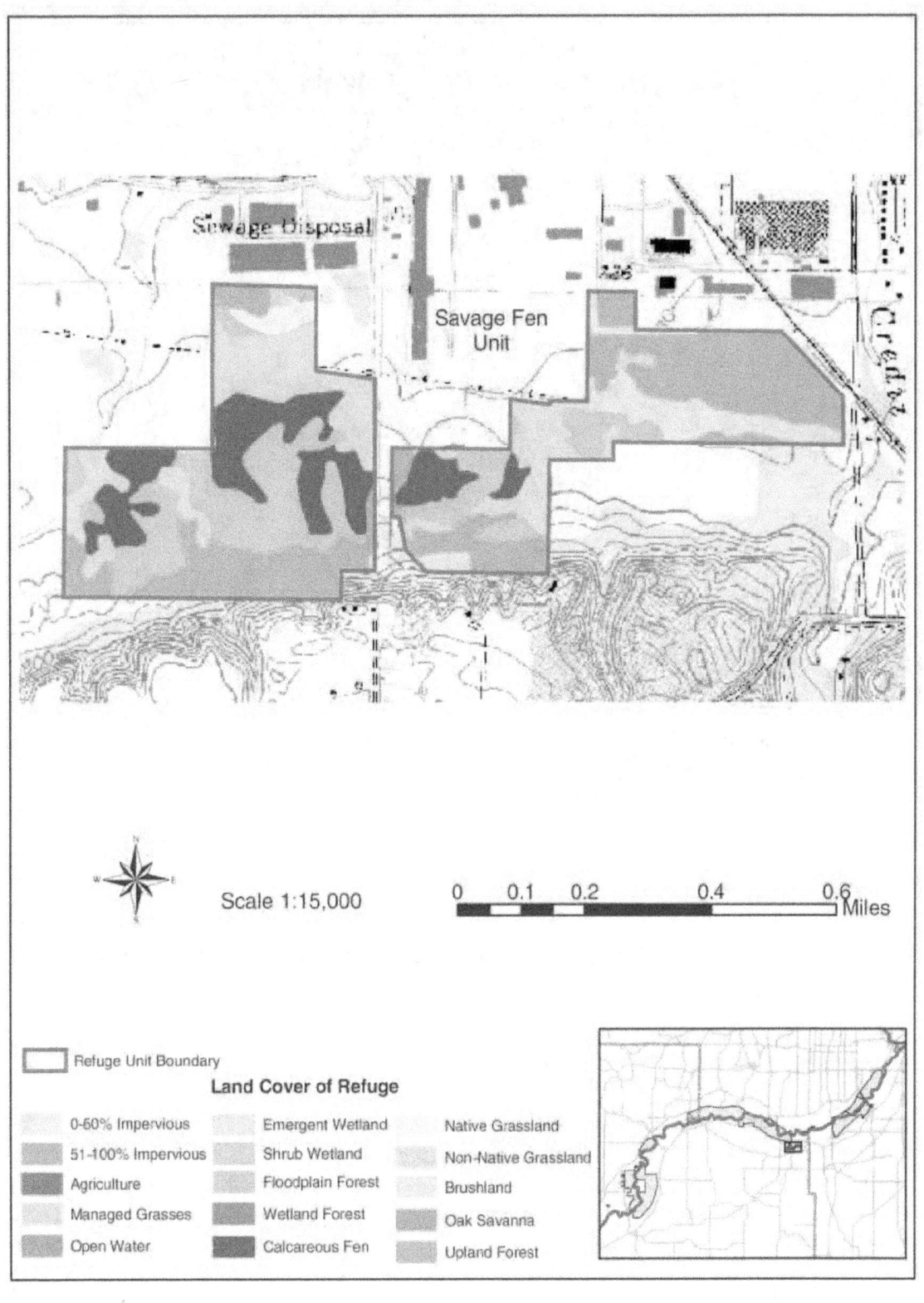

Figure 7: Existing Habitat (2002), Chaska Unit

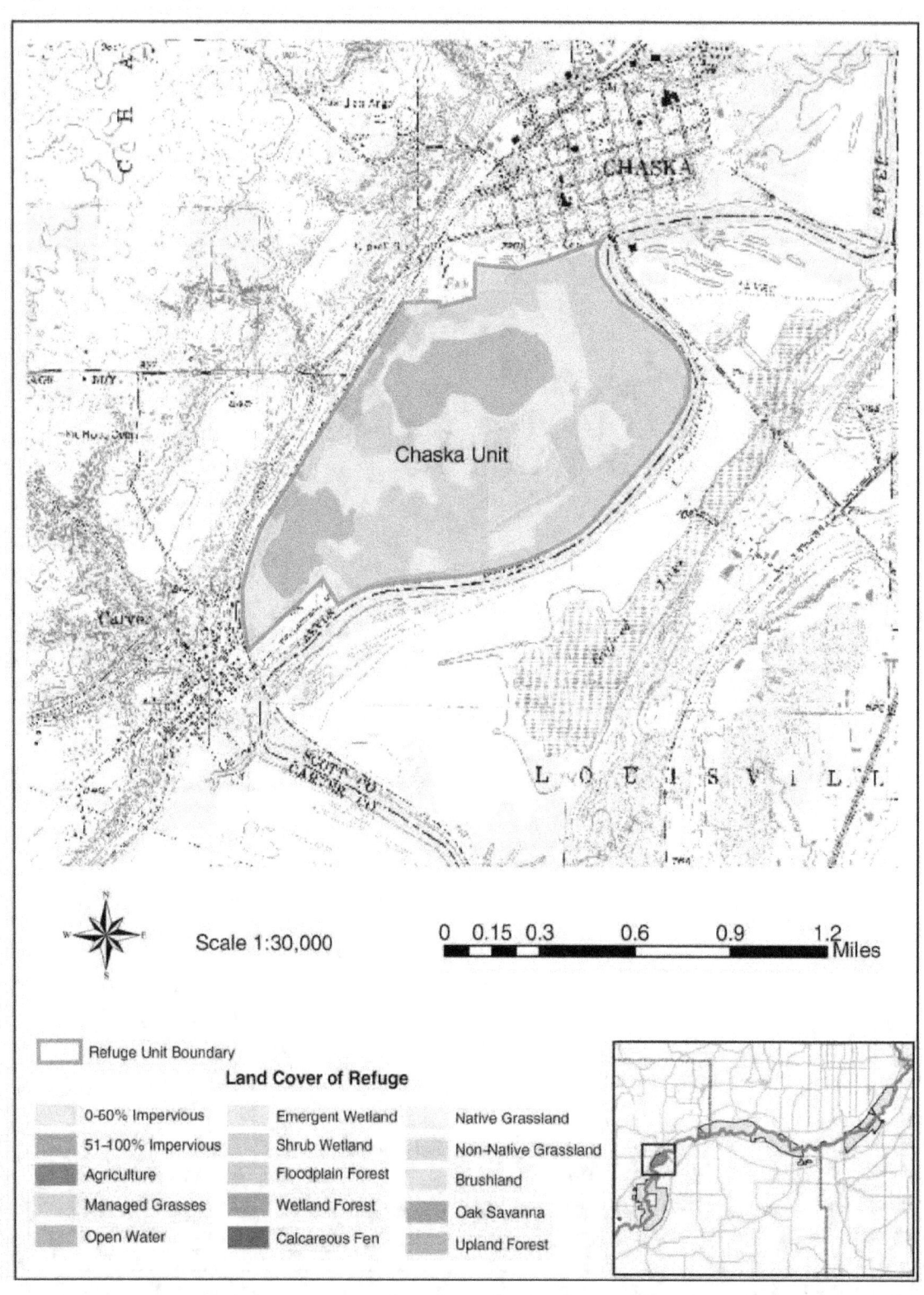

Chaska Unit

Scale 1:30,000

0 0.15 0.3   0.6   0.9   1.2
Miles

Refuge Unit Boundary

Land Cover of Refuge

0-50% Impervious	Emergent Wetland	Native Grassland
51-100% Impervious	Shrub Wetland	Non-Native Grassland
Agriculture	Floodplain Forest	Brushland
Managed Grasses	Wetland Forest	Oak Savanna
Open Water	Calcareous Fen	Upland Forest

Figure 8: Existing Habitat (2002), Rapids Lake and Louisville Swamp Units

Rapids Lake
Unit

Louisville Swamp
Unit

Scale 1:55,000

0   0.25 0.5   1   1.5   2
Miles

Refuge Unit Boundary

Land Cover of Refuge

0-50% Impervious	Emergent Wetland	Native Grassland
51-100% Impervious	Shrub Wetland	Non-Native Grassland
Agriculture	Floodplain Forest	Brushland
Managed Grasses	Wetland Forest	Oak Savanna
Open Water	Calcareous Fen	Upland Forest

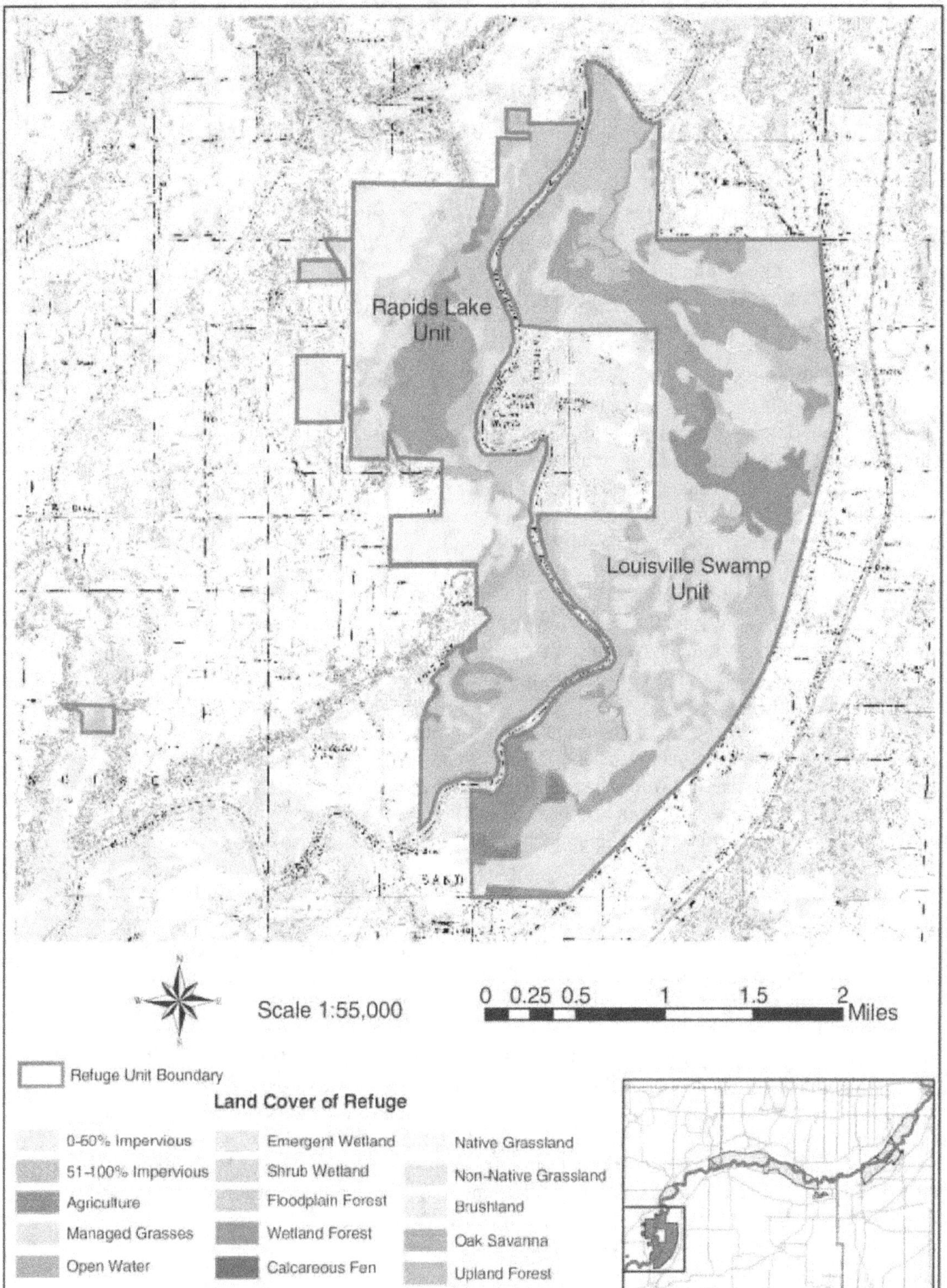

feeding, and/or migration habitats for a host of resident and migratory species. They also provide good quality spawning and nursery habitat for fish that inhabit the Minnesota River.

Water level management is the primary technique used to maintain the diversity and productivity of Refuge wetlands. Through periodic drawdowns, followed by subsequent reflooding, they support a variety of aquatic emergents and expose mudflats that attract good concentrations of waterfowl, waterbirds, and shorebirds.

Photograph by Scott Sharkey

Frequent fluctuations of the Minnesota River sometimes complicate the management of these large wetlands. For example, high river elevations during late spring and summer can prevent drawdowns and the germination of emergent vegetation. Likewise, prolonged or frequent flooding can destroy beneficial aquatic plants and convert the area from a "hemi-marsh" community to open water wetland habitats with limited plant diversity. Fortunately, however, the long-term productivity of these wetlands can be maintained with a committed effort that is prepared to take advantage of drawdowns and other management opportunities when they occur. Water control structures designed to keep the low bounces of the Minnesota River out of these wetlands also enhance the success of this management. An active water management program also helps to decrease rough fish populations that exist in many of these riverine wetlands.

As indicated earlier, three moist soil management units have been constructed on the Refuge since its inception. All of these units were constructed as mitigation for a development project that impacted Refuge lands to some degree. Unfortunately, these units have not functioned as planned due to a number of factors, including permeable soils upon which they were constructed. The long-term plan for these units is to convert them to green tree reservoirs as the adjacent floodplains are reestablished to a forest cover.

Management of calcareous and sedge fens that occur on the Refuge consists of periodic prescribed burning with hand removal of invading shrubs. Management is needed on these units to maintain favorable conditions for the rare and unique species that occur in these important ecological communities.

A water control structure and outlet ditch has also been installed on the Round Lake Unit, which is located in Arden Hills. The sediments of Round Lake include high concentrations of boron and chromium. Because of the potential to disturb these sediments and introduce heavy metal contaminants into the food chain, no active water level management of Round Lake is occurring at this time. In addition, many lakefront homeowners prefer a more open water management regime instead of widespread emergent vegetation. However, the Service should maintain the option of actively managing the water levels in the future upon assurances that periodic drawdowns and reflooding would not cause undue risk to the ecosystem.

Floodplain Forests

No active management techniques, such as cutting for timber stand improvement, are planned for floodplain forested areas other than those that will perpetuate the development of old growth forest. As indicated previously, all former agricultural lands within the floodplain will be converted to forested habitat. Unbroken blocks of forest minimizes the "edge" effect, a fragmented habitat condition that leads to increased predation rates for some nesting birds. Continuous forest also provides for a wildlife movement corridor along the Minnesota River.

Hillside Forests

The mixed deciduous forests that exist along the bluffs of the Minnesota River have an overstory of ash, elm, maple, white oak and basswood with an understory of dogwood, choke berry and other shrubs including European buckthorn, an exotic species. No active management techniques are planned in this plant community other than control measures for exotic species. The community will be allowed to continue to age into an old growth forest. Prescribed fire will be used only in those locations where there is an understory of grassland.

Oak Savanna

The Refuge contains some areas that were historically oak savanna. Nearly 200 acres of historic oak savanna exists on the Louisville Swamp Unit alone. With the cessation of wildfires, the open canopies of the oak savannas were gradually replaced with a closed canopy mixed deciduous forest. Upon removal of all but the bur oaks, and a series of prescribed burns, these oak savannas begin to take on their historic character. Long-term management of these areas includes periodic prescribed burns combined with occasional mechanical removal of unwanted trees and brush.

Bernie Angus

Grasslands

Refuge grasslands are limited primarily to remnant native prairie along the Minnesota River Bluffs and restored native grasses in former agricultural fields. The largest block of remnant native prairie on the Refuge exists along the Eden Prairie Bluffs and is characterized by a diversity of native grasses and forbs. Most of the Refuge's restored native prairie is located on the Rapids Lake Unit (~300 acres) and on Waterfowl Production Areas.

Prescribed fire is the primary tool used to periodically invigorate these native communities and discourage the invasion of introduced cool season grass, noxious weeds, and shrubs. Over the past 10 years, Refuge staff have conducted well over 150 prescribed burns within an urban/wildland interface without a major accident or incident. However, the prescriptions for timing of these burns are very narrow because of safety concerns. Sometimes, delays due to unfavorable weather means that units cannot be burned on schedule. Grassland habitat quality can suffer because of subsequent fuel buildup and woody plant species invasion.

A Fire Management Plan for the Refuge and District was prepared in 2002. These plans are required before conducting either prescribed burning or wildfire suppression. The plan describes in detail fire management objectives, strategies, responsibilities, personnel and public safety, monitoring of effects, fire planning, air quality and smoke management, and compliance with Fish and Wildlife Service fire management policies, including Section 7 of the Endangered Species Act. The plan is available at the Refuge Office for public review. In addition to the Fire Management Plan, each prescribed burn must have an individual plan that describes in detail the unit to be burned, objectives, weather parameters, safety, crew size, equipment, contingencies, and smoke management.

Smoke and the risk of fire escaping onto private property is a major concern for the public regarding the Service's use of prescribed fire. As noted, smoke management is a part of each unit burn plan and burns are not conducted if smoke drift will cause a safety hazard to traffic or adjacent private dwellings. Neighbors are notified prior to burns to ensure precautions in the event that some smoke drifts over residences. Burn plans are designed to minimize escape of fires onto private property through the use of fire breaks, and burning within strict weather parameters and fire behavior models. Each plan also describes contingency plans in case of fire escape, including pre-burn notification of local fire departments and other units of government such as MnDNR fire crews.

Exotic Species Control

Several exotic species exist on Refuge lands and have the potential to significantly affect the diversity and quality of important wildlife habitats. Most notable among these are leafy spurge, which has invaded Refuge grasslands, purple loosestrife in a few of the wetlands, and European buckthorn, which is prevalent in the understory of the oak savanna on top of the bluff and in the floodplain forest. Other exotics include Phragmites, Reed's canary grass, and a small amount of spotted knapweed.

An Exotic Species Management Plan was developed in 2000 and serves to document and organize Refuge efforts to control these species. Consistent with this plan, biological control is used wherever possible followed by mechanical removal of the plants. Chemical control of these exotics is only used as a last resort. Due to the widespread distribution of these exotics, the Refuge has chosen to place emphasis on the control of leafy spurge followed by purple loosestrife and European buckthorn.

To date, leafy spurge beetles have been released on the Upgrala Unit in cooperation with the U.S. Department of Agriculture and the Minnesota Department of Agriculture. Beetles have been released on most spurge sites on the Refuge. In addition, purple loosestrife beetles, including several different species, have been released on Refuge sites. Finally, European buckthorn has been removed by cutting on a limited basis.

Habitat Management on the Wetland Management District

The 14-county Wetland Management District is in the transition zone between the eastern deciduous forest and the tallgrass prairie. Consequently, lands acquired contain a variety of wetland, grassland, and forest habitats. Our primary objective for waterfowl production areas and easements is to restore and manage diverse, productive, and sustainable native plant

USFWS File Photograph

communities. As with Refuge lands, these habitats will be periodically managed to maintain their value to waterfowl as well as other wildlife species. It should be noted that several of the waterfowl production areas in the District are former agricultural lands that contained deciduous forests. Where this occurs, these lands are being restored to grassland-wetland complexes and primarily managed for waterfowl production and grassland nesting birds.

Wetlands
A variety of wetlands occur on the Waterfowl Production Areas and easements within the District and provide important habitat for waterfowl, waterbirds, and associated species. Where possible, these wetlands are being restored to their historic levels. Due to challenging logistics associated with these scattered tracts, water control structures are only installed in rare instances.

Grasslands
All former agricultural fields are converted to grassland to provide for good waterfowl and grassland bird nesting cover. A mixture of six species of native grass and 30 species of native forbs are generally used for these sites. Once established, prescribed burns are used to maintain the areas' vigor and value to wildlife.

Oak Savanna
A small amount of oak savanna occurs on a few Waterfowl Production Areas. Most of these areas have been identified and will be restored to historic communities as time and resources permit. As with grasslands, prescribed burns will be used on these areas periodically to maintain their diversity and wildlife values.

Forests
Small stands of eastern deciduous forest occur on some Waterfowl Production Areas that provide some limited habitat for forest birds. No active management is contemplated in the foreseeable future for these forests.

Habitat Management: Private Lands Program

The Partners for Fish and Wildlife Program is very important to Minnesota Valley National Wildlife Refuge and its District since significant wetland, riparian and grassland habitats have been restored throughout the area. The seamless implementation of Refuge, District, and Partners programs also serve to restore and protect an array of wildlife habitat located in uplands as well as in the floodplain. These restorations provide excellent production and migration habitat for area wildlife and serve to strengthen community support for wildlife conservation issues.

Since 1987, more than 10,000 acres of habitat have been restored by Refuge staff through the Partners program. This program has fostered excellent relationships between the Service and many local partners including the MnDNR, the Natural Resource Conservation Service, the Metropolitan Council, soil and water conservation districts, conservation clubs and organizations and, most importantly, private landowners. Refuge private lands biologists serve to "broker" the programs of others with the common goal of restoring and protecting additional wildlife habitats on private lands.

Fish, Wildlife, and Plant Monitoring

The monitoring of fish, wildlife, and their habitats at the Refuge and District is conducted to provide information that is used to make management decisions and support statewide and national conservation efforts. The Resource Inventory Plan, which contains protocols for all monitoring, inventories, surveys and investigations, is the foundation of the biological program for the Refuge and District. Among other items, each protocol describes its purpose, methods, study area, data analysis, and data storage. Within the Plan, the protocols are organized into one of three categories. These categories are Baseline Information, Management Monitoring, and Cooperative Projects. It should be noted that the Resource Inventory Plan is a living document that is constantly subject to change and improvement. Fish, wildlife, and plant monitoring activities currently existing on the Refuge and District are summarized in the following paragraphs.

Bald Eagle Inventory: All Bald Eagle nests on the Refuge are monitored monthly by staff and volunteers to obtain basic habitat and phenology data. All information is shared with the MnDNR Nongame Program, which monitors nesting activity throughout the state.

Colonial Bird Surveys: The Wilkie Unit supports a large Great Blue Heron/Great Egret colony on the west shore of Blue Lake. Winter nest and summer nestling counts are conducted annually to monitor trends in the breeding population and reproductive success of the colony. The number of Double-crested Cormorant, Green Heron, and Black-crowned Night Heron nests are also recorded.

Point Counts for Songbirds: This protocol was developed to document the non-game bird species that are using mature floodplain forest located on the Refuge.

Frog and Toad Calling Survey: Frog/toad calling surveys are conducted annually at specific Refuge units to determine population status and diversity. The survey methods were adopted from the North American Amphibian Monitoring Program. The data collected is shared with Minnesota Frog Watch, which administers the Minnesota frog/toad survey efforts.

Marsh Birds: These species are surveyed using a modified version of the Marsh Monitoring Program developed by Bird Studies Canada. Every 5 years play back is used to detect the presence of Virginia Rails, Sora, Least Bitterns, American Bitterns, Pied-billed Grebes, King Rails, Common Moorhens, and American Coots.

Muskrat and Beaver Lodge Index: Muskrat numbers are monitored annually on select Refuge Unit marshes using winter ground count methods to estimate reproductive success. House counts are conducted and occupancy confirmed, via temperature probes, during winter months when ice thickness permits safe foot travel. Beaver lodges are also noted during the muskrat surveys.

Waterfowl: Waterfowl surveys are conducted monthly (biweekly during migration) on specific wetlands throughout the Refuge. The data are used to provide managers and the public with current information on the distribution and abundance of waterfowl using the Refuge, and to identify annual trends in waterfowl use.

Waterbird Inventory: Waterbird counts are conducted in conjunction with waterfowl surveys and provide information about distribution and relative use of Refuge wetlands.

Invertebrates: Recently, Refuge volunteers began compiling a list of lepidopterans (butterflies) and moths found in the Refuge as well as a voucher collection to be used in the Refuge Visitor Center. Most of the survey data and collecting efforts were conducted on the Louisville, Upgrala, and Rapids Lake units with hopes to expand the effort to other parts of the Refuge.

Vegetative Cover Mapping: Refuge units and District lands have been mapped according to the Minnesota Land Cover Classification System that was recently developed by the MnDNR in cooperation with many others. The classification system is a five-level hierarchial design, permitting a gradation of refinement relevant to any land cover mapping project. This system is valuable in an urban interface because it combines vegetative cover mapping with the mapping of artificial and impervious features.

Floodplain Forest Restoration Effectiveness: This protocol was designed to test a variety of floodplain forest restoration techniques to identify which technique or techniques successfully reduces the cover of reed canary grass. In addition, the survivability of planted trees and the natural regeneration of seedling trees into the restoration area will be investigated. This information will help management focus on a technique that is most effective for restoring floodplain forest.

Louisville Swamp Oak Savanna: A long-term monitoring plan is in place to track changes in the flora and fauna communities before and after management actions are conducted. The purpose is to assist in determining the success of the oak savanna restoration efforts on Louisville Swamp.

Rapids Lake Oak Savanna: A long-term monitoring plan is in place to track the vegetative changes that occur in response to oak savanna restoration efforts on the Rapids Lake Unit.

Purple Loosestrife: The Refuge has developed a monitoring protocol to evaluate the success of *Galerucella* beetles released on wetlands within areas of high purple loosestrife infestations. This monitoring will continue as additional beetles are released wherever this exotic plant occurs.

Native Prairie Fire Management: This monitoring protocol is used to assess the effectiveness of fire management on select samples of original native prairie. The method was initially used to collect baseline and postburn information on the Upgrala Bluff, but the same method can be used to monitor changes at other prairie sites.

Restored Prairie Fire Management: This protocol is currently being developed and it will monitor the effects of prescribed burning on a select sample of restored prairie habitat.

Leafy Spurge Biological Control: This protocol was developed to monitor the effects of releasing beetles as biological agents for the control of leafy spurge.

Water Quality: In fiscal year 2002, we decided to initiate a new wetland health protocol that is known as the Wetland Health Evaluation Project. This protocol uses invertebrate and vegetative indices developed by staff at the Minnesota Pollution Control Agency to help determine the health of wetlands. This method and basic water quality monitoring will focus on obtaining baseline information and long-term water quality trends of wetlands throughout the Refuge.

White-tailed Deer Surveys: In an effort to determine the distribution and density of whitetail deer in the Twin Cities area, the MnDNR conducts an annual winter deer survey; a portion of this survey is conducted on Refuge lands. This information is used to estimate Refuge deer populations and to determine the effectiveness of deer control efforts.

Gypsy Moth Trapping: In cooperation with the U.S. Department of Agriculture, gypsy moth traps at several locations on the Refuge are used to determine the occurrence of this species. No gypsy moths have been discovered on Refuge lands since this cooperative program was initiated in 1991.

Mid-Winter Waterfowl Survey: In cooperation with the MnDNR, Refuge staff conduct a mid-winter waterfowl survey to assist in determining waterfowl distribution and habitat utilization throughout the nation. A total of 63 sites located throughout the Twin Cities area are surveyed in January of each year.

Predator and Furbearer Scent Post Surveys: This survey is conducted annually to determine the relative distribution and abundance of these species on Refuge lands. In addition, this information is provided to the MnDNR for incorporation into that agency's statewide database.

Refuge Public Recreation, Environmental Education and Outreach

The second component of the Refuge's mission identifies the need to develop high quality wildlife-dependent recreation and interpretive programs for Twin Cities residents. Consequently, a variety of hiking trails, interpretive trails, and related facilities have been developed over the years. Most of the river units of the Refuge are connected to the Minnesota Valley State Trail, which is authorized to be constructed from Fort Snelling upstream to LeSueur. At the time of this writing, there is a movement among conservation organizations and trail users to extend the Minnesota Valley State Trail along the full length of the Minnesota River. This proposal will likely be considered by the Minnesota State Legislature in the near future.

The visitor center, which is located in Bloomington, is a main attraction of the Refuge and serves as a welcoming and orientation site for Refuge visitors. The 32,000-square-foot facility was opened to the public in September 1990 and contains nearly 8,000 square feet of exhibit space, a 120-seat auditorium, two multi-purpose educational classrooms, a resource library, a hearth room, a bookstore, administrative offices, a service garage and storage space. An observation deck is located opposite the main entry of the building. Parking is provided for 125 cars and buses.

An art gallery is also administered within the Visitor Center for local artists to display their natural resource related works. On an annual basis, approximately 10 artists are provided this opportunity.

In addition to environmental education and interpretive programming, the Visitor Center and its equipment are used to a limited degree by non-profit organizations for their monthly meetings. These groups include the Friends of the Minnesota Valley, the Minnesota River Valley Audubon Chapter, the Minnesota Nature Photography Club, and the Native Plant Society.

Estimated Refuge visitation ranges between 250,000 and 300,000 each year. Visitors enjoy a variety of activities including priority public uses such as hunting, fishing, wildlife observation, wildlife photography, wildlife interpretation, and environmental education. General visitation at the Visitor Center peaked out at nearly 53,000 in 1991 but has since declined to less than 25,000 each year.

Hunting
Various forms of hunting are allowed in selected units of the Refuge. Portions of the Wilkie Unit and all of the Louisville Swamp and Rapids Lake units are open to archery deer hunting. Public hunting for waterfowl, small game, and turkey is permitted south of the Middle Road on the Louisville Swamp Unit. Waterfowl hunting is allowed on Rice Lake in the Wilkie Unit. In addition, the Rapids Lake Unit is open to public hunting in accordance with state regulations.

Youth Waterfowl Program
The Refuge in cooperation with the Minnesota Waterfowl Association and other partners sponsors a youth waterfowl hunting program each year. The purpose of this program is to teach youth how to hunt waterfowl both ethically and safely. In addition to teaching young people waterfowl hunting techniques, the instructors also provide information about wildlife conservation, wetland ecology, and regulations. Following classroom instruction, the youth are provided the opportunity to trap shoot with their patterned shotguns, and to hunt on Refuge lands in the presence of their mentor. This is a popular program its goal is to instruct 30 young people annually in the art and science of waterfowling. A wild game recognition dinner is normally held each winter following the hunt.

Hunting Opportunities for Persons with Disabilities
For several years, Capable Partners, Inc. has been granted a special use permit to conduct waterfowl hunting on the north shore of Rice Lake of the Upgrala Unit for hunters with disabilities. The Refuge has provided wheel-chair accessible blinds, a boat dock, and an access road. In 2001, the Refuge expanded opportunities for this group by establishing two wheelchair-accessible turkey blinds on the Raids Lake Unit. Over the years, this partnership has provided some unique experiences to outdoor enthusiasts who normally do not have the opportunity to hunt or access to public hunting lands.

Fishing
The Refuge offers a variety of opportunities for anglers. The most popular spots are from the banks of the Minnesota River on the Long Meadow Lake and Black Dog units where catfish and carp are the most common catch. The Bass Ponds also offer anglers an opportunity to try their luck. Over the past few years, the Refuge has seen a significant increase in fishing by immigrants. Hispanics in particular commonly use the Refuge in addition to members of the Russian and Hmong communities. Due to significant sources of contamination, Refuge signage and officers inform the Minnesota River anglers about the dangers of eating fish caught from these waters. Spanish language fishing regulations as well as consumption advisories are available to assist with this effort.

Since 1994, two wheelchair accessible fishing docks have been constructed, one at Cedar Pond and one at Youth Fishing Pond. These facilities provide an opportunity for members of the disabled community to participate in fishing activities.

Youth Fishing Day
The Refuge and several of its partners host an annual Youth Fishing Day at the Bass Ponds for inner city and community youth. This is a very popular program in which 200 young people and their families enjoy learning about proper and ethical angling techniques. Many partners, including the Red Lake Nation and Gander Mountain, Inc., have helped make this event successful year after year.

Wildlife Observation
The Refuge is a popular destination for visitors seeking opportunities for observing wildlife in their native habitats. The Minnesota River Valley, including the Refuge, is regionally known as an excellent bird watching location, especially during spring and fall migrations. Species ranging from warblers to Wood Ducks to Bald Eagles are commonly observed in the Refuge's diverse habitats. Other visitors enjoy observing resident wildlife such as white-tailed deer, beaver and, on occasion, river otter.

To the degree possible, the Refuge cooperates with the Minnesota River Valley Audubon Chapter and others to promote wildlife observation activities. Several members of this Chapter organize bird watching trips that involve visits to various portions of the Refuge. Likewise, the Refuge is working with Audubon and others in establishing a Minnesota River Birding Trail, which will have several stops on or near the Refuge.

Wildlife Photography
Consistent with the opportunities to view wildlife, many visitors also take the opportunity to photograph these critters and their associated habitats. These photographers, who have access to most portions of the Refuge, take advantage of early mornings and late evenings to shoot photographs. Due to periodic flooding of most Refuge lands, no permanent photo blinds have been constructed. With funds donated by North American Nature Photography Associated and labor provided by the Tree Trust, Inc., two portable photo blinds were constructed in 2001. These blinds will be used in subsequent years to promote wildlife photography on the Refuge.

Photograph by Scott Sharkey

Over the years, numerous volunteers and neighbors have obtained some extraordinary photographs of Refuge wildlife and scenery. These people have graciously shared their photographs with the Refuge and they have become invaluable in the development of brochures and publications.

Wildlife Interpretation
The primary interpretive theme for the Refuge is described by asking the pivotal question of "How Should We Live Together?" This concept was formulated in 1992 under contract and explored the relationship of this urban refuge to its surrounding communities. This concept and the history, conservation, and importance of wildlife to our society

are interpreted through a variety of mediums. The approximately 125 special programs conducted by Refuge staff or volunteer interpreters annually is the foundation of this interpretation. These programs, combined with Refuge brochures, Visitor Center exhibits, and interpretive nature trails, help the visiting public connect their lives with their natural environment. Nationally recognized special events such as International Migratory Bird Day, National Wildlife Refuge Week, and Earth Day are also conducted by Refuge staff to advance the public's understanding and knowledge of wildlife.

Environmental Education
Environmental education is a very important Refuge activity and is conducted year-round in the Visitor Center, on the Refuge and, at times, in off-site classrooms. Public, private, and home schools from throughout the Twin Cities participate in these environmental education programs. In addition, the Refuge has provided programs to schools as far away as Stillwater, Rochester, and St. Cloud. Approximately 10,000 students participate each year with the majority of the students coming from elementary and middle schools. All programs are free of charge and they can be led by staff (park rangers) or by teachers. The curriculums consist of a variety of subject matters and are tailored to meet the needs of youth in pre-school on up to 12th grade. Refuge staff have also hosted educator workshops designed to assist teachers in meeting their school's environmental educational needs. A brief summary of the environmental education curriculum is summarized below.

Pre-school
Since its inception in 1997, the pre-school program has been very popular with area daycare centers and pre-school facilities. More than 2,000 children, plus their parents and guardians, have enrolled in this program each year. The 1.5-hour programs expose the children to concepts such as migration, squirrel behaviors, wildlife habitat such as trees, and wildlife tracks and sign. Each program includes a story or activity, a take home craft project, and a hike.

Kindergarten – 3rd Grade
Created in 1999, the programs are curriculum-based with pre- and post-site activities. The curriculum contains five days of activities, one day being an 1.5-hour visit to the Refuge with a park ranger. Programs cover four topics: birds, insects, habitats, and the earth.

4th – 12th Grade
These 11 field-based programs focus on resource management issues and explore the Refuge from a wildlife biologist's perspective through biological surveys and observations. Among other activities, students learn how water quality affects the health of the Refuge by comparing the chemical, physical, and biological characteristics of Refuge wetlands through macro invertebrate and water sampling. Other topics include wildlife monitoring, prairie interrelationships, etc.

Volunteer Contributions
Public interest in and concern for the natural environment are the seeds that grew into Minnesota Valley National Wildlife Refuge, and public commitment has proven lasting. Over the years, numerous volunteers have made significant contributions to the development, operations, and maintenance of the Refuge and its facilities. Most of these individuals share a great deal of passion for the fish, wildlife, and plant communities of this area.

Volunteers have contributed in many different ways that range from teaching pre-schoolers the concept of migration, to inventorying reptiles and amphibians, and to the clean-up of building sites through the operation of backhoes and bulldozers. It almost goes without saying that volunteers are very important to the Refuge and the District and will continue to be for a very long time.

Wetland Management District Public Recreation, Environmental Education and Outreach

The Waterfowl Production Areas located in the District also provide local communities with the opportunity to participate in wildlife-dependent recreation and environmental education. All Waterfowl Production Areas are open to hunting and fishing consistent with state regulations. Soberg Waterfowl Production Area is closed to the use of single projectiles (rifles and shotgun slugs) due to safety concerns and a City of Lakeville ordinance.

To a limited degree, Waterfowl Production Areas are used by the general public for bird watching, wildlife interpretation, and environmental education. A good potential exists to develop quality environmental education curriculums, consistent with State graduation standards, for use by rural schools on nearby Waterfowl Production Areas.

The Minnesota Valley Wetland Management District is one of seven Districts within Minnesota that combined administer nearly 800 Waterfowl Production Areas. The visiting public, neighbors, local units of government, and the MnDNR benefit when management and permitted uses on Waterfowl Production Areas are consistent from one end of the state to the other. This Comprehensive Conservation Plan provides the opportunity to articulate policies that have been in place for many years but have not always been consistently applied or communicated. New national policies and regulations governing management and use of the Refuge System also prompted a review and fine tuning of what uses will and will not be allowed, and the stipulations all Districts will follow when allowing certain uses.

A summary of generally prohibited and permitted uses and activities on Waterfowl Production Areas in Minnesota is provided below. For each of the permitted activities, the reader is encouraged to review the separate compatibility determinations found in Appendix D. Stipulations or operating guidelines are provided in most compatibility determinations. Except where noted, these rules also apply to lands within the Refuge Units.

Public Uses Generally Prohibited
- Off-road vehicle use, including snowmobiles and ATVs (except on State Trail)
- Camping
- Open fires
- Discharge of firearms except during State hunting seasons
- Use of motorized water craft
- Dog trials
- Horseback riding (except on State Trail)
- Commercial bait collecting
- Beekeeping

Public Uses Permitted
(See Compatibility Determinations in Appendix D)
- Hunting in accordance with Refuge-specific seasons and regulations
- Wildlife observation
- Photography
- Fishing in accordance with State seasons and regulations
- Environmental education
- Interpretation for individuals or groups
- Trapping in accordance with State seasons and regulations (permit required on Refuge)
- Berry and nut collecting for personal use
- Limited plant and seed collection for decorative purposes

(Note: These uses include the use of non-motorized means of access including hiking, snowshoeing, cross-country skiing, or where appropriate, bicycling on existing trails.)

Generally Permitted Management Activities Done by Others, and Miscellaneous Activities/Programs
- Haying for grassland management
- Farming for grassland management
- Timber or firewood harvest
- Food plots and feeders for resident wildlife
- Wildlife nesting structures
- Archaeological surveys
- Special access for disabled users
- Irrigation travelways across easement wetlands
- Temporary road improvement outside of existing right-of-way
- Special dedications/ceremonies
- Wetland access facilities
- WPA parking facilities
- Local Fire Department Training – Prescribed Burning
- Local Fire Department Training – Burning of Surplus Buildings on New Acquisitions

Other Reoccurring Uses Handled on Case-by-Case Basis
- Grazing for grassland management
- New or expanded rights-of-way requests
- Ditch or channel maintenance to facilitate waterflow
- Major new facilities associated with public uses
- Commercial filming
- Special events
- Animal collecting requests
- Other requests for uses not listed above

Refuge Mitigation Projects

Background
Beginning in 1989, the Metropolitan Airports Commission (MAC) began to explore alternatives for expanding the operations of the Minneapolis-St. Paul International Airport. This action lead to the preparation of an environmental impact statement that

considered building a brand new airport or expanding the existing facility. Ultimately, the Minnesota State Legislature weighed in on this issue and directed MAC to construct a new north-south runway on existing airport property.

The new runway will be constructed on the west side of the airport roughly parallel to Cedar Avenue. Although the south threshold of the runway will be nearly 1 mile away from Refuge lands, the use of this runway will result in overflights, on average, every other minute between 500 and 1,000 feet above the river valley. The impact of these overflights to the Refuge and its various programs is significant. Although current literature is not conclusive concerning the impacts of overflights on area wildlife, there is no question that the noise generated from these flights will significantly affect noise-sensitive public use activities such as bird watching, environmental education, and nature hikes.

Following prolonged negotiations, the U.S. Fish and Wildlife Service agreed to a cash settlement of $26,090,000 to compensate for damages associated to Refuge facilities and programs. As specified in the Minnesota Valley National Wildlife Refuge Funding Agreement dated September 14, 1999, a non-profit organization would be established to administer these funds and to serve as a mitigation agent to work on behalf of MAC. In close coordination and cooperation with the Service, mitigation activities to be accomplished include but are not limited to:

(1) Acquisition of a minimum of 4,090 acres of lands within the area identified as appropriate, and making such lands available for Refuge environmental education and wildlife-dependent recreational opportunities either through donation to the United States to be administered by the Service or its successor as part of the Refuge, or through a cooperative or other agreement for such use at no cost to the United States;

(2) Construction and development of a visitor and education center on the Rapids Lake Unit or another suitable location approved by the Service or its successor for the Refuge; and

(3) Construction of visitor access, environmental education, and wildlife interpretive facilities at suitable locations approved by the Service or its successor on Refuge lands.

Consistent with the Agreement, the final components of the Refuge Mitigation Plan have been developed by the Service and are included in this Plan as Appendix L. In developing this Plan, the Service sought to replace the public use and wildlife values that will be affected on the Refuge by future aircraft overflights. In addition, the Service sought to provide mechanisms for the long-term administration and management of the new lands and facilities that will be acquired with Refuge Mitigation Funds.

On August 31, 2000, the Minnesota Valley National Wildlife Refuge Trust, Inc. (Trust) was formally established for the primary purpose of administering these funds and completing Refuge mitigation projects. Consistent with prior agreements, MAC transferred $26,090,000 into the account of the Trust. The Trust's Board of Directors includes a representative of the following organizations: Friends of the Minnesota Valley, Minnesota Department of Natural Resources, National Audubon Society, Minnesota Waterfowl Association, and the Minnesota River Joint Powers Board.

<u>Specific Mitigation Projects</u>
Included as strategies within this CCP are projects that have been designated as airport
mitigation projects. They include the acquisition of lands, the construction of the environmental education center and interpretive facilities, plus intern housing. These projects
are described in greater detail in Appendix L.

Archaeological and Cultural Resources

The Refuge Manager is responsible for applying several historic preservation laws and
regulations to ensure that historic properties are identified and are protected to the
extent possible within the Refuge's established purposes and the Refuge System mission.
Early in project planning for all construction projects and other ground-disturbing
actions, the Refuge Manager contacts the Regional Historic Preservation Officer to

initiate the Section 106 process. The Refuge Manager
also will inform and request comments from the public
and local officials through presentations, meetings,
and media notices. Public involvement may also be
achieved as part of the environmental planning
required by the National Environmental Policy Act of
1969.

Archeological investigations and collecting on Refuge
and District lands are performed only in the public
interest by qualified archeologists or persons recommended by the Governor working under an Archaeological Resources Protection Act permit issued by the
Service's Regional Director. The Refuge Manager must also issue a special use permit.
As of 2001, five archeological investigations have produced 4,000 artifacts from Refuge
and District lands. Artifacts are or will be stored at the Minnesota Historical Society
under a cooperative agreement. Artifacts are owned by the Federal Government and can
be recalled by the Service at any time.

Refuge staff take steps to prevent unauthorized collecting and violators are cited or
other appropriate action is taken. Violations are reported to the Regional Historic
Preservation Officer.

Law Enforcement

Enforcement of Federal wildlife laws, as well as regulations specific to the Refuge
System, is an integral part of Refuge and District operations. Law enforcement plays a
crucial role in ensuring that natural and cultural resources are protected and that visitors
encounter a safe environment, even within a major metropolitan area. The Refuge
currently has two employees, one full-time and one collateral duty, who are commissioned
to conduct law enforcement duties on Federal property. However, Federal law enforcement is a cooperative effort by many agencies in the region. Cooperative relationships
and strategies have been developed with state conservation officers and all county sheriff
departments in the area.

USFWS Photograph

Wilderness Review

As part of the CCP process, we reviewed lands within the legislative boundaries of the Refuge for wilderness suitability. No lands were found suitable for designation as Wilderness as defined in the Wilderness Act of 1964. The Refuge does not contain 5,000 contiguous roadless acres nor does it have any units of sufficient size to make their preservation practicable as Wilderness. Lands acquired for the Refuge have been substantially affected by humans, particularly through agriculture and transportation infrastructure.

Future Management Direction: Where We Want To Go Tomorrow

Goals, Objectives and Strategies

Goals, objectives and strategies for the Minnesota Valley National Wildlife Refuge and Wetland Management District were developed with the participation of many citizens, cooperating agencies, conservation organizations, and Refuge staff. The following pages describe the goals established for major management areas, objectives for achieving those goals, and the specific strategies that will be employed by Refuge staff. The goals are organized into the broad categories of Biological, Land Protection, and Public Use.

USFWS File Photograph

Biological Goals:

Goal 1. Floodplain Forest:
To restore, protect, and maintain natural species diversity while emphasizing priority wildlife and plants characteristic of floodplain forests within the northern tallgrass prairie ecosystem.

Discussion: The forested floodplain of the Minnesota River Valley provides migration and production habitat for several bird species that are significant locally or are included in the Region 3 Regional Conservation Priority list. These include the Red-headed Woodpecker, Red-shouldered Hawk and Wood Duck. Numerous songbird species nest within or migrate along floodplain forests. Bald Eagles also use floodplain forests on the Refuge or throughout the Wetland Management District for either migration or nesting habitat. Wading birds, such as the Great Blue Heron and Black-crowned Night-Heron, nest in colonies within the floodplain. These colonial nesting sites are vulnerable to human disturbance and destruction by high winds. The endangered dwarf trout lily also occurs in floodplain forests within part of the Wetland Management District.

1.1 Objective: By 2017, provide 4,700 acres of floodplain forest along the Minnesota River and major tributaries to benefit Bald Eagles, cavity-nesting birds such as Wood Ducks, colonial-nesting wading birds and rare plant communities (Figures 9-12).

Figure 9: Future Habitat Conditions (2017) Long Meadow Lake and Black Dog Units

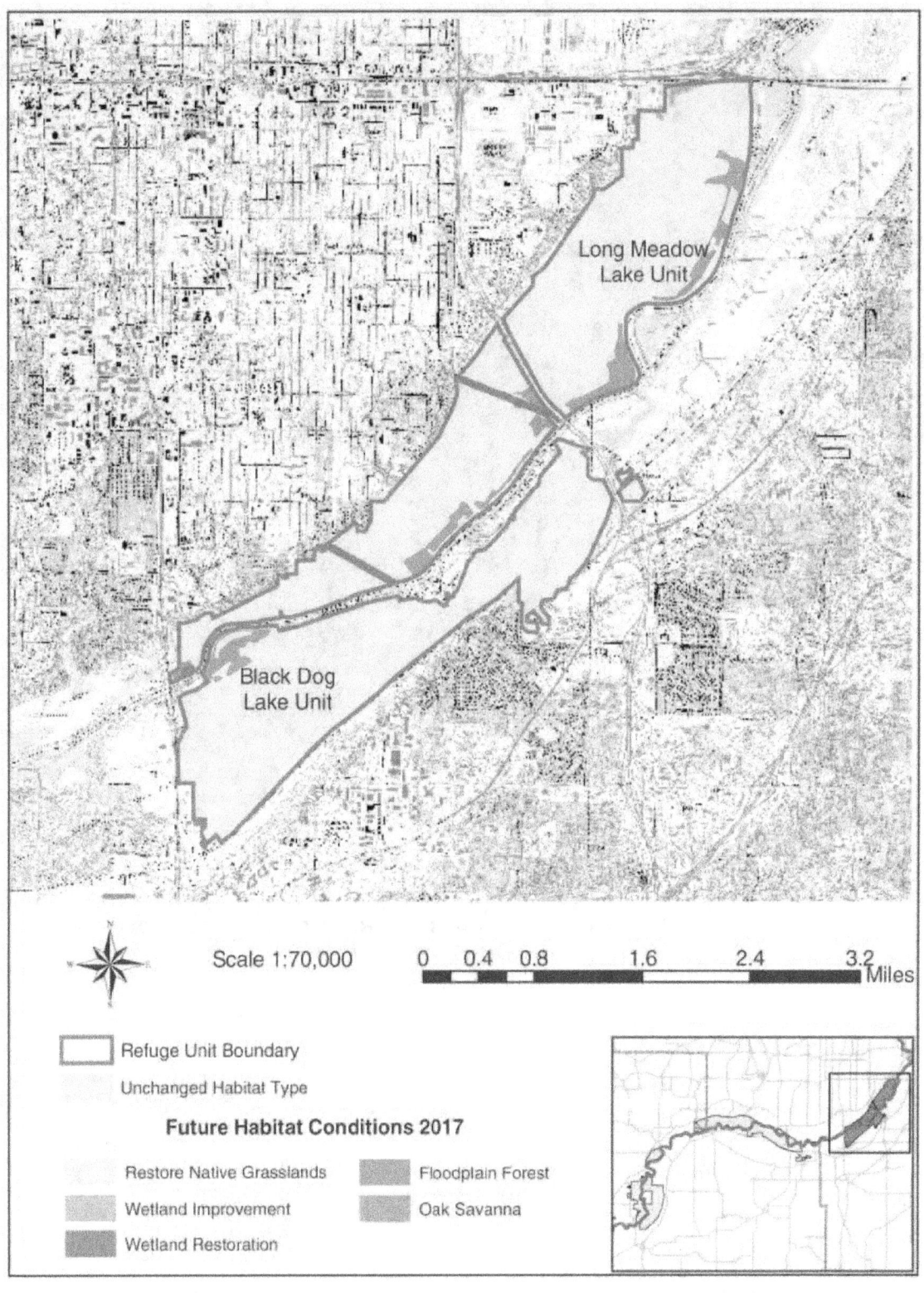

Figure 10: Future Habitat Conditions Upgrala, Wilkie and Bloomington Ferry Units

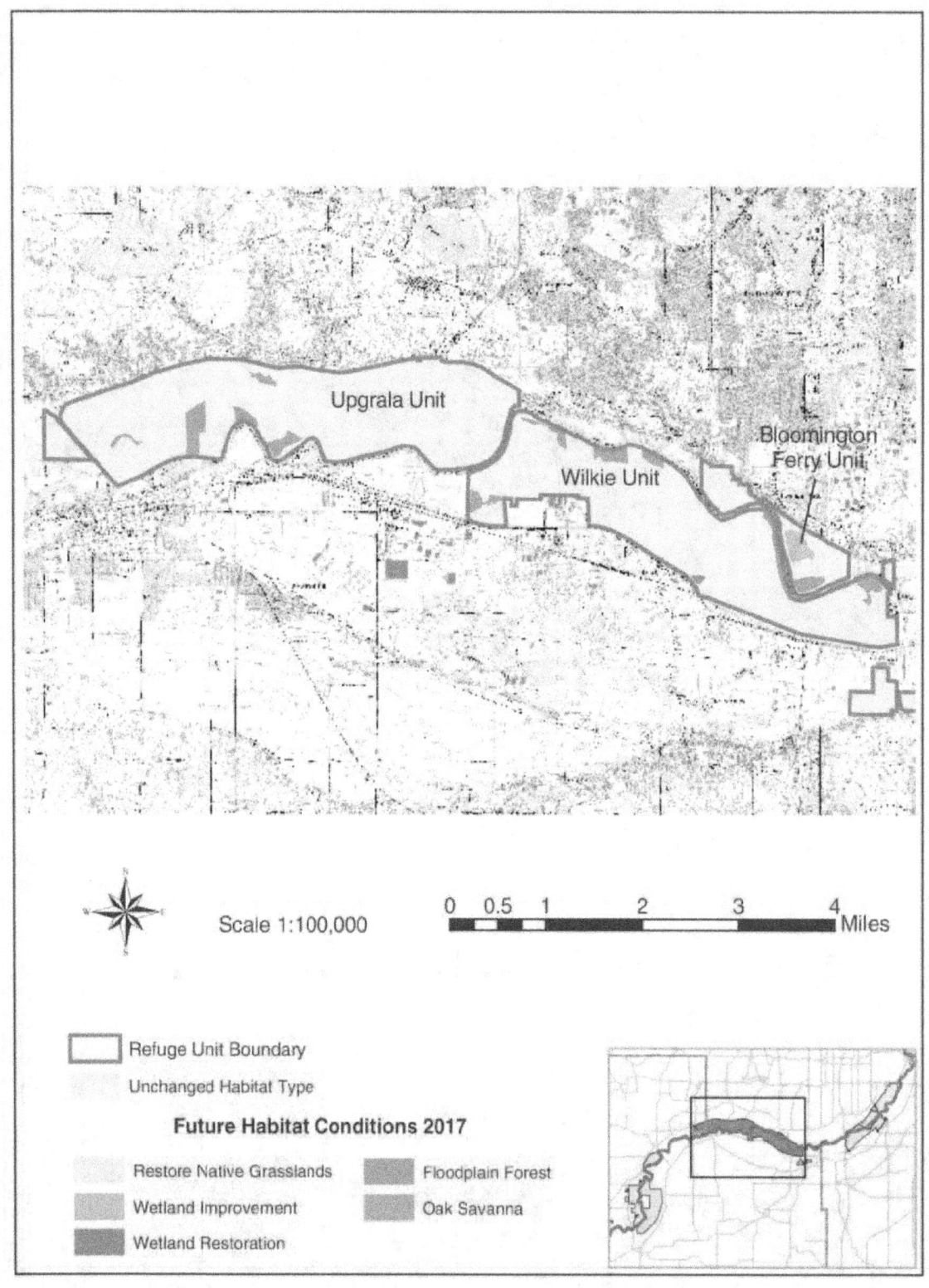

Figure 11: Future Habitat Conditions Chaska Unit (2017)

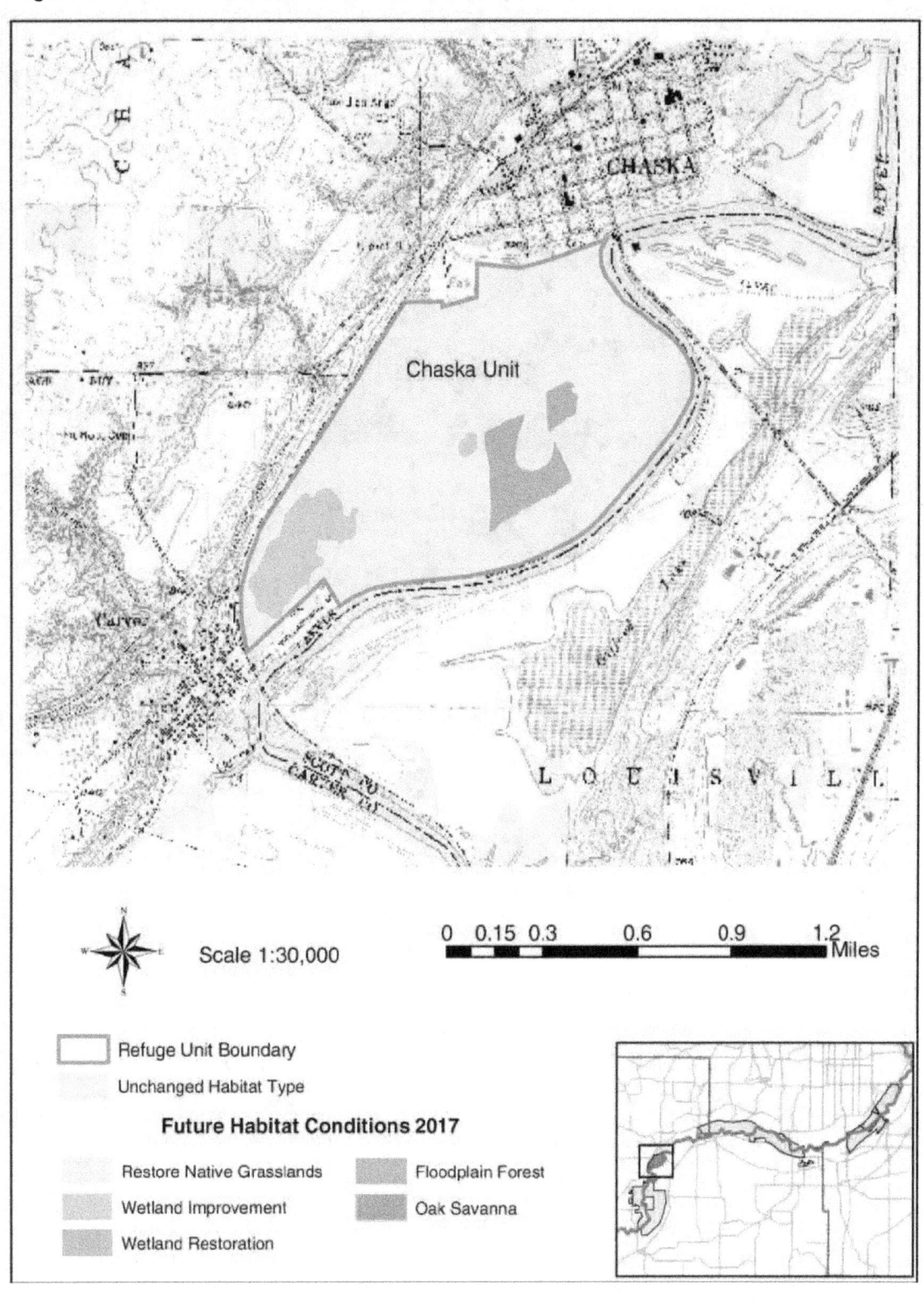

Chaska Unit

Scale 1:30,000

0   0.15 0.3   0.6   0.9   1.2
                                                    Miles

☐ Refuge Unit Boundary

  Unchanged Habitat Type

Future Habitat Conditions 2017

  Restore Native Grasslands   Floodplain Forest

  Wetland Improvement   Oak Savanna

  Wetland Restoration

Figure 12: Future Habitat Conditions Rapids Lake and Louisville Swamp Units (2017)

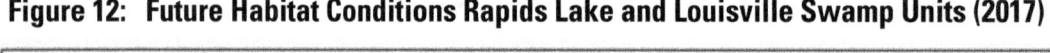

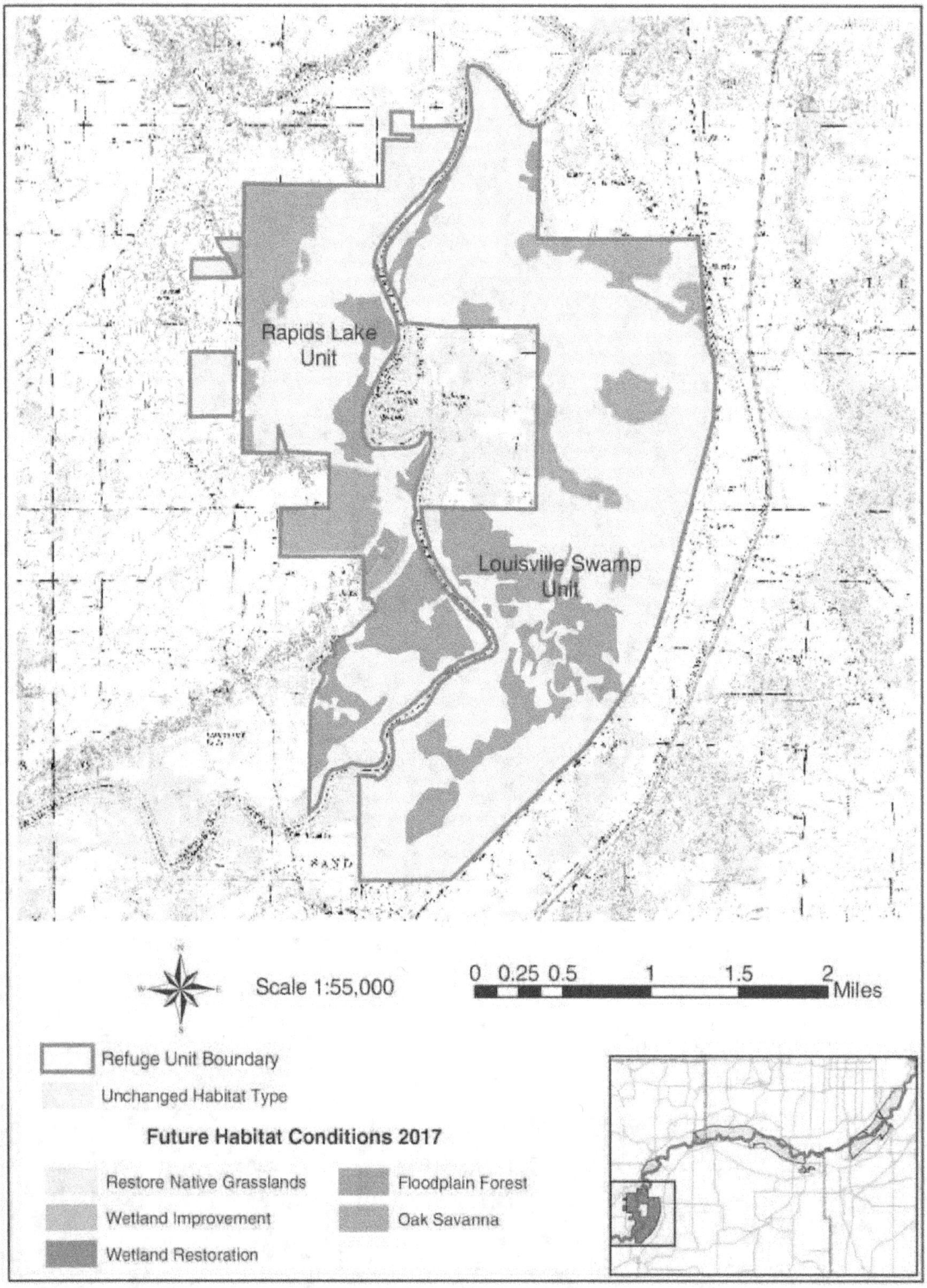

Rapids Lake Unit
Louisville Swamp Unit
SAND
N
S
Scale 1:55,000
0 0.25 0.5 1 1.5 2
Miles
Refuge Unit Boundary
Unchanged Habitat Type
Future Habitat Conditions 2017
Restore Native Grasslands
Wetland Improvement
Wetland Restoration
Floodplain Forest
Oak Savanna

Note: The acreage estimate includes lands within the authorized boundary of the Refuge only. New Refuge Units along the Minnesota River would provide additional floodplain forest habitats.

Strategies:

1.1.1   Through research and investigation, determine the long-term viability of the floodplain forest community that exists on Refuge lands.

1.1.2   Employ a senior wildlife biologist (GS 11/12). This position will benefit all of the biological goals set forth in this CCP.

1.1.3   Continue to acquire important floodplain forests that provide valuable wildlife habitats within the Minnesota River Valley and throughout the Wetland Management District. Where possible, block sizes greater than 100 acres should be acquired.

1.1.4   Protect existing Bald Eagle nests and heron and egret nesting colonies from human disturbance throughout the breeding season.

1.1.5   Complete a forest management plan by 2005 that establishes long-term objectives for each block of floodplain forest that exists on Refuge Units.

1.1.6   Using native species from a tree nursery and root propagation methods, continue to restore no fewer than 100 acres of floodplain forest each year until all potential floodplain forest is restored.

1.1.7   Develop a root propagation nursery using local sources of tree species.

1.1.8   Develop and implement a floodplain forest monitoring protocol designed to assess restoration success, vegetative changes, and wildlife response.

Goal 2. Wetlands:

To restore, protect, and maintain natural species diversity while emphasizing priority fish, wildlife and plants characteristic of wetlands within the northern tallgrass prairie ecosystem.

Discussion: Refuge and District wetlands contribute migration and production habitat for waterfowl, waterbirds, and shorebirds. Several of these key species are regional conservation priorities including the Mallard, Blue-winged Teal, Canvasback, Wood Duck, American Bittern, and Black Tern. Other wildlife species of local significance that use these wetlands include Great Blue Heron, Great Egret, river otter, mink, muskrat and several amphibian species. Floodplain and riverine wetlands located on the Refuge also provide important spawning and nursery habitats for resident fish.

2.1 Objective: By 2017, provide 7,400 acres of wetlands within the floodplain of the Minnesota River and 4,600 acres of prairie pothole wetlands in the Wetland Management District to benefit priority waterfowl species, marsh, shore and wading birds and healthy aquatic ecosystems.

Note: The acreage estimates include lands within the authorized boundary of the Refuge and existing and future Waterfowl Production Areas. New Refuge units along the Minnesota River would provide additional wetland acres.

Strategies:

2.1.1   Maintain the productivity of Refuge wetlands through the installation of water control structures and the active management of water levels through an annual water management plan.

2.1.2   Continue to actively manage wetlands, wet meadows, and fens located on Refuge and Wetland Management District lands through periodic prescribed burning to control invasion of brush and other woody vegetation.

2.1.3   Continue to seek Environmental Management Program funding and other sources of funding to improve, maintain, restore, and manage wetland habitats on Refuge.

2.1.4   Develop monitoring protocols to determine effectiveness of wetland management actions upon vegetative diversity and use by wildlife.

2.1.5   Continue to acquire important wetlands and associated habitats for both the Refuge and Wetland Management District.

2.1.6   Manage and protect the Savage Fen Unit, in cooperation with the MnDNR and others, for as long as the Refuge administers the area.

2.1.7   Inventory aquatic species (fish and macro-invertebrates) in Refuge streams, creeks and lakes using volunteers, students, and Refuge staff. Biologists from the Service's Fishery Resource Office in LaCrosse, Wisconsin, will conduct sampling surveys at least once every 5 years to detect trends in fish abundance and distribution.

2.1.8   Restore Continental Grain berm along Eagle Creek to prevent creek degradation.

2.1.9   Develop and implement a comprehensive water quality monitoring program designed to obtain baseline information and document impacts of storm water events and other adjacent land uses upon Refuge wetland flora and fauna.

2.1.10   Work with partners and continue to identify and seek funding for a variety of research and monitoring projects associated with the Refuge and WMD. More specifically, support the 3-year study entitled "Land Stewardship, Habitation Protection, and Avian Occurrence in the Minnesota Valley National Wildlife Refuge and Wetland Management District." Likewise, continue to support the development of a multi-faceted GIS for the Refuge and WMD.

2.1.11   Seek operational funds to employ up to two biological technicians (GS-404-5/7) to address the District's workload.

2.1.12   Obtain operational funds to employ a maintenance worker (WG-4749-6/7) to assist in restoring and maintaining Wetland District fee and easement lands.

2.2 Objective: Control and ultimately reduce the distribution of exotic plant species on wetlands primarily through biological control methods.

Strategies:

2.2.1   Continue to monitor and release purple loosestrife beetles into Refuge wetlands where purple loosestrife exists.

Photograph by Scott Sharkey

2.2.2   Control the spread of purple loosestrife using biological control methods such as purple loosestrife beetles (*Galerucella* sp.). In cooperation with others, establish a purple loosestrife field nursery to be used as a source of beetles for release on Refuge, Wetland Management District, and other suitable locations.

2.2.3   Within staff and time limitations, seek methods to reduce and control the presence of giant reed grass (Phragmites) that exists on Refuge lands.

2.3 Objective: Control wildlife populations at levels consistent with available habitat to address public safety concerns and to allow effective management of wetlands.

Strategies:

2.3.1   For aircraft safety reasons, continue to cooperate with the Metropolitan Airports Commission in the removal of Canada Geese from the Long Meadow Lake Unit.

2.3.2   Continue to use trapping as a management tool to control beaver populations.

2.4 Objective: Maintain Round Lake at full basin water level (2001 level) to provide migration habitat for Bald Eagles, waterfowl such as Canvasbacks, and Common Loons. Maintain the capability to actively manage water levels in the future upon assurances that periodic drawdowns and reflooding would not cause undue risk to the ecosystem.

Discussion: The 152-acre Round Lake Unit is adjacent to the dismantled Twin Cities Army Ammunition Plant in Arden Hills, Minnesota. The Unit is bounded on the west by industrial development and on the south and east by private homes. The deep sediments of the 120-acre permanent wetland have elevated concentrations of heavy metals including zinc, chromium, and cadmium. In addition, two storm water sewers enter Round Lake which may impact water quality.

The shallow lake is an open body of water and aquatic emergent plants are limited to a narrow fringe of cattail, slender bulrush, and water lily. An existing water control structure provides water level management capabilities and the potential for periodic drawdowns to enhance emergent plant growth for wildlife food and cover. However, water levels for Round Lake have been maintained at a constant level over the past 15 years due to concerns of neighboring landowners and the potential for exposing contaminated sediments.

Strategies:

2.4.1　Assist the U.S. Army and other agencies with studies to determine the threat, if any, of contaminants on aquatic communities.

2.4.2　Develop partnership with educational institutions in the area, such as the nearby Bethel College, to monitor water quality, migratory bird use and collect baseline wildlife data.

2.4.3　Maintain year-round closure of lake to fishing and boating.

2.4.4　Maintain the existing partnership with the City of Arden Hills to provide trail connection through the west side of the unit to complement the City's trail system and to facilitate wildlife observation.

Goal 3. Upland Forest:
To restore, protect, and maintain natural species diversity while emphasizing priority wildlife and plants characteristic of upland forests within the northern tallgrass prairie ecosystem.

Discussion: Upland forests, primarily those located along the bluffs of the river valley, provide migration and production habitat for several species of songbirds that are significant locally or are included in the Region 3 RCP list. Among these species are Red-headed Woodpecker, Northern Flicker, and Wood Thrush. Several locally or regionally significant raptors also use upland forests on the Refuge or throughout the Wetland Management District for either migration, nesting, and in some cases wintering habitat. These species include the Bald Eagle, Red-shouldered Hawk, and Long-eared Owl. The endangered dwarf trout lily also occurs in upland forests within part of the Wetland Management District.

3.1 Objective:　By 2017, provide 1,000 acres of upland forest along the Minnesota River, in 50-acre or larger blocks throughout the Wetland Manage-

Photograph by Scott Sharkey

ment District, to ensure migration and nesting habitat for Bald Eagles, Red-headed Woodpeckers and songbirds.

Note: The acreage estimates include lands within the authorized boundary of the Refuge and existing and future Waterfowl Production Areas. New Refuge Units along the Minnesota River would provide additional upland forest habitats.

Strategies:

3.1.1 Through research and investigation, determine the long-term viability of the upland forest community that exists on Refuge lands.

3.1.2 Continue to acquire upland forest habitats within the Minnesota River Valley and throughout the Wetland Management District. Block sizes greater than 100 acres should be a priority for acquisition.

3.1.3 Complete a forest management plan by 2005 that sets long-term objectives for each block of hillside forest that exists on Refuge Units.

3.1.4 Plant a shrub understory using native species from a tree nursery and/or root propagation nursery.

3.2 Objective: Control and ultimately reduce the distribution of exotic plant species on upland forests primarily through biological control methods.

Strategy:

3.2.1 To the extent possible, and with the use of volunteer and youth groups, seek to control and reduce the distribution of European buckthorn in forested areas through hand cutting and treatment with chemicals.

3.3 Objective: Control wildlife populations at levels consistent with available habitat to address public safety concerns and to allow effective land management.

Strategy:

3.3.1 In cooperation with the MnDNR and local communities, maintain whitetail deer populations at levels consistent with the carrying capacity of available habitat. Allow public hunting where feasible and sharpshooting when needed to maintain populations of 15-25 deer per square mile.

Goal 4. Grasslands and Oak Savanna:
To restore, protect, and maintain natural species diversity while emphasizing priority grassland-dependent wildlife and plants characteristic of the northern tallgrass prairie ecosystem.

Discussion: Refuge and Wetland District grasslands, especially those within the uplands of Waterfowl Production Areas, have the potential to provide benefits for birds that require large blocks of grasslands for nesting success and population viability. Oak savannas, historically found throughout the Minnesota River Valley, also afford critical habitat for some of these birds. This is important because populations of many Region 3 Regional RCP "grassland" bird species, such as Bobolink, Grasshopper Sparrow and Eastern Meadowlark have shown steady declines over the last 35 years. Large grassland patches (over 250 acres), or smaller connected grasslands or those in proximity to other non-forested habitats, provide the best nesting conditions for many area-sensitive bird species. Larger grassland blocks will also increase the nesting success of RCP waterfowl such as Mallards and Blue-winged Teal. In addition, several reptile and butterfly species of Special Concern in the State of Minnesota, such as five-lined skink, racer, gopher snake and western hognose snake, and the Arogos, Leonardus, and Powesheik Skippers will benefit from native grassland management.

4.1 Objective: By 2017, provide 800 acres of original native prairie and 8,700 acres of restored native grasses in block sizes of over 50 acres and with varying grass height, density and grass/forb ratios to benefit grassland-dependent wildlife such as Boblinks, Grasshopper Sparrows and five-lined skinks.

Note: The acreage estimates include lands within the authorized boundary of the Refuge and existing and future Waterfowl Production Areas. New Refuge Units along the Minnesota River would provide additional native grasslands.

Strategies:
4.1.1   Maintain the vigor and productivity of Refuge grasslands by emphasizing the use of a progressive prescribed burning regime under the Fire Management Plan. On an annual basis, burn no less than 1,500 acres located on the Refuge and District.

4.1.2   Assess newly-acquired lands as to their suitability for conversion to native grassland and initiate appropriate conversion practices.

4.1.3   Monitor wildlife and vegetation response using procedures developed in the Refuge's Inventory and Monitoring Plan.

4.1.4   Initiate or continue oak savanna restoration efforts on the Louisville Swamp, Wilkie and Rapids Lake units through removal of unwanted trees and a progressive prescribed burning regime.

4.1.5   Establish prairie and forb nurseries using local ecotype seeds for harvesting and use in restoration of native prairie.

4.1.6   Identify hillside "goat" prairies on the Refuge and maintain or restore as necessary. Methods would include brush removal by volunteers and prescribed burning by trained staff.

4.2 Objective: Control spread and ultimately reduce the distribution of exotic or nuisance plant species on grasslands and oak savannas primarily through biological control methods.

Strategies:
4.2.1   Control spread of invasive woody plant species and noxious weeds using accepted methods such as mechanical, chemical and biological control.

4.2.2   Consistent with the Exotic Species Management Plan prepared for the Refuge, identify and map locations of all existing exotic species infestations.

4.2.3   Continue to release and monitor leafy spurge beetles at sites infested with leafy spurge.

4.2.4   Control the spread and distribution of spotted knapweed through the use of biological control methods.

4.2.5   In cooperation with the U.S. Department of Agriculture and the Minnesota Department of Agriculture, collect leafy spurge beetles that are not needed by the Refuge for release at non-Refuge locations.

Goal 5. Land Protection:
To enhance the integrity of lands within the authorized boundary of the Refuge and contribute to the protection and restoration of fish and wildlife habitats within the Minnesota River watershed.

5.1 Objective: By 2017, achieve the appropriate conservation status necessary for permanent protection and management viability of any remaining lands within the original authorized boundary. This will also address existing and future threats to resources within the authorized Refuge boundaries.

Strategies:
5.1.1   Seek Congressional appropriations and other sources of funds to purchase the Upgrala tract plus any remaining lands within the original authorized Refuge boundary.

5.1.2   In cooperation with the State of Minnesota, seek to transfer the 54-acre Minnesota Department of Transportation (former Northwest Airlines) tract into the Refuge.

5.1.3   Consistent with early correspondence between the Regional Director and the Commissioner of Minnesota Department of Natural Resources, explore the possibility of exchanging Service ownership of the Savage Fen with other lands administered by the MnDNR.

5.1.4   Continue to work cooperatively with cities, counties, developers, and others to address external threats and to avoid future impacts to Refuge flora and fauna due to development of neighboring lands.

5.2 Objective: By 2017, and in cooperation with many others, contribute to the restoration of the Minnesota River by acquiring fee or conservation easements on up to 10,737 additional acres of high quality fish and wildlife habitat within or adjacent to the Minnesota River Valley beyond the existing Refuge boundary and proceeding upstream to Mankato, Minnesota.

Photograph by Scott Sharkey

Discussion: Local communities and state agencies have worked together for years to restore and protect the unique natural qualities of the Minnesota River Valley. Efforts within the last decade have focused on reducing the sediment and pollutant load within the river to make it "swimmable and fishable" as soon as possible. The Service would like to contribute to that effort. The river and its riparian habitat is important to Federal trust species such as waterfowl, migratory songbirds and endangered plants. Land acquisition for new refuge units, either in fee or through conservation easements, and subsequent habitat restoration is one way the Service can contribute to the collective goal of a clean river and abundant and healthy fish, wildlife and plant communities.

Numerous participants during the CCP public scoping process encouraged us to consider land acquisition upriver. The environmental assessment included with this CCP (Appendix A) and Land Protection Plan (Appendix I) provide agency decision makers and the public with an analysis of management alternatives, including refuge expansion. **Please see the Land Protection Plan for descriptions and maps of proposed new Refuge units.**

Strategies:
5.2.1   From the amount identified above, use Trust funds to acquire no less than 4,090 acres in order to satisfy airport mitigation settlement requirements.

5.2.2   Make a concerted effort to leverage all land acquisition funding with those of other programs such as the Wetland Restoration Program, North American Wetlands Conservation Act (NAWCA), Conservation Reserve Enhancement Program, and Reinvest in Minnesota.

5.2.3 Work with the City of Bloomington to fully develop City property along the Minnesota River into good quality wildlife habitat.

5.2.4 Enhance Refuge GIS capability for assessing impacts of adjacent or upstream land use on Refuge flora and fauna.

5.2.5 Work with Friends of the Minnesota Valley to increase landowner participation in private land stewardship through the Heritage and Corporate Registry programs.

5.3 Objective: Continue to acquire, restore, and manage fee and easement lands within the Wetland Management District.

Discussion: The Waterfowl Production Areas, wetland conservation easements and Farmer's Home Administration easements of the 14-county District provide habitat for nesting waterfowl and grassland songbirds, as well as public recreation opportunities, in areas that are often under widespread agricultural production or are subject to suburban growth. Established in 1994, the District is relatively new and opportunities abound for growth. The working relationship with local governments, conservation organizations and private landowners is very solid. The District grew an average of 500 to 1,000 acres per year through fee and easement acquisitions during the 5-year period ending in 2001. The District should strive to maintain the top end of this growth rate, if measured on a 5-10 year average, if adequate funding is available.

Strategies:

5.3.1 In cooperation with the MnDNR and private conservation organizations, delineate and submit acquisition proposals for no fewer than 750 acres annually.

5.3.2 In cooperation with the Natural Resource Conservation Service, identify high quality habitats where Wetland Reserve Program funds can be combined with Duck Stamp funds for the purchase of Waterfowl Production Areas.

5.3.3 Pursue all available sources of funds for land acquisition and habitat restoration including the Migratory Bird Conservation Fund, North American Wetland Conservation Act grants and private donations. A limited amount of Refuge Mitigation funds could be made available for specific acquisitions.

5.4 Objective: On an annual basis, and in partnership with others, restore 1,000 acres of habitat located on private lands though the Partners for Fish and Wildlife Program.

Strategies:

5.4.1　Continue to work with other agencies and organizations in the restoration and protection of wildlife habitats. Where possible, continue to broker and assist with programs of others including the Wetland Reserve Program, Conservation Reserve Enhancement Program, Conservation Reserve Program, and the Reinvest in Minnesota Program.

5.4.2　Continue to closely work with Soil and Water Conservation Districts to assist in restoring and protecting wildlife habitats on private lands.

5.4.3　Continue to work directly with landowners on habitat restoration projects through the use of the Service's private landowner agreements.

5.4.4　Seek opportunities to obtain financial assistance and administrative support for field biologists within the Partners program through creative partnerships with conservation organizations and others.

5.5 Objective:　Protect the cultural, historic, and prehistoric resources of federally-owned lands within the Refuge and District.

Discussion: The overview study (Godfrey 1999) drew upon a substantial yet limited number of cultural resources reports for the Minnesota River Valley. Some 31 other studies cover portions of the Wetland Management District. Completed cultural resources surveys as reported in some of these studies have covered 1,500 acres of Refuge and District land. Eighty cultural resources sites have been identified or recorded on Refuge and District land. The vast majority of Refuge and District land has never been subject to a cultural resources survey and many more sites are expected to be located on this land.

The large land base and the presence of two large cities make a search of and comparison with the list of National Register properties a meaningless exercise for this purpose. Nevertheless, the Refuge is surrounded by numerous properties on the National Register including some right adjacent to the boundary. No sites in the Refuge have been nominated but several have been determined eligible and most of the others are considered eligible until determined otherwise.

Strategies:

5.5.1　Describe, identify and take into consideration all archeological and cultural values prior to implementing construction or other ground-disturbing projects. Notify the Regional Historic Preservation Officer early in project planning or upon receipt of a request for permitted activities.

5.5.2   By 2006, develop a step-down plan for surveying lands to identify archeological resources and for developing a preservation program to meet the requirements of Section 14 of the Archaeological Resources Protection Act and Section 110(a)(2) of the National Historic Preservation Act.

5.6 Objective: Protect Refuge lands and resources from damaging uses adjacent to Refuge boundaries.

Discussion: Outdoor amphitheaters: Written comments were received from representatives of a citizens group opposed to the construction of outdoor amphitheaters in the Minnesota River valley. The group requested that we address the potential impacts of proposed amphitheaters on Refuge resources. At the time of this writing, two amphitheater proposals are being considered by local governments within the river valley: the Black Dog Amphitheater in Burnsville and the Q-Prime Amphitheater adjacent to the Louisville Swamp Unit.

The Service has publicly gone on record opposing the use of the Refuge as a "noise dump" for large outdoor concert arenas. We do not believe that the construction and use of amphitheaters that intentionally direct noise toward Refuge lands is consistent with Congress' intent in establishing the Refuge. We also do not believe that these facilities are in the best long-term interest of citizens who enjoy wildlife-dependent recreational opportunities within the Minnesota Valley.

Concert events will project significant amounts of amplified music and related crowd noise. Without question, public use activities at the Black Dog and Louisville Swamp units such as bird watching and wildlife interpretation will be affected by these noise generating facilities. In addition, these facilities have great potential to affect the use and distribution of wildlife on Refuge lands. Just as the State of Minnesota has determined that noise is a pollutant subject to regulation, we classify noise as pollutant and that the dissipation of noise from amphitheaters as proposed is an inappropriate use of National Wildlife Refuge System lands.

Strategy:
5.6.1   Continue to monitor amphitheater proposals and actively participate in any public hearings, focus group discussions, and/or provide written comments to appropriate local government agencies. If constructed, retain a working relationship with amphitheater owners and local regulatory agencies to reduce impacts to Refuge users and resources.

<u>Goal 6. Public Use:</u>

To provide high quality wildlife-dependent recreational and environmental education opportunities to a diverse audience. These activities will promote understanding, appreciation and support for Minnesota Valley National Wildlife Refuge and the Wetland Management District as well as the entire National Wildlife Refuge System.

Hunting

6.1 Objective:　Provide no less than 14,000 high quality hunting experiences for area residents per year. Seventy-five percent of hunters will report no conflicts with other users, a reasonable harvest opportunity and satisfaction with the overall experience.

USFWS File Photograph

Discussion: Providing opportunities for hunting is consistent with the Refuge and District mission and the National Wildlife Refuge System Improvement Act of 1997. Service-owned lands in the Refuge and District will be open to hunting, subject to state and local regulations and public safety concerns, where conflicts with other users will not occur, and where biologically feasible. Waterfowl Production Areas are open to hunting subject to state regulations unless there is a significant safety issue. Where needed, Refuge staff will seek ways to ensure that hunters have the opportunity for high quality experiences.

Strategies:

6.1.1　By 2005 and in cooperation with the MnDNR, develop a plan to improve waterfowl hunting on Rice Lake of the Wilkie Unit. The plan will explore alternatives such as hunter education and the use of limited permits to improve the quality of hunting at this location.

6.1.2　By 2005, through revision of the Refuge Hunting Plan, examine opportunities to expand bow hunting for deer on the Refuge to assist in maintaining deer densities between 15-25 deer per square mile. Coordinate efforts with the MnDNR and cities adjacent to the Minnesota River Valley.

6.1.3　Maintain disabled hunting opportunities in cooperation with Capable Partners or another suitable organization. Expand disabled hunting opportunities to include turkey and deer in designated areas on the Refuge.

6.1.4　Continue to improve the Refuge's youth waterfowl hunting program. Provide this opportunity to no fewer than 25 young people each year and seek to enroll disabled and disadvantaged youth plus youth of single-parent households located in urban areas.

6.1.5　Enhance public understanding of Refuge hunting opportunities by increasing the quality of maps, signs and wording within brochures and on the Refuge web page.

6.1.6　Increase the visibility of Refuge law enforcement and hunter adherence to federal and state regulations to ensure high quality, ethical hunting.

6.1.7　At least one parking lot will be developed on each Waterfowl Production Area to allow for hunting, fishing, and other wildlife-dependent activities.

6.1.8　Where appropriate, a Waterfowl Production Area entrance sign will be erected to recognize contributions from private conservation organizations and agencies.

6.1.9　Obtain operational funding amounting to approximately $100,000 a year to employ a full-time law enforcement officer to enhance the Refuge's law enforcement and public use programs.

6.1.10　Each Waterfowl Production Area will be clearly posted to avoid any potential landowner/visitor conflicts.

Fishing

6.2 Objective:　By 2005, provide for 6,000 high quality fishing visits per year to the Refuge by Twin Cities residents. Seventy-five percent of anglers will report no conflicts with other users and will recollect awareness that they were fishing on a national wildlife refuge.

Discussion: Bank fishing will be allowed on all Refuge lands where this activity does not interfere with wildlife conservation. Boating will continue to be restricted on Refuge-interior waterways other than the Minnesota River to reduce disturbance of migratory birds. The public will be encouraged to practice catch and release in light of the fish consumption advisories for the Lower Minnesota River.

Strategies:
6.2.1　Promote catch and release fishing opportunities on Refuge waters through the development and maintenance of good quality maps, signs, multilingual brochures, and the Refuge's web page. Ensure that the fishing public clearly understands the fish consumption advisories for the Lower Minnesota River through signs and brochures.

6.2.2　In cooperation with the MnDNR and the City of Bloomington, maintain existing boat ramp and parking facilities located at Lyndale Avenue. Likewise, cooperate with the City of Shakopee, the MnDNR, and others to develop an additional boat ramp near State Highway 101.

6.2.3   In cooperation with the MnDNR and Federal fish hatcheries, optimize Refuge fishing opportunities for youth and the disabled by annually stocking, in order of priority, Youth Fishing Pond, Cedar Pond, and Hogback Ridge Pond. Maintain the two existing accessible fishing piers at these locations.

6.2.4   In cooperation with other partners, continue to promote fishing opportunities for disadvantaged persons and others through activities such as Youth Fishing Day.

Wildlife Observation

6.3 Objective: By 2005, provide for 180,000 wildlife observation visits per year to the Refuge and Waterfowl Production Areas. Ninety percent of all visitors will report a memorable wildlife observation and that it occurred on land managed by the U.S. Fish and Wildlife Service.

Strategies:
6.3.1   Promote public use of the new Audubon-sponsored Minnesota Valley Birding Trail. The trail includes wildlife observation stops on the Refuge.

6.3.2   With Refuge staff and/or volunteers, conduct no fewer than six birdwatching/wildlife observation programs for the public each year. In addition, conduct no fewer than two birdwatching/wildlife observation tours for disabled visitors per year. A portion of these wildlife observation tours will be conducted from canoes or other suitable water craft.

6.3.3   Explore the possibility of developing a wildlife observation tour of the Minnesota River Valley using a van or motorized tram.

6.3.4   Modify the Refuge web site to include current and accurate information about wildlife observations and opportunities available to the public. Link Refuge web site to other important wildlife observation web sites.

USFWS File Photograph

6.3.5   Maps and information describing Waterfowl Production Areas and their appropriate uses will be continuously updated on the Refuge's web site.

6.3.6   Establish state-of-the-art bird feeding stations at existing and future Refuge visitor centers. Manage these stations as dynamic exhibits that promote wildlife observation opportunities to the public.

6.3.7   Maintain strong partnership with the Minnesota River Valley
         Audubon Chapter and the Native Plant Society and continue
         to provide them monthly meeting space. Seek ways to
         coordinate organized wildlife and plant observation activities
         with those of the Refuge.

6.3.8   Enhance wildlife observation opportunities on Refuge
         wetlands by designing, constructing and installing elevated
         observation decks at several locations. at a minimum,
         observation decks will be installed at Fisher lake, Rapids
         Lake, and Long meadow Lake at locations that would
         enhance visitor opportunities to view waterfowl and
         waterbirds.

Wildlife Photography

Discussion: The Refuge will encourage wildlife photography at locations and times that
do not conflict with wildlife conservation needs. Access to sensitive wildlife habitats and
seasonal concentration areas, such as wading bird nesting colonies and Bald Eagle nest
sites, will continue to be restricted to reduce disturbance to wildlife.

6.4 Objective: On an annual basis, provide for 3,000 high quality wildlife photogra-
                  phy visits to the Minnesota River Valley and adjacent areas.

        Strategies:
        6.4.1   Provide the public with no fewer than two portable photog-
                 raphy blinds to be used at specific sites throughout the
                 Refuge. In addition, allow the public to use existing hunting
                 blinds during off-season for additional wildlife photography
                 sites.

        6.4.2   In cooperation with the Minnesota Nature Photography
                 Club and others, enhance and promote the annual Refuge
                 photography contest and display winning photos in Refuge
                 Visitor Center for a 45-day period each year.

        6.4.3   Maintain strong partnership with the Minnesota Nature
                 Photography Club and continue to provide monthly meeting
                 space for this organization.

Wildlife Interpretation

Discussion: Several of the strategies presented in the following five objectives were
developed to address the issue of eliminating confusing rules and regulations, which was
highlighted in Chapter 2. Due in part to the land ownership patterns within the Minnesota River Valley, there is some public confusion about what type of recreation is appropriate on Refuge lands and where this recreation is allowed. Some additional strategies
aimed at this issue can be found under the Public Use Facilities and Land Protection
Goal.

6.5 Objective: By 2004, provide for 30,000 high quality wildlife interpretive visits per year to the Refuge and Waterfowl Production Areas. Fifty percent of visitors will independently report that "wildlife comes first" on System lands and understand the need for seasonal closures on sensitive wildlife habitats.

Discussion: Through the use of brochures, kiosks, web sites, and interpretive programs, the Refuge and District have a great opportunity to interpret the value of wildlife and their habitats to historic cultures and today's society. Interpretive products will be dynamic, of high quality, and will articulate the importance of Service lands to local and national conservation efforts. The foundation of these programs and activities will be a revised and upgraded interpretive plan for the Refuge that will address both on-site and off-site opportunities.

Strategies:

6.5.1 By 2004, review, revise, and upgrade the Refuge's Interpretive Plan to reflect Refuge contribution to local and national conservation efforts. The plan will identify a Refuge theme that will be promoted in all interpretive products.

6.5.2 Upgrade and/or replace Refuge Visitor Center exhibits consistent with the Refuge theme. New exhibits need to be dynamic, affordable, and easy to repair and replace if needed.

6.5.3 Upgrade and replace all interpretive and information panels that exist on Refuge kiosks consistent with the Refuge theme. The panels and kiosks will conform to U.S. Fish & Wildlife Service, Region 3, policy and will be environmentally sensitive in their design and placement.

6.5.4 Develop appropriate signs and materials which interpret the cultural and historic sites located on the Refuge and their relationship with historic wildlife populations. Six kiosks that serve this purpose have been identified in the current Refuge Sign Plan.

6.5.5 In cooperation with Refuge volunteers and others, conduct no fewer than 125 high quality interpretive programs annually. Keep interpretive programming fresh by continually upgrading, improving, and/or replacing individual programs.

6.5.6 In cooperation with the Friends of the Minnesota Valley, upgrade the interpretive and educational materials offered for sale in the Blufftop Bookshop.

6.5.7 Upgrade audio visual equipment in the Visitor Center auditorium, update the content of the orientation slide show and offer a variety of wildlife-related videos for the visiting public.

6.5.8   Write and distribute no fewer than 24 news releases each year that increase the public's understanding and knowledge of the Refuge and its programs.

6.5.9   In cooperation with many partners, sponsor no fewer than 10 special events annually that engage the public in Refuge activities and increase people's knowledge and understanding of wildlife conservation and associated issues.

Environmental Education

6.6 Objective: By 2004, provide environmental education programing to no less than 12,000 students per year followed by 2 percent annual growth until 2017. Eighty percent of students will report an increased desire to protect fish and wildlife habitats as a result of the programs.

Discussion: Consistent with the Refuge Mission, Refuge staff will provide high quality environmental education services to teachers and school districts throughout the urban and suburban Twin Cities Metropolitan Area. The curriculum will directly relate to Refuge management activities and it will meet the State of Minnesota environmental education graduation requirements. In order to keep it fresh and dynamic, the curriculum will be continually improved in concert with area teachers.

Strategies:
6.6.1   The Refuge's environmental education curriculum will be thoroughly reviewed by 2003 and every 4 years thereafter with the assistance of local educators. Ensure curriculum is fresh and dynamic and meets the needs of students in preschool on up to high school seniors.

6.6.2   Effectively promote the environmental program through a number of mediums including an annual syllabus, maintaining current information on the Refuge's web page, and periodic distribution of CDs for use on computes.

6.6.3   Refine and expand the use of Partnership Agreements with area schools in order to clearly articulate program goals and objectives and to build strong educational partnerships.

6.6.4   Emphasize the delivery of environmental education services to inner-city schools with both on-site and off-site programing. Secure funding through partnerships for busing for those schools that do not have the ability to assume those costs on their own.

6.6.5   Develop and strengthen internships/work study opportunities through partnerships with academic institutions. In partnership with local universities, hire interns in the natural resource field using funds provided to the Refuge annually through the Jack Lynch Endowment. Where possible, leverage these funds with those provided by the universities.

6.6.6   Following completion of a new environmental education facility, expand environmental education programing to suburban and rural schools and incorporate the use of waterfowl production areas in curriculum.

6.6.7   Administer the Regional Resource Center as an integral component of the Refuge's environmental education program by providing appropriate educational and interpretive materials to area schools.

Inappropriate Recreational Uses:

The Refuge Improvement Act established six priority uses of the Refuge System (which includes Waterfowl Production Areas). These priority uses all depend on the presence of, or expectation of the presence, of wildlife, and are thus called wildlife-dependent uses. These uses are hunting, fishing, wildlife observation, photography, environmental education, and interpretation. As outlined in Chapter 2, unauthorized biking on Refuge lands and horseback riding beyond the State Trail have been identified as two uses that are not wildlife-dependent and will be evaluated in this plan.

<u>Mountain Biking</u>

6.7 Objective: By 2005, working with the MnDNR, the City of Bloomington, mountain biking organizations and others, eliminate inappropriate biking on Refuge lands and concentrate this activity on authorized and designated trails only.

Photograph by Rick Schultz

Discussion: For a number of reasons, including a collective inability to complete the State Trail, portions of the river valley and the Bloomington Bluffs have been used for several years by mountain biking enthusiasts. This area is very popular and, due to extensive and virtually unrestricted mountain bike use, considerable bluff and trail erosion has occurred over time. Unfortunately, significant unauthorized mountain biking currently occurs on Refuge lands. This situation must be corrected in the near future if we are to remain responsible natural resource managers.

Strategies:
6.7.1   If possible, and in cooperation with the City of Bloomington, eliminate mountain biking on the Bloomington Bluffs between Indian Mounds School and I-35W. In addition, develop

and implement a plan to address the environmental degradation that currently exists throughout this area.

6.7.2   In cooperation with others, monitor and enforce appropriate trail usage on Refuge lands.

Horseback Riding

6.8 Objective: By 2003, eliminate horseback riding on all Refuge and District lands and trails except on the State Trail.

Discussion: A limited amount of horseback riding occurs on Refuge lands beyond the State Trail. It occurs on specific trails on both the Wilkie and Louisville Swamp units consistent with the 1984 Master Plan. The National Wildlife Refuge System Improvement Act of 1997 called for a focus on wildlife-dependent activities and a re-examination of other recreational uses. Horseback riding is not considered to be a wildlife-dependent activity and may conflict with other priority recreational uses. In light of the Act, the Refuge will limit horseback riding to lands that are part of the State Trail System.

Strategies:

6.8.1   Following appropriate public notice, and the installation of signs, restrict horseback riding to the State Trail within the Louisville Swamp Unit.

6.8.2   Consistent with the Refuge web site and its brochures, ensure that good quality information about horseback usage on Refuge/State Trail lands is provided to the public.

6.8.3   In cooperation with the MnDNR and the horseback riding community, monitor and, if needed, strictly enforce appropriate trail usage of the Louisville Swamp Unit.

Volunteer and Intern Programs:

6.9 Objective: Provide a highly visible and dynamic volunteer and intern work force to assist in all aspects of Refuge and District operations including environmental education, habitat improvement and visitor facility maintenance.

Strategies:

6.9.1   Seek opportunities to increase coordination between Refuge volunteers and Friends of the Minnesota Valley.

6.9.2   Enhance communication with Refuge volunteers through various forums including periodic newsletters, a volunteer hotline, the Refuge's web site, and recognition picnics, dinners and socials.

6.9.3   Renew efforts to provide high quality training to Refuge volunteers so they are able to effectively and efficiently complete projects and responsibilities.

6.9.4   Expand efforts to provide volunteer opportunities to members of the disabled public.

6.9.5   Continue to provide Refuge projects for kids at risk through a variety of programs including the Twin Cities Tree Trust, Skills for Tomorrow, and community programs like Sentenced to Serve.

6.9.6   Seek to expand volunteer opportunities for retired citizens and explore the possibility of developing trailer pads and a septic system for seasonal retiree volunteers with recreational vehicles.

6.9.7   Employ interns as needed through the use of the Jack Lynch Endowment Fund. Leverage the use of these funds by entering into agreements with universities and colleges.

Public Use Facilities

6.10 Objective: By 2005, develop new and maintain existing facilities to promote public advocacy and use of the Refuge and Waterfowl Production Areas. Ninety percent of visitors will report satisfaction with the safety, comfort and functionality of these facilities and express a desire for a return visit.

Discussion: Public use facilities will be developed and maintained at a high standard ensuring public safety and a positive reflection upon the Service. Included on this list of facilities are Refuge trails and parking lots, the existing and future visitor centers, the Rapids Lake historic home, historic buildings and structures, and the Minnesota Valley State Trail. To the extent practical, all facilities will be made accessible to disabled Refuge visitors. Please note that Strategies 3, 4, and 5 will be completed with Refuge Mitigation funds. Existing and proposed trails, parking lots and facilities are depicted in Figures 13-16.

Strategies:
6.10.1   By 2004, submit a major Visitor Center upgrading package that addresses current outstanding maintenance needs and that will serve to keep this facility in excellent condition for the next 10 years.

6.10.2   By 2004, all Refuge facilities will be reviewed to determine what measures need to be taken to make them more accessible to disabled persons. Following this review, an implementation plan will be developed and funding will be sought to upgrade these facilities.

Figure 13: Existing and Proposed Trails and Facilities: Long Meadow Lake and Black Dog Units

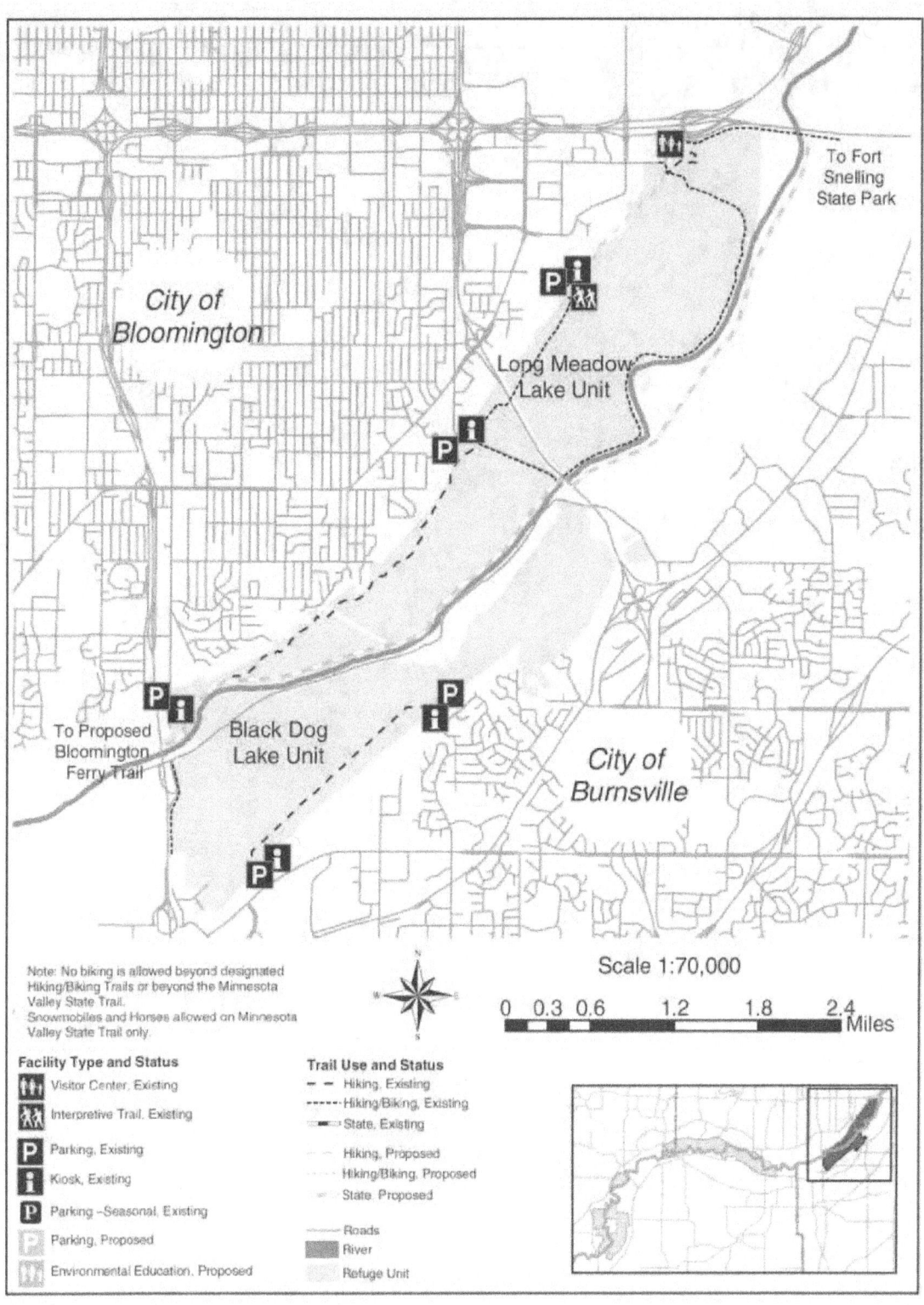

Note: No biking is allowed beyond designated Hiking/Biking Trails or beyond the Minnesota Valley State Trail.
Snowmobiles and Horses allowed on Minnesota Valley State Trail only.

Scale 1:70,000

0 0.3 0.6   1.2   1.8   2.4 Miles

Facility Type and Status

- Visitor Center, Existing
- Interpretive Trail, Existing
- P Parking, Existing
- i Kiosk, Existing
- P Parking –Seasonal, Existing
- P Parking, Proposed
- Environmental Education, Proposed

Trail Use and Status

- – – Hiking, Existing
- ------- Hiking/Biking, Existing
- State, Existing
- Hiking, Proposed
- Hiking/Biking, Proposed
- State, Proposed
- Roads
- River
- Refuge Unit

Figure 14: Existing and Proposed Trails and Facilities: Upgrala, Wilkie and Bloomington Ferry Units

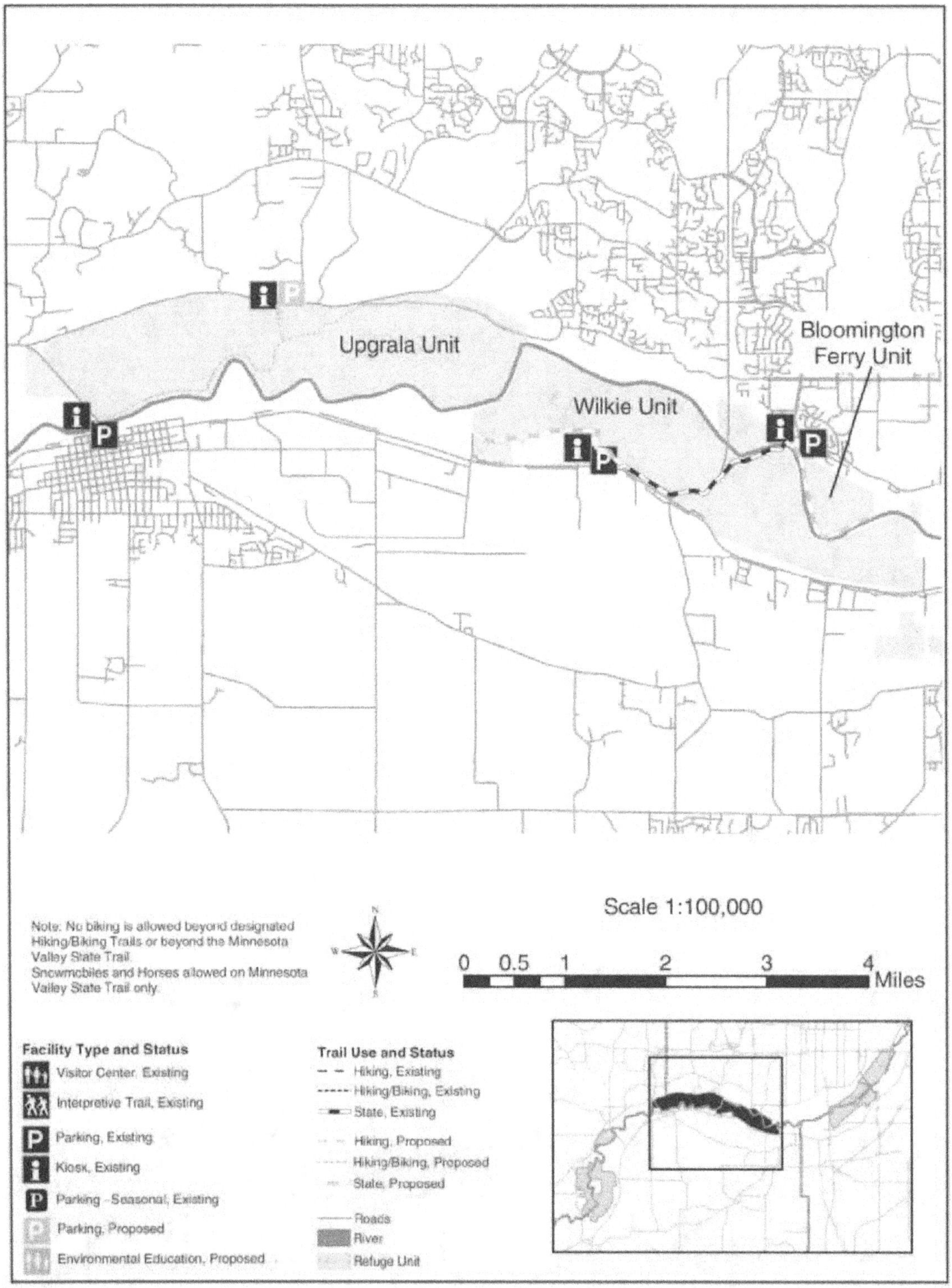

Upgrala Unit

Bloomington Ferry Unit

Wilkie Unit

Note: No biking is allowed beyond designated Hiking/Biking Trails or beyond the Minnesota Valley State Trail.
Snowmobiles and Horses allowed on Minnesota Valley State Trail only.

Scale 1:100,000

| 0 | 0.5 | 1 | 2 | 3 | 4 |

Miles

Facility Type and Status

- Visitor Center, Existing
- Interpretive Trail, Existing
- P Parking, Existing
- i Kiosk, Existing
- P Parking - Seasonal, Existing
- Parking, Proposed
- Environmental Education, Proposed

Trail Use and Status

- – – Hiking, Existing
- ----- Hiking/Biking, Existing
- State, Existing
- Hiking, Proposed
- Hiking/Biking, Proposed
- State, Proposed
- Roads
- River
- Refuge Unit

Figure 15: Existing and Proposed Trails and Facilities: Chaska Unit

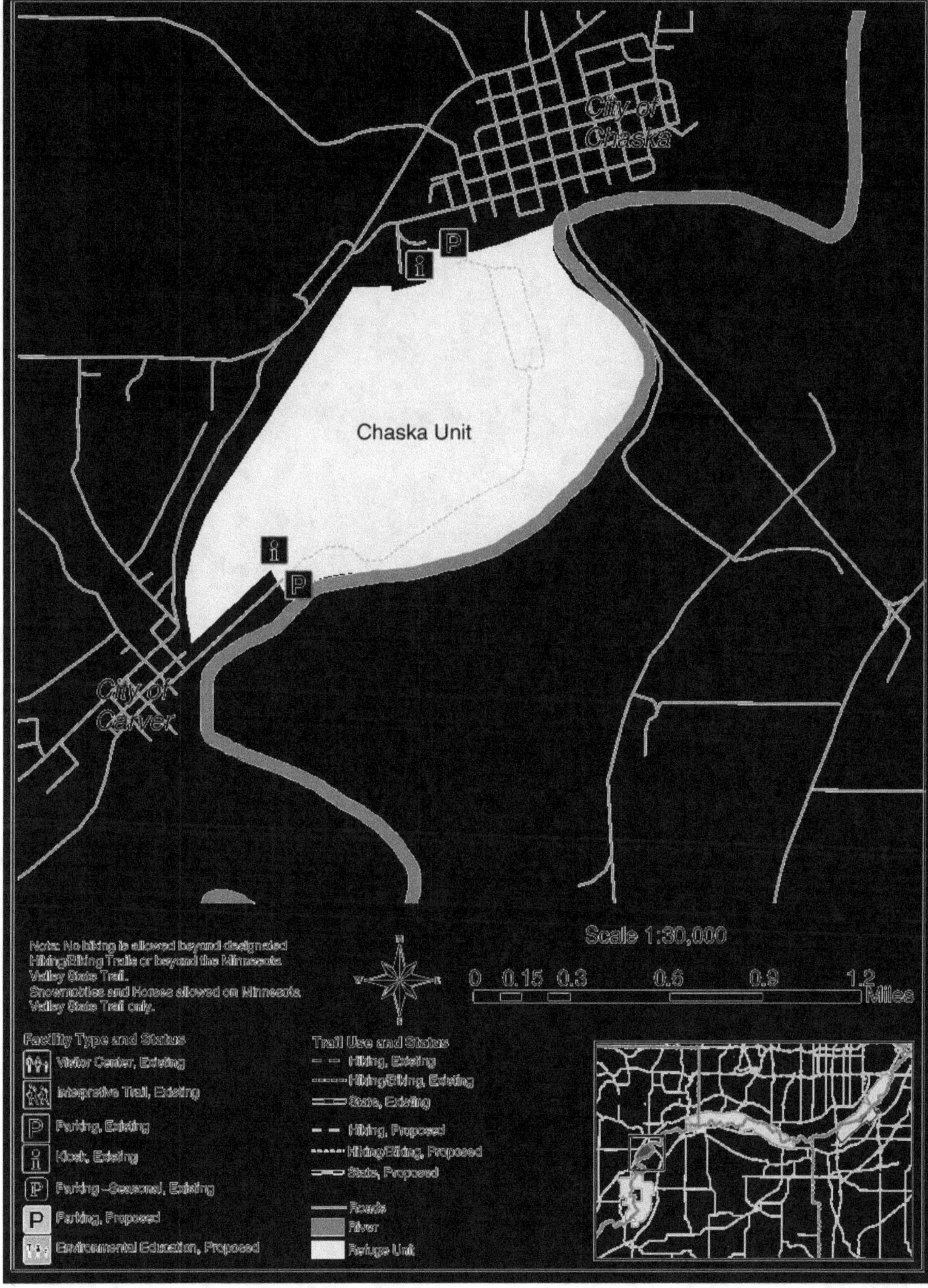

City of Chaska

Chaska Unit

City of Carver

Note: No biking is allowed beyond designated Hiking/Biking Trails or beyond the Minnesota Valley State Trail.
Snowmobiles and Horses allowed on Minnesota Valley State Trail only.

Scale 1:30,000

0   0.15   0.3   0.6   0.9   1.2
                                              Miles

Facility Type and Status
- Visitor Center, Existing
- Interpretive Trail, Existing
- Parking, Existing
- Kiosk, Existing
- Parking—Seasonal, Existing
- Parking, Proposed
- Environmental Education, Proposed

Trail Use and Status
- Hiking, Existing
- Hiking/Biking, Existing
- State, Existing
- Hiking, Proposed
- Hiking/Biking, Proposed
- State, Proposed
- Roads
- River
- Refuge Unit

Figure 16: Existing and Proposed Trails and Facilities: Rapids Lake and Louisville Swamp Units

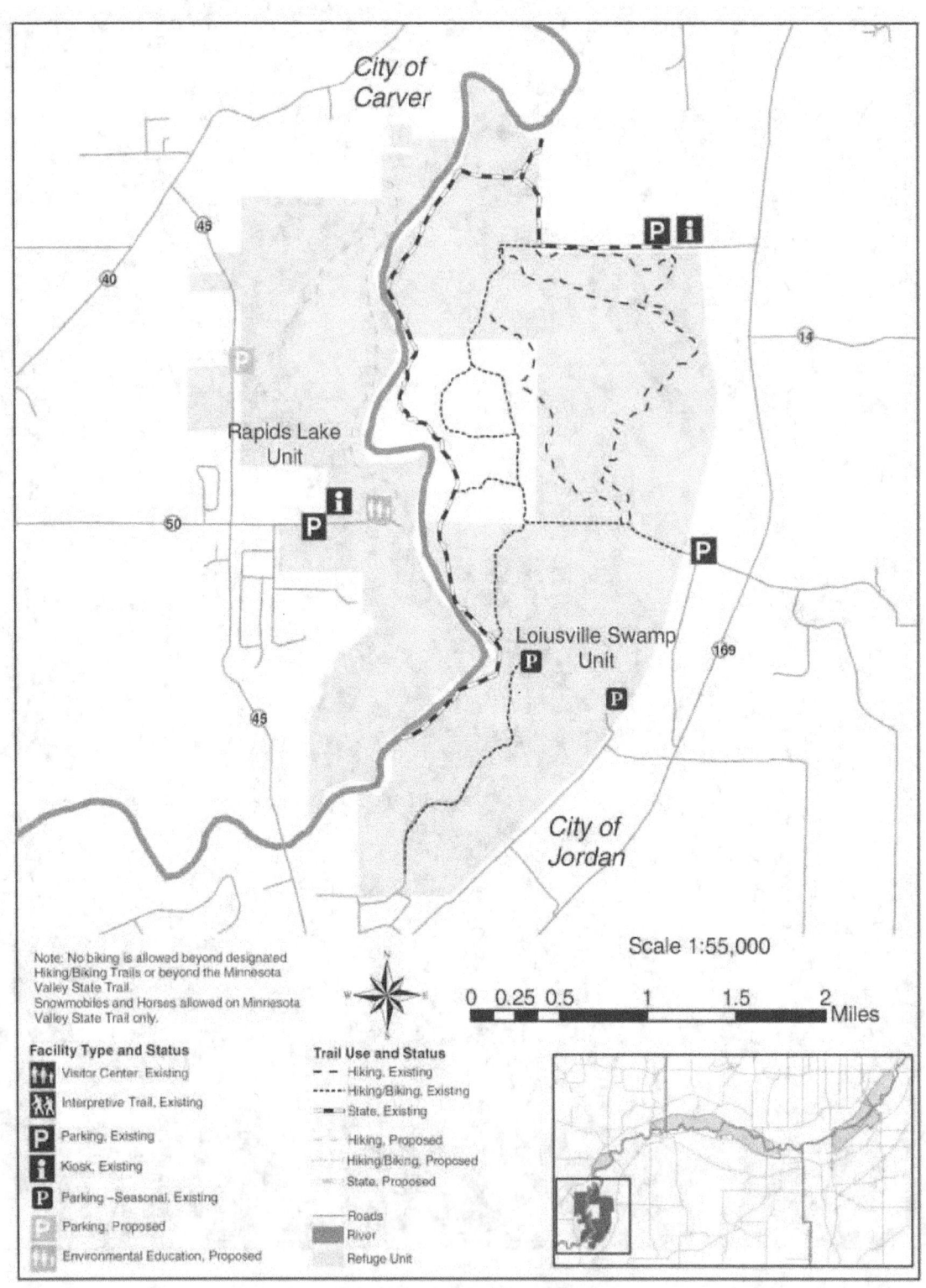

Minnesota Valley National Wildlife Refuge and Wetland Management District

6.10.3   By 2004, begin the conversion of the historic Rapids Lake home into an environmental education and interpretive site. As part of this effort, design and build trails, interpretive kiosks, and parking lots in support of this project. Upon completion, allow this site to be used by local governments, non-profit organizations and others for meetings and natural resource-related workshops and conferences.

6.10.4   Obtain or construct intern housing on or near the Rapids Lake Unit to meet expanded responsibilities for wildlife interpretation and environmental education as well as to attract candidates of diverse backgrounds, cultures, and experiences.

6.10.5   Stabilize the historic buildings on the Jabs and Ehmiller farm sites to ensure their longevity and their historic interpretive value.

6.10.6   Obtain operational funding to employ a maintenance worker (WG- 4749-6/7) to enhance the Refuge's capability to address its maintenance needs.

6.10.7   Establish a hard surfaced trail open to hiking and bicycling between the Refuge Visitor Center and the Bass Ponds.

6.10.8   In cooperation with the cities of Chaska and Carver, develop a plan for the Chaska Unit and nearby city lands that addresses wildlife interpretive trails, public parking, and related interpretive facilities and programming.

6.10.9   Seek a sufficient increase in operational funds to maintain, to a high standard, the existing Refuge Visitor Center, parking lots, kiosks, and signing.

6.10.10 Seek annual funding to enter into contracts for routine mowing, snow plowing, and custodial services for the Refuge's visitor centers, parking lots, and nature trails.

6.10.11 Using Trust funds, employ a supervisory park ranger (GS-025-11/12) who will initiate early planning for new environmental education center(s) and associated facilities. Following completion of the center, this employee will assume responsibility for operations of these facilities.

6.10.12 Using Trust funds, employ up to two park rangers (GS-025-5/7/9) and one maintenance worker (WG-4749-6/7/8) to assist in planning and conducting environmental education programming and in the management of new Refuge units.

6.10.13 Seek construction funding to replace the existing Shakopee shop facility with a combination cold storage/heated staff building. The new building would also contain a small office suitable for two staff. The commercial lot owned by the Service near the Savage Fen would be a likely location for this facility.

6.10.14 Seek construction funding to replace the existing Rapids Lake maintenance facility. The new facility would contain office space suitable for three Refuge maintenance staff and three District employees.

6.10.15 Enhance the Refuge's capability to reduce the amount of vandalism and arson that occurs on Refuge facilities. Seek funding for installation and use of remote sensors designed to detect damage to facilities and apprehend those responsible for such activities.

6.11 Objective: To work in partnership with the MnDNR, cities, and other organizations to finish the Minnesota Valley State Trail and to provide appropriate public access to the trail from Refuge lands.

Discussion: This objective addresses the issue of completion of the Minnesota Valley State Trail, a primary issue highlighted in Chapter 2. We hope that preparation of this CCP will prompt a renewed effort by citizens, public agencies, private conservation organizations, and recreational users of the valley to place a high priority on the completion of the Minnesota Valley State Trail. Upon its completion, there is great potential for recreational users of this trail to develop an enhanced appreciation for the cultural and natural resource values of the Refuge as well as the greater Minnesota River Valley.

Strategies:
6.11.1 In cooperation with the MnDNR, identify the State Trail corridor across the Wilkie Unit, which will connect this part of the Refuge with the City of Shakopee.

6.11.2 In cooperation with the MnDNR, identify the State Trail corridor across the Long Meadow Lake Unit between Old Cedar Avenue and Lyndale Avenue. Seek sources of funding to construct access across at least two large gullies that occur along this section of the trail.

6.11.3 Working with partners, seek sources of funding (TEA-21, etc.) for the replacement of the Old Cedar Avenue Bridge with a pedestrian bridge that will connect Old Cedar Avenue with the State Trail.

6.11.4 Working with partners, acquire in fee or easement remaining lands on the Bloomington Ferry Unit that will allow the completion of the State Trail between I-35W and the Bloomington Ferry Bridge. Work with the City of

Bloomington and the MnDNR to specifically identify the corridor on this section of the State Trail.

6.11.5　In cooperation with the City of Eden Prairie, develop a hiking and bicycling trail on the north side of the Minnesota River connecting River View Road with the Bloomington Ferry Bridge.

6.11.6　Following Service acquisition of the Upgrala Unit, develop a hiking and bicycling trail connecting River View Road with the City of Shakopee trail facilities located near U.S. Highway 101. This work will be completed in cooperation with the cities of Eden Prairie and Shakopee.

6.11.7　As soon as practicable and in cooperation with all appropriate parties, develop a brochure that specifically identifies all trails within the Lower Minnesota River Valley and their allowed uses. This information will also be made available on the Refuge's web site.

Chapter 5: Plan Implementation

New and Existing Projects

This Comprehensive Conservation Plan outlines an ambitious course of action for the future management of Minnesota Valley National Wildlife Refuge and Wetland Management District. It will require considerable staff commitment as well as funding commitment to acquire more wildlife habitats, to maintain existing public use facilities and to develop additional high-quality public use facilities. The Refuge will continually need appropriate operational and maintenance funding to implement the objectives in this plan.

The following paragraphs provide a brief description of the highest priority Refuge and District projects, as determined by the Service. The projects may be funded through the traditional source, the Refuge Operating Needs System (RONS), or through financial support of the Minnesota Valley National Wildlife Refuge Trust. However, under no circumstances should funds from the Trust be used to replace or supplant the Refuge's existing operational funds. A full listing of unfunded Refuge and District projects and operational needs can be found in Appendix C.

Refuge Operating Needs (Highest Priority)

Improve Maintenance of Visitor Facilities: The Refuge administers a state-of-the art visitor and education center within a one hour drive of 3 million people. In addition, the Refuge manages a variety of outdoor facilities such as kiosks, boardwalks, nature trails, parking lots, and environmental education shelters. Funding is needed to hire a full-time maintenance worker to maintain public use facilities. Better public facilities maintenance will help ensure a top quality experience for refuge visitors. Estimated cost: $65,000 annually.

Inventory and Control Spread of Exotic Species: Consistent with the Exotic Species Control Plan, we are seeking to control the spread of exotic species such as leafy spurge, purple loosestrife, and European buckthorn on Refuge lands. Among other items, the project will inventory and monitor the presence of invasive species. Where possible, exotics will be controlled using integrated pest management. Mechanical and limited use of chemical treatment will supplement the use of biological control agents. This will be an ongoing effort and will be completed in partnership with the MnDNR and others. Estimated cost: $75,000 annually.

Construct Rapids Lake Environmental Education Center or Classroom Modules on Refuge Units: Through use of Trust funds, an environmental education center will be planned and developed for the Rapids Lake Unit or individual classroom modules will be built on several Refuge Units. As of February 2002, Refuge staff and local educators were discussing the advantages of either option. An education facility would include two classrooms, exhibit space, a multi-purpose room, a small theater, and office space for no fewer than six employees and six volunteers and/or interns. The classroom module option would include smaller facilities on at least the Bloomington Ferry, Upgrala and Rapids Lake units. These classrooms would be used by local educators on a more informal basis and would not house permanent staff. Estimated cost: $3,000,000

Construct Residence at Rapids Lake Unit: A modern home will be constructed on the Rapids Lake Unit to ensure the safety and well being of facilities and equipment located on the site. Although the area is near a large urban population, the site is remote and subject to a variety of problems including theft, vandalism and arson. Local law enforcement personnel do not have ready access to this property to provide any major deterrent to illegal trespass and activities. The home would be occupied by a Refuge employee with law enforcement authority who would oversee the area and provide the extra margin of safety and protection. Estimated cost: $175,000

Convert Historic Home into Environmental Education Site: Through use of Trust funds, the Rapids Lake historic home will be converted into an environmental education site. Included in this project will be the replacement of the structure's utilities and the flood proofing of its basement. Upon completion, the home will be used by school groups and others for programs and meetings. Estimated cost: $350,000

Construct Intern Housing on or near Rapids Lake Unit: To support the Refuge's expanded environmental education and wildlife interpretive programs, intern housing capable of accommodating 16 individuals will be constructed on or near the Rapids Lake Unit. Both interns and volunteers will be housed in this facility. Estimated cost: $350,000

Hire Park Ranger and Staff for Rapids Lake Environmental Education Center: Through the use of Trust funds, one employee will be hired to plan and coordinate the construction of the Rapids Lake Environmental Education Center and support facilities. Following their construction, up to two additional staff will be employed to provide environmental education programs to area schools. Estimated cost: $250,000 annually.

Wetland District Operating Needs (Highest Priority)

Hire a Full-time Maintenance Worker: This individual will assist in restoring over 500 acres of wildlife habitat each year on existing and future Refuge and District lands. Likewise, the employee will assist in managing approximately 3,000 acres of restored grasslands on Waterfowl Production Areas and easements. Weed control on these lands will benefit many species of wildlife as well as providing public hunting opportunities. Habitat restoration will be completed in partnership with many local conservation organizations and challenge grant programs. Estimated cost: $65,000 annually.

Improve Visitor Access to District Lands: A maintenance worker will be hired to construct and maintain entrance signs, boundary signs, parking lots and boundary fences for Waterfowl Production Areas. Construction of these facilities will improve visitor access to these District units. Estimated cost: $65,000 annually.

Table 2: New Positions Needed to Fully Implement the CCP

Position	Full-time Equivalent (FTEs)
Refuge Operations Specialist	1.0
Senior Wildlife Biologist	1.0
Private Lands Wildlife Biologist	0.5
Contract Specialist	1.0
Administrative Technician	0.5
Park Ranger–EEI	2.0
Park Ranger–LE	2.0
Maintenance Worker	3.0
Total	11.0

Hire a Senior Wildlife Biologist: This employee will be responsible for all biological programs and activities of the Refuge and the District. The biologist will conduct a new, long-term monitoring program to determine the response of grassland-dependent species to native grass restoration on waterfowl production areas and easements in the District. The biologist will make recommendations for future management, restoration and acquisition of important grasslands and other habitats. Estimated cost: $90,000 annually.

Hire a Full-time Law Enforcement Officer: The addition of this position will improve public education and understanding of Refuge laws and regulations relating to migratory bird management. Through this project, a law enforcement officer will work on the Refuge and with easement landowners and WPA neighbors to ensure that they understand their role in protecting the migratory bird habitat on these important lands. The officer will also be responsible for increased migratory waterfowl enforcement. Estimated cost: $100,000 annually.

Future Staffing Requirements

Implementing the vision set forth in this CCP will require changes in the organizational structure of the Refuge and District. Existing staff will direct their time and energy in new directions and new staff members will be added to assist in these efforts. The following are organizational charts and tables of the current staff of the Refuge and District, Fiscal Year 2002, as well as and a staff needed to fully implement this plan by Fiscal Year 2017 (Table 2, Figure 18, and Figure 19).

Partnership Opportunities

Partnerships have become an essential element for the successful accomplishment of Minnesota Valley National Wildlife Refuge goals, objectives, and strategies. The objectives outlined in this Comprehensive Conservation Plan need the support and the partnerships of federal, state and local agencies, non-governmental organizations and indi-

Figure 17: Minnesota Valley NWR Organizational Chart, 2002

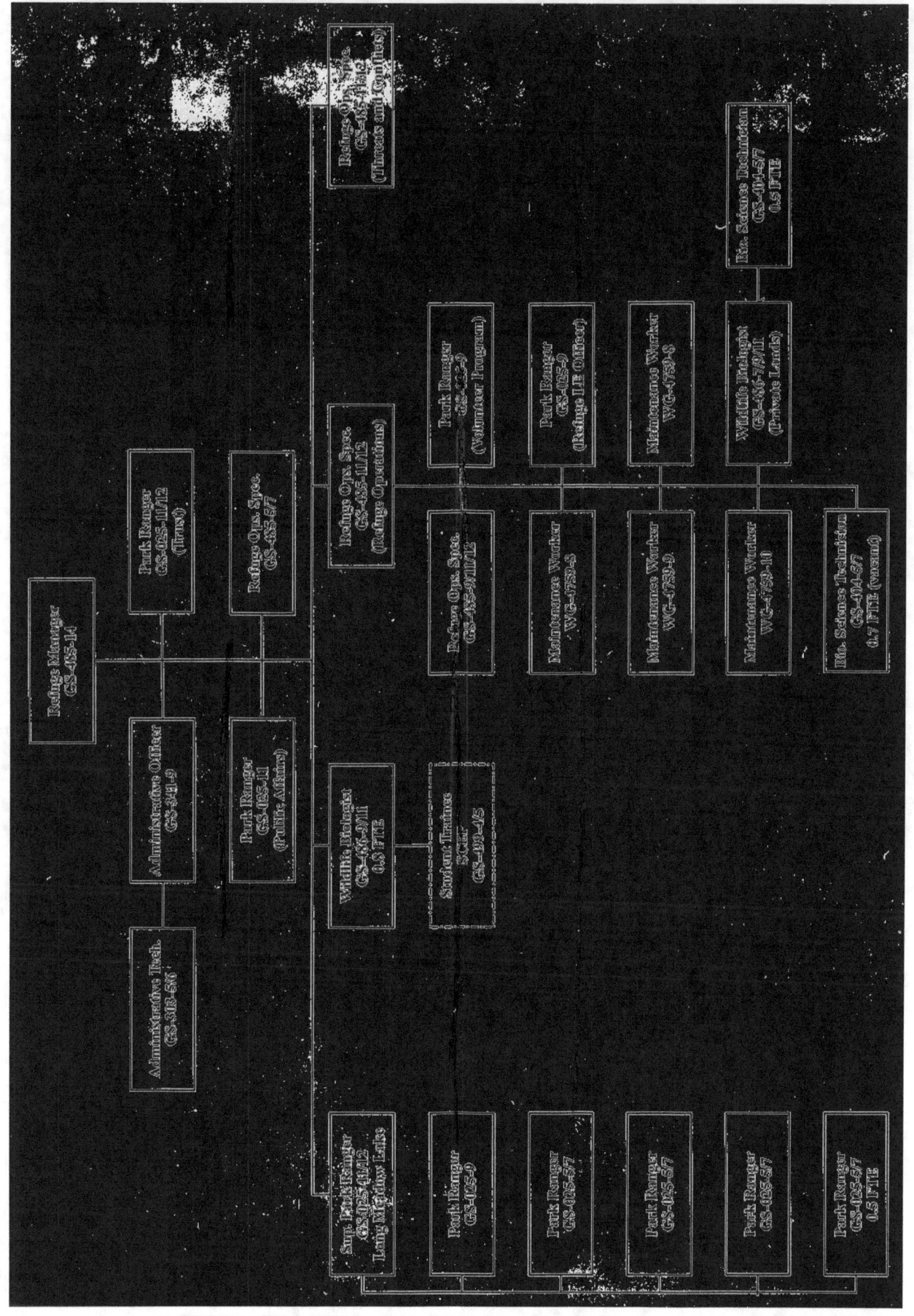

Figure 18: Minnesota Valley National Wildlife Refuge Organizational Chart, 2017

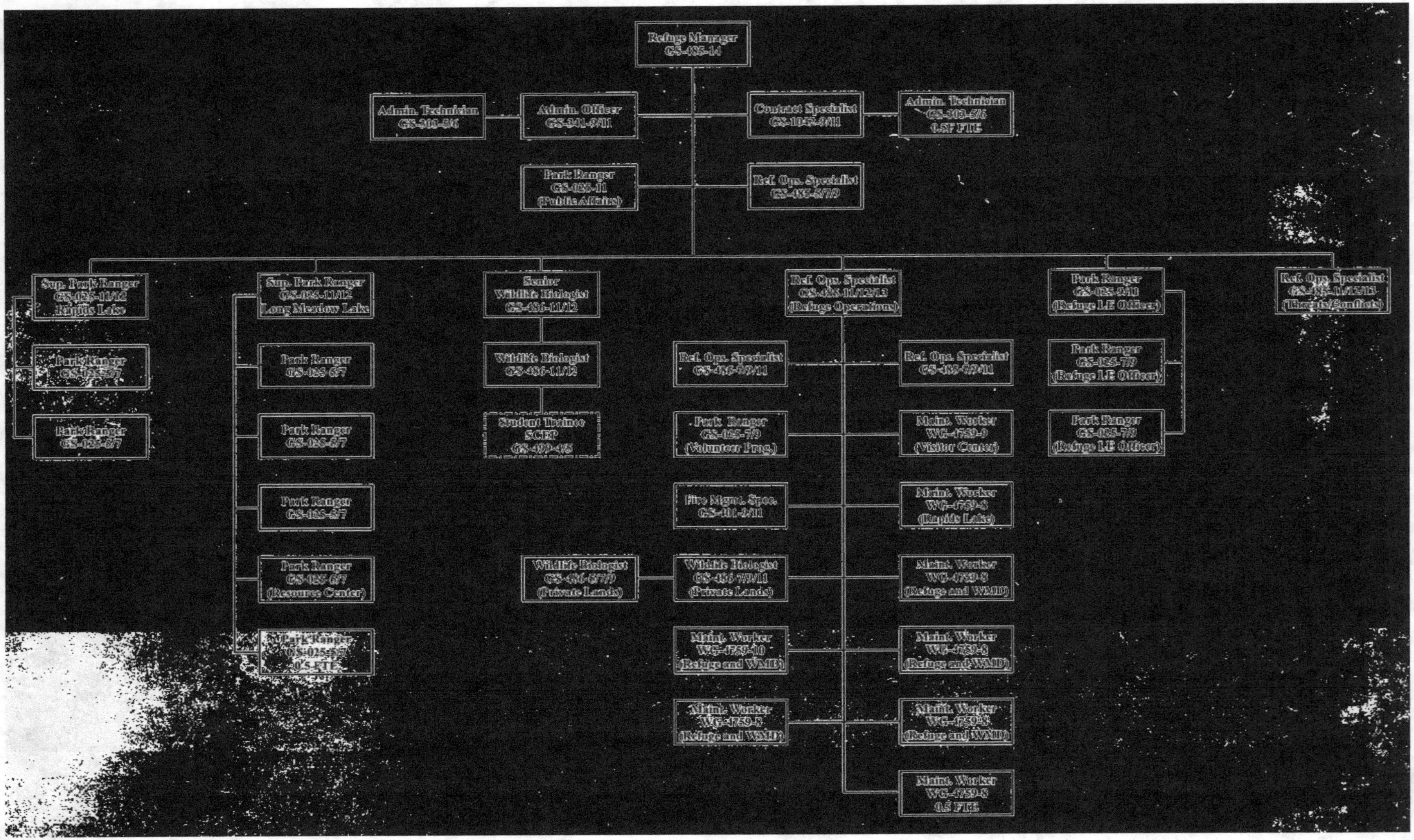

Table 3: Step-down Management Plan Schedule

Plan	Date Completed	Anticipated Revision
Resource Inventory Plan	2000	Dynamic document – Revisions Ongoing
Refuge Interpretive Plan	1994	2003
Law Enforcement Plan	2000	2005
Water Management Plan	1999	2004
Forest Management Plan	–	2005
Hunting Plan	1986	2005
Fire Management Plan	2002	2007
Accessibility Plan	–	2004
Cultural Resources Management Plan	–	2006

vidual citizens. This broad-based approach to managing fish and wildlife resources extends beyond social and political boundaries and requires a foundation of support from many organizations and people. Minnesota Valley National Wildlife Refuge will continue to seek creative partnership opportunities to achieve its vision for the future.

The Friends of the Minnesota Valley, a non-profit organization comprised of Refuge supporters from many walks in life, has been an important ally and Refuge advocate in the past and will become an increasingly important partner in the future. This association has demonstrated its ability to reach out to the community for support and assistance for Refuge projects and conservation issues. Refuge staff will continue to seek guidance, support, and assistance from the Friends into the foreseeable future.

Other notable partners include the Minnesota River Valley Audubon Chapter, the Minnesota Waterfowl Association, the Minnesota River Joint Powers Board and the MnDNR. Conservation organizations and agencies who have been very supportive of habitat restoration efforts on both private and public lands in the District include Minnesota Pheasants, Pheasant Forever chapters, and the Metropolitan Council.

Step-down Management Plans

Several step-down management plans describe specific actions that support the accomplishment of Refuge objectives. The management plans identified in Table 3 will be reviewed and revised as necessary to achieve the results anticipated in this Comprehensive Conservation Plan.

Monitoring and Evaluation

The direction set forth in this CCP plus specifically identified strategies and projects will be monitored throughout the life of this plan. On a periodic basis, the Regional Office will assemble a station review team to visit Minnesota Valley National Wildlife Refuge and evaluate current Refuge activities in light of this plan. The team will review all aspects of Refuge and District management, including direction, accomplishments and funding. The goals and objectives presented in this CCP will provide the baseline from which this field station will be evaluated.

Plan Review and Revision

The CCP for the Minnesota Valley National Wildlife Refuge is meant to provide guidance to refuge managers and staff over the next 10-15 years. However, the CCP is also a dynamic and flexible document and several of the strategies contained in the plan are subject to such things as drought, floods, windstorms and other uncontrollable events. Likewise, many of the strategies are dependent upon Service funding for staff and projects. Because of all these factors, the recommendations in the CCP will be reviewed periodically and, if necessary, revised to meet new circumstances.

Photograph by Scott Sharkey

Appendices

Appendix A: Environmental Assessment

Contents

Finding of No Significant Impact

Environmental Assessment and Comprehensive Conservation Plan for the Minnesota Valley National Wildlife Refuge and Wetland Management District, Minnesota

An Environmental Assessment has been prepared to identify management strategies to meet the conservation goals of the Minnesota Valley National Wildlife Refuge (Refuge) and Wetland Management District (District). The Environmental Assessment examined the environmental consequences that each management alternative could have on the quality of the physical, biological, and human environment, as required by the National Environmental Policy Act of 1969 (NEPA). The Environmental Assessment presented and evaluated four alternatives for managing fish, wildlife and plant habitats, as well as visitor services, on the Refuge and District over the course of the next 15 years:

Alternative A: Public Use Emphasis

This alternative would encourage a minimal approach to managing habitats while allowing for significantly more public recreational uses and an expanded environmental education program. Staff time, emphasis and resources would be shifted to allow for more public activities in all areas of the Refuge and District. No land for Refuge units would be acquired outside of the current boundaries. Waterfowl Production Area acquisitions would proceed at current or reduced levels.

Alternative B: Current Situation (No Action)

The Current Situation alternative would favor existing, or status quo, refuge management and public outreach practices. Refuge staff would continue to restore and maintain existing wetland, grassland, forest and oak savanna habitats. New Refuge lands would be acquired to complete the current approved boundary. Waterfowl Production Area acquisitions would proceed at current levels. The environmental education program would receive minor improvements in existing facilities, exhibits and interpretive materials.

Alternative C: Balanced Public Use and Habitat Management (Preferred)

This alternative would promote active management of existing habitats, higher quality recreational experiences for visitors and improved public outreach strategies. Up to 10,000 acres of additional Refuge lands would be acquired beyond the current boundaries. The District=s Waterfowl Production Area program would also expand as worthy sites are identified. The environmental education program could see a new visitor education facility upriver with needed improvements in existing exhibits and interpretive materials. Additional staff, along with volunteers and interns, would be essential to implement an expanded public use program.

Alternative D: Habitat Management Emphasis

Alternative D would emphasize the pro-active management of existing habitats such as prescribed burning of grasslands and oak savannas, planting trees in converted bottomland forests and invasive plant control. Up to 20,000 acres of additional Refuge lands would be acquired beyond the current boundaries. The District=s Waterfowl Production Area program would also expand as worthy sites are identified. The environmental education program would receive minor improvements in existing facilities, exhibits and interpretive materials.

The alternative selected for implementation is *Alternative C*. The strategies presented in the Comprehensive Conservation Plan (CCP) were developed as a direct result of the selection of this alternative. Restoration of wetlands, grassland, oak savanna, and floodplain forest habitat would benefit a variety of fish and wildlife plant species identified as Resource Conservation Priority species by the Service. Habitats would be managed for nesting and migrating songbirds, waterfowl and shorebirds. Visitors to the refuge will also benefit through an expanded environmental education program, new facilities, and improved signage and displays.

For reasons presented above and below, and based on an evaluation of the information contained in the Environmental Assessment, we have determined that the action of adopting Alternative C as the management alternative for the Refuge and District CCP is not a major federal action which would significantly affect the quality of the human environment, within the meaning of Section 102 (2)(c) of the National Environmental Policy Act of 1969.

Additional Reasons:

1. Future management actions will have a neutral or positive impact on the local economy.
2. A cultural resource inventory completed prior to this CCP included recommendations for the protection of cultural, archaeological and historical resources.
3. This action will not have an adverse impact on threatened or endangered species.

Supporting References:

Environmental Assessment
Comprehensive Conservation Plan

ACTING Regional Director   9/15/04
                            Date

Environmental Assessment

Minnesota Valley National Wildlife Refuge and
Wetland Management District
Comprehensive Conservation Plan

Chapter 1 – Purpose and Need

Purpose

The purpose of the proposed action is to specify a management direction for Minnesota Valley National Wildlife Refuge (Refuge) and Wetland Management District (District) for the next 15 years. This management direction will be described in detail through a set of goals, objectives, and strategies in a Comprehensive Conservation Plan.

Photograph by Scott Sharkey

The action is needed because adequate, long-term management direction does not exist for the refuge. Management is now guided by a Comprehensive Plan that was published in 1984 and by several general policies and short-term plans. Also, the action is needed to address current management issues and to satisfy the legislative mandates of the National Wildlife System Improvement Act of 1997, which requires the preparation of a Comprehensive Conservation Plan for all national wildlife refuges.

The purposes for the Refuge were established by Congress in 1976 through the Minnesota Valley National Wildlife Refuge Act *(Public Law 94-466; October 8, 1976).* In general, its purposes are to (1) provide habitat for a large number of migratory waterfowl, fish, and other wildlife species; (2) to provide environmental education, wildlife recreational opportunities, and interpretive programs for hundreds of thousands of Twin Cities residents; (3) to protect important natural resource areas from degradation; and to (4) protect the valley's unique social, educational, and environmental assets.

We prepared this Environmental Assessment (EA) using guidelines established under the National Environmental Policy Act of 1969. The Act requires us to examine the effects of proposed actions on the natural and human environment. In the following sections we describe four alternatives for future Refuge management, the environmental consequences of each alternative, and our preferred management direction. We designed each alternative as a reasonable mix of fish and wildlife habitat prescriptions and wildlife-dependent recreational opportunities, and then we selected our preferred alternative based on their environmental consequences and their ability to achieve the refuge's purpose.

Need for Action

The CCP ultimately derived from this EA will set the management direction for the

Refuge and the District for the next 15 years. The Refuge is currently guided by a Master Plan published in 1984 and the District has no long-term management plan. Management actions are now mostly guided by general policies and short-term plans. This EA will present four management alternatives for the future of the Refuge and District. The preferred alternative will be selected based on its ability to meet identified goals. These goals may also be considered as the primary need for action. Goals for the Refuge and District were developed by the planning team and encompass all aspects of Refuge and District management including public use, habitat management and maintenance operations. Each of the four management alternatives described in this EA will be able to at least minimally achieve these goals.

Floodplain Forest: To restore, protect, and maintain natural species diversity while emphasizing priority wildlife and plants characteristic of floodplain forests within the northern tallgrass prairie ecosystem.

Discussion: The forested floodplain of the Minnesota River Valley provides migration and production habitat for several bird species that are significant locally or are included in the Region 3 Regional Conservation Priority list. These include the Red-headed Woodpecker, Red-shouldered Hawk and Wood Duck. Numerous songbird species nest within or migrate along floodplain forests. Bald Eagles also use floodplain forests on the Refuge or throughout the Wetland Management District for either migration or nesting habitat. Wading birds, such as the Great Blue Heron and Black-crowned Night-Heron, nest in colonies within the floodplain. These colonial nesting sites are vulnerable to human disturbance and destruction by high winds. The endangered dwarf trout lily also occurs in floodplain forests within part of the Wetland Management District.

Wetlands: To restore, protect, and maintain natural species diversity while emphasizing priority fish, wildlife and plants characteristic of wetlands within the northern tallgrass prairie ecosystem.

Discussion: Refuge and District wetlands contribute migration and production habitat for waterfowl, waterbirds, and shorebirds. Several of these key species are regional conservation priorities including the Mallard, Blue-winged Teal, Canvasback, Wood Duck, American Bittern, and Black Tern. Other wildlife species of local significance that use these wetlands include Great Blue Heron, Great Egret, river otter, mink, muskrat and several amphibian species. Floodplain and riverine wetlands located on the Refuge also provide important spawning and nursery habitats for resident fish.

Upland Forest: To restore, protect, and maintain natural species diversity while emphasizing priority wildlife and plants characteristic of upland forests within the northern tallgrass prairie ecosystem.

Discussion: Upland forests, primarily those located along the bluffs of the river valley, provide migration and production habitat for several species of songbirds that are significant locally or are included in the Region 3 RCP list. Among these species are Red-headed Woodpecker, Northern Flicker, and Loggerhead Shrike. Several locally or regionally significant raptors also use upland forests on the Refuge or throughout the Wetland Management District for either migration, nesting, and in some cases wintering habitat. These species include the Bald Eagle, Red-shouldered Hawk, and Long-eared Owl. The endangered dwarf trout lily also occurs in upland forests within part of the Wetland Management District.

Grasslands and Oak Savanna: To restore, protect, and maintain natural species diversity while emphasizing priority grassland-dependent wildlife and plants characteristic of the northern tallgrass prairie ecosystem.

Discussion: Refuge and Wetland District grasslands, especially those within the uplands of Waterfowl Production Areas, have the potential to provide benefits for birds that require large blocks of grasslands for nesting success and population viability. Oak savannas, historically found throughout the Minnesota River Valley, also afford critical habitat for some of these birds. This is important because populations of many Region 3 Regional RCP "grassland" bird species, such as Bobolink, Grasshopper Sparrow and Eastern Meadowlark have shown steady declines over the last 35 years. Large grassland patches (over 250 acres), or smaller connected grasslands or those in proximity to other non-forested habitats, provide the best nesting conditions for many area-sensitive bird species. Larger grassland blocks will also increase the nesting success of RCP waterfowl such as Mallards and Blue-winged Teal. In addition, several reptile and butterfly species of Special Concern in the State of Minnesota, such as five-lined skink, racer, gopher snake and western hognose snake, and the Arogos, Leonardus, and Powesheik Skippers will benefit from native grassland management.

Land Protection: To enhance the integrity of lands within the authorized boundary of the Refuge and contribute to the protection and restoration of fish and wildlife habitats within the Minnesota River watershed.

Discussion: Local communities and state agencies have worked together for years to restore and protect the unique natural qualities of the Minnesota River Valley. Efforts within the last decade have focused on reducing the sediment and pollutant load within the river to make it "swimmable and fishable" as soon as possible. The Service would like to contribute to that effort. The river and its riparian habitat is important to Federal trust species such as waterfowl, migratory songbirds and endangered plants. Land acquisition for new refuge units, either in fee or through conservation easements, and subsequent habitat restoration is one way the Service can contribute to the collective goal of a clean river and abundant and healthy fish, wildlife and plant communities.

Public Use: To provide high quality wildlife-dependent recreational and environmental education opportunities to a diverse audience. These activities will promote understanding, appreciation and support for Minnesota Valley National Wildlife Refuge and the Wetland Management District as well as the entire National Wildlife Refuge System.

Discussion: Under the National Wildlife Refuge System Improvement Act of 1997, the Service must provide opportunities for six priority uses: hunting, fishing, wildlife observation, wildlife photography, environmental education, and environmental interpretation. These uses will be encouraged where they do not conflict with the primary purposes of the Refuge and Management District.

Decision Framework

The Regional Director for the Great Lakes-Big Rivers Region will need to make two decisions based on this EA: (1) select an alternative and (2) determine if the selected alternative is a major Federal action significantly affecting the quality of the human environment, thus requiring preparation of an Environmental Impact Statement. The planning team has recommended Alternative C to the Regional Director. The Draft CCP was developed for implementation based on this recommendation.

Authority, Legal Compliance, and Compatibility

The National Wildlife Refuge System includes federal lands managed primarily to provide habitat for a diversity of fish, wildlife and plant species. National wildlife refuges are established under many different authorities and funding sources for a variety of purposes. The purposes for the Refuge were established by specific legislation and are listed in the previous section. The District's Waterfowl Production Areas are also part of the Refuge System and are acquired using receipts from the Migratory Bird Conservation Fund (Duck Stamp Fund).

Additional authority delegated by Congress, federal regulations, executive orders and several management plans guide the operation of the Refuge and Wetland District. The appendix of the CCP contains a list of the key laws, orders and regulations that provide a framework for the proposed action.

Scoping of the Issues

The planning process began in October 1998 when a team comprised of Service employees and a representative each from the Minnesota Department of Natural Resources and the Friends of the Minnesota Valley met to review the original Comprehensive or Master Plan (1984) and identify a number of issues and concerns that would likely affect the future of the Refuge and the District. The team agreed to a process for obtaining public input and for completion of the Refuge and District CCP. Public input was obtained using several methods including open houses, issue-based focus groups, public use surveys, and personal contacts. Please see Chapter 2 of the CCP for more detail on the scoping of issues.

Issues and Concerns

An array of issues, concerns, and opportunities were addressed during the planning process. Numerous discussions among citizens, focus group participants, resource specialists, and Refuge planning staff brought to light several recurring themes. In general, themes centered on appropriate recreational uses, confusing rules and regulations on public lands in the valley, land protection and watershed activities, and maintenance of Refuge and District facilities. Some of the issues raised during internal and public scoping included:

- Degradation of Minnesota River Water Quality
- Land Use and Development Adjacent to Refuge
- Loss in Quality of Visitor Facilities
- Completion of the Minnesota Valley State Trail
- Control of Exotic/Invasive Plants
- Mountain Biking
- Horseback Riding
- Low Public Awareness of Refuge and Resource Protection Goals

A complete listing and further discussion of these issues and concerns can be found in Chapter 2 of the CCP and Chapter 2 of this EA.

Chapter 2 – Description of the Alternatives

Formulation of Alternatives

Four management alternatives were developed by the planning team based on issues, concerns and opportunities presented during the CCP scoping process. The issues that are discussed came from individuals, cooperating agencies, conservation organizations and Refuge staff. A summary of the four alternatives is provided in Table 1 on page 113.

The following four management alternatives were developed to generally fit within the current Refuge and Wetland District budget. In other words, the alternatives were formulated under the assumption that a large budget increase for refuge operations is unlikely during the life of the plan. If an alternative calls for one program to increase significantly in size or scope other refuge programs would need to be reduced. However, we did provide for the possibility of new private resources (volunteers, grant funds, etc.) and a modest refuge program and/or staff funding increase. In addition, the airport mitigation Trust Fund established in 2000 will be able to contribute toward land acquisition, new facilities and some program increases.

The four management alternatives were developed to address most of the issues, concerns and opportunities identified during the CCP planning process. Specific impacts of implementing each alternative will be examined in seven broad issue categories;

Habitat: What level of habitat restoration and maintenance is appropriate given funding constraints and desired future conditions?

Fish, Wildlife and Plants: How should we deal with the overpopulation of some wildlife species, such as carp, white-tailed deer and beaver, that can cause negative impacts to vegetation and habitat management capabilities? Can we protect critical migratory bird habitats, such as heron colonies and Bald Eagle nests? Will the proposed management scenario benefit natural biodiversity?

Recreation: What is the appropriate level of recreational activities on Refuge and District lands? Does the Refuge adequately meet the mandate to provide quality wildlife-dependent recreation?

Secondary Recreational Uses: What are appropriate non-wildlife dependent recreational activities on Refuge and District lands?

Resource Threats: What aspects of surrounding land uses threaten the integrity of ecological processes on the Refuge and Waterfowl Production Areas? What can the refuge do to control or reduce negative impacts?

Land Protection: Will the Refuge and District continue to grow and for what reasons? Can the Refuge, and the U.S. Fish and Wildlife Service, play a larger role in resource conservation in the Minnesota River watershed?

Environmental Education: Will the quality of environmental education, both on-site and through outreach, be improved in the future? How can the airport mitigation Refuge Trust Fund be used to replace lost opportunities and/or expand the environmental education program?

Alternative A. Public Use Emphasis

This alternative would encourage a minimal approach to managing habitats while allowing for significantly more public recreational uses and an expanded environmental education program. Staff time, emphasis and resources would be shifted to allow for more public activities in all areas of the refuge. Additional wetlands, grasslands or oak savannas would not be restored on existing refuge lands. No land for Refuge units would be acquired outside of the current boundaries. Waterfowl Production Area acquisitions would proceed at current or reduced levels. Control of exotic plant or nuisance wildlife populations would be kept to a minimal and reactive level.

No new restrictions on recreational uses such as canoeing, horseback riding and mountain biking would occur under this alternative. The environmental education program could see a new visitor education facility, exhibits and interpretive materials. Additional staff and/or volunteers would be added in an effort to increase on-site public contacts throughout the Refuge.

Further site-specific detail, public involvement and planning under the National Environmental Policy Act will occur prior to construction of a visitor education facility or other major facility.

Alternative B. Current Situation–2002 (No Action)

The No Action alternative would favor existing, or status quo, refuge management and public outreach practices. Refuge staff would continue to restore and maintain existing wetland, grassland, forest and oak savanna habitats. New Refuge lands would be acquired to complete the current approved boundary. Biological controls and harvest methods would be used to control exotic plant or nuisance wildlife species. Current restrictions or prohibitions remain in place on canoeing, snowmobiling, horseback riding and off-trail biking. The environmental education program could see a new visitor education facility upriver but only minor improvements in existing exhibits and interpretive materials.

Alternative C. Balanced Public Use and Habitat Management (Preferred Alternative)

The Service planning team has identified Alternative C, a balanced public use and habitat management approach, as the preferred alternative. Alternative C was selected and developed based on public input and the best judgement of the planning team. The strategies presented in the CCP were developed as a direct result of the selection of Alternative C.

The preferred alternative would promote active management of existing habitats, higher quality recreational experiences for visitors and improved public outreach strategies. Refuge staff would continue to restore and maintain existing wetland, grassland and floodplain forest areas. Oak savanna habitats could receive new and intensive maintenance applications. New Refuge lands could be acquired up to 10,737 acres (see Appendix I: Land Protection Plan). The District's Waterfowl Production Area program would also expand as worthy sites are identified. Integrated biological controls and harvest methods would be used to control exotic plant or nuisance wildlife species. Horseback riding and

Table 1: Summary of Management Alternatives for the Minnesota Valley National Wildlife Refuge and Wetland District.

Issues	Alternative A Public Use Emphasis	Alternative B Current Situation (No Action)	Alternative C Balanced Public Use and Habitat Management (Preferred Alternative)	Alternative D Habitat Management Emphasis
Habitat				
Wetlands	No active management.	Mitigative management.	Manage intensively with new water control structures	Same as Alt. C.
Grasslands / Oak Savanna	No active management.	Restoration and management (hydro-ax and burn).	Prairie eco-type planting scheme and intensive management.	Restoration with component of native trees, shrubs and forbs.
Floodplain Forest	No active management.	Natural regen-eration.	Intensive restor-ation (plant trees).	Intensive restor-ation with full complement of native trees and shrubs.
Upland Forest	No active management.	Natural regen-eration.	Intensive restor-ation (tree planting).	Intensive restor-ation with full complement of native trees and shrubs.
Fish, Wildlife and Plants				
Exotic Plant Species	No control measures.	Limited control (2 species), minimal biological control.	Control of target species and integrated biological control.	Full control of all species and int-egrated biological control.
Nuisance Wildlife Control	Reactive control and public education.	Proactive control (i.e. deer hunts and beaver control).	Same as Alt. B.	Same as Alt. B, but consider adding species to active control list.
Critical Migratory Bird Nesting Areas	Enforce minimum legal protection.	Limited access and protection (some nesting areas not closed).	Minimum level of protection as stated under MnDNR guide-lines (case-by-case).	Maximum level of protection as stated under MnDNR guidelines.
Endangered and Threatened Species (Federal)	Possible limited disturbance of Bald Eagle nests.	Limited closures to protect Bald Eagle nests.	Limited closures to protect Bald Eagle nests.	Increased closures to protect Bald Eagle nests.

Table 1: Summary of Management Alternatives for the Minnesota Valley National Wildlife Refuge and Wetland District (Continued)

Issues	Alternative A Public Use Emphasis	Alternative B Current Situation (No Action)	Alternative C Balanced Public Use and Habitat Management (Preferred Alternative)	Alternative D Habitat Management Emphasis
Recreation				
Hunting	Allow on all refuge units upstream of of I-35W consistent with state regulations.	Allow within select units/areas (identified in hunting brochure).	Hunting program designed to improve quality (limited permits system).	Significantly decrease hunting on refuge.
Fishing (Minnesota River, side-channels and Refuge lakes)	Open to all fishing (non-motorized boats only). Improved or new boat and shore-line access.	Bank fishing only on Minnesota River.	Improve quality of fishing and access with active manage-ment (i.e., Long Meadow and Chaska lakes.	Bank fishing with seasonal closures near sensitive wildlife habitats.
Recreational Trail System	Complete trails as proposed in 1984 Master Plan	Same as Alt. A plus maintain existing trails.	Partner with DNR to help complete State Trail. Possible trail development for all refuge units. Provide trail maps.	Same as Alt. B
Secondary Recreational Uses				
Bicycling	Allowed on State Trail and existing refuge trails.	Allowed on State Trail and existing refuge trails.	Limited access routes to State Trail and designated refuge trails.	Allowed on State Trail only.
Horseback Riding	State Trail, Fisher Lake, Rice Lake and Blue (unregulated).	State Trail, Fisher Lake, Rice Lake and Blue (unregulated).	Allowed on State Trail and across limited access routes.	Same as Alt. C
Canoeing (excluding Minnesota River, non-motorized only)	Unregulated (will be allowed on all Refuge waters).	No canoeing.	Increase in canoe trip interpretive programs.	No canoeing.
Resource Threats				
Storm water, spills and persistent contaminants	No action.	Reactive actions only with minimal monitoring.	Proactive, work with cities and include routine monitoring.	Same as Alt. C.
Land use and development adjacent to Refuge	No action.	React to immediate threats to Refuge resources.	Proactive. Work with partners and decision-makers.	Same as Alt. C.

Table 1: Summary of Management Alternatives for the Minnesota Valley National Wildlife Refuge and Wetland District (Continued)

Issues	Alternative A Public Use Emphasis	Alternative B Current Situation (No Action)	Alternative C Balanced Public Use and Habitat Management (Preferred Alternative)	Alternative D Habitat Management Emphasis
Land Protection				
Land Protection: Wetland Management District	No new WPA acquisitions.	Average 500-1,000 acres per year in fee and easements.	Acquire approximately 750 acres per year.	Acquire 25,000 acres in total.
Land Protection: Existing Refuge and Beyond	No or limited acquisitions. Only manage lands within existing Refuge boundary.	Acquire and manage lands only within existing Refuge boundary (14,000 acres total).	Add up to 10,737 acres to Refuge	Protect up to 100,000 acres up-river based on 1994 Citizens Advisory Committee recommendations.
Environmental Education				
Need for New Facilities	Add visitor education facility, possibly at Chaska, Rapids Lake, or Louisville.	Add visitor education facility, possibly at Chaska, Rapids Lake, or Louisville.	Add visitor education facility, possibly at Chaska, Rapids Lake, or Louisville.	Decrease effort directed toward public education and use of Refuge.
Underused Existing Facilities and Interpretive Media	Improve outreach media and interpretive materials.	No change in quality and quantity of outreach efforts.	Same as Alt. A.	Decrease effort directed toward public education and use of Refuge.
Outdated Exhibits	Replace and actively maintain exhibits. Create a multi-purpose room.	Minimal maintenance with occasional improvements.	Replace and actively maintain exhibits. Create a multi-purpose room.	Minimal maintenance with occasional improvements.
Low Public Awareness of Refuge and Protection Goals	Increase in staffing. Explore new techniques for outreach and enforcement.	No increase in outreach or law enforcement.	Increase in staffing. Explore new techniques for outreach and enforcement.	No increase in outreach or law enforcement.

the use of snowmobiles and mountain bikes would be limited to authorized segments of the Minnesota Valley State Trail. The environmental education program could see a new visitor education facility upriver with needed improvements in existing exhibits and interpretive materials. Additional staff, along with volunteers and interns, would be essential to implement an expanded public use program.

Alternative D. Habitat Management Emphasis

Alternative D would emphasize the pro-active management of existing habitats. Available staff and discretionary funding would be applied to fish and wildlife habitat enhancements such as prescribed burning of grasslands and oak savannas, planting trees in converted bottomland forests and invasive plant control. The biological research and monitoring program would also receive more attention. In contrast to the expanding habitat work, new recreational opportunities for visitors would not be pursued and environmental education and outreach programs would remain at the year 2001 level or below.

Refuge staff would restore and maintain existing wetland, grassland and floodplain forest areas. Oak savanna habitats would receive intensive maintenance applications including hand cutting of woody plant invasives. New Refuge lands could be acquired up to a 100,000-acre maximum (see Appendix I: Land Protection Plan). The District's Waterfowl Production Area program would also expand as worthy sites are identified. Integrated biological controls and harvest methods would be used to control exotic plant or nuisance wildlife species. Horseback riding and the use of snowmobiles and mountain bikes would be limited to authorized segments of the Minnesota Valley State Trail. The environmental education program could see a new visitor education facility upriver but only minor improvements in existing exhibits and interpretive materials.

Chapter 3 – Affected Environment

Minnesota Valley National Wildlife Refuge is located along 40 miles of the lower Minnesota River from Minneapolis, Minnesota, upstream to the town of Jordan, Minnesota. The Refuge, with a current approved boundary of 14,000 acres, was established by Congress in 1976. The Minnesota Valley Wetland Management District was established in 1994 and the 14-county District includes conservation easements and fee ownership of over 5,000 acres. The following section briefly describes the Minnesota River Valley downstream from the Cottonwood River at New Ulm to its confluence with the Mississippi River at Fort Snelling. More detail is included in Chapter 3 of the CCP.

Lower Minnesota River: Major vegetation community types found within the Refuge and the lower Minnesota River Valley include floodplain forest, upland forest, oak savanna and native prairie. The floodplain forests, which can flood in the spring or after a heavy rainfall, are dominated by water tolerant tree species such as silver maple, cottonwood and black willow. The upland forests consist of oak forest in well drained areas and maple-basswood forests in wetter sites such as ravines and moist terrace slopes. Existing oak savannas are primarily grazed pastures with scattered bur and northern pin oak trees. Remnant prairies, with a mix of warm season grasses and forbs, are generally found at sites along the river bluff (known locally as goat prairies) or are maintained on state and county park lands.

Middle Minnesota River: From the air, the midsection of the Minnesota River appears as a ribbon of green stretching through a vast patchwork of crop fields, roads and prairie settlements. The river corridor, at the historic juncture of the Northern Tallgrass Prairie and the Big Woods, still includes remnant prairies, deciduous upland forests, floodplain forests, oak savannas, and at least eight types of wetlands. Downstream from the City of New Ulm, numerous small streams and several major tributaries, including the Le Sueur, Blue Earth and Cottonwood Rivers enter the Minnesota River. These rivers flow slowly as the range of elevations in the Minnesota River Valley and surrounding uplands, some of the lowest in the State, varies only from 600 to 800 feet.

Photograph by Scott Sharkey

More than 260 species of birds use the area during migration and 100-150 of these species nest in the Minnesota River Watershed. Bald Eagles use the area for nesting and feeding each spring and fall. Every year, 30,000-40,000 waterfowl congregate in the lower portion of the Minnesota River Valley prior to fall migration. This avian diversity is complemented by approximately 50 species of mammals and 30 species of reptiles and amphibians. At least 10 game fish species are found in the river and tributaries including walleye, sauger, largemouth bass and channel catfish.

Threatened and Endangered Species

One federally listed species (Bald Eagle) and two state-listed species (Loggerhead Shrike and Common Tern) bird species use the Minnesota River Valley during part of their life cycle. Blanding's turtle, a state-listed reptile, is also found in suitable habitat.

Four more federally listed species have historically occurred on or near the Refuge or District, or are undocumented but may be found in suitable habitat. The Karner blue butterfly (*Lycaeides samuelis*), a federally listed threatened species, and its larval host plant, wild blue lupine (*Lupinus perennis*) have not been found but, although they are rare, could exist in the region. The dwarf trout lily (*Erythronium popullans*), a federally listed endangered species, occurs in Rice County and so may be found within the Refuge or District. Prairie bush clover (*Lespedeza leptostachya*), a federally listed threatened species, may occur in the western portion of the District since suitable habitat exists. The Higgins eye pearly mussel (*Lampsilis higginsi*), a federally listed endangered species, historically occurred in large rivers and, although it is listed as rare or absent, could occur in the Minnesota River.

Archeological and Cultural Values

Archeological records show evidence of the presence of all cultural periods from the retreat of the glaciers to the present day on the Refuge and the District. Known and potential sites include prehistoric isolated finds, camps, villages, subsistence and procurement stations, quarries, and mounds and human burials; and post contact (Western culture) Indian villages, trading posts, homesteads, farmsteads (buildings and land), other rural buildings and structures, cemeteries, trails, roads, and railroads, ferries, conservation projects, drainage ditches, open pit mines (e.g., gravel), sacred sites, cultural hunting and gathering areas, and battlefields.

To date, archeological investigations have covered about 1,500 acres of Refuge and District land. Through these studies and from other sources, 80 cultural resource sites have been identified. Most Refuge and District lands are in close association with larger bodies of water and permanent streams, the same landforms that appear to have been preferred by prehistoric inhabitants as well as more recent settlers. The number of reported sites is expect to be a small fraction of the total number of sites actually present on Service land.

Chapter 4 – Environmental Consequences

Effects Common to all Alternatives

Specific environmental and social impacts of implementing each alternative are examined in the seven broad issue categories; habitat, fish/wildlife/plants, recreation, secondary recreational uses, resource threats, land protection and environmental education. However, a few potential effects will be the same under each alternative and are summarized below:

Air and Water Quality: Habitat management involving prescribed burning may occur and only under ideal conditions of weather. Smoke management practices will be implemented during all burning events. Refuge management activities and visitor use should not negatively affect water quality. Future land acquisition in erosion-prone areas and encouraging municipal storm water treatments will improve water quality in the Minnesota River and tributaries.

Cultural Resources: The U.S. Fish and Wildlife Service is responsible for managing archeological and historic sites found on federal land. At the start of the CCP planning process, the Service contracted with U.S. West Research, Inc. to produce a Cultural Resource Management Plan for the Refuge and the District's Waterfowl Production Areas (Godfrey 1999). The three volume plan was delivered in June 1999. There are 77 known historical sites located on Service lands. Sites include ferry/steamboat landings, farmsteads, trading posts, bridges, townsites, etc. Many sites have not been evaluated regarding their eligibility for the National Register of Historic Places. However, at least 24 sites have been determined to be ineligible.

The Cultural Resource Management Plan will be used by Refuge managers to ensure compliance with relevant federal, tribal, state and local laws and regulations. Prior to all habitat and facility maintenance activities, appropriate efforts will be made to identify known and possible cultural resources within the area of potential impact. Avoidance of cultural resources would be the preferred treatment.

Environmental Justice: Executive Order 12898 "Federal Actions to Address Environmental Justice in Minority Populations and Low-Income Populations" was signed by President Clinton on February 11, 1994, to focus Federal attention on the environmental and human health conditions of minority and low-income populations with the goal of achieving environmental protection for all communities. The Order directed Federal agencies to develop environmental justice strategies to aid in identifying and addressing disproportionately high and adverse human health or environmental effects of their programs, policies, and activities on minority and low-income populations. The Order is also intended to promote nondiscrimination in Federal programs substantially affecting human health and the environment, and to provide minority and low-income communities access to public information and participation in matters relating to human health or the environment.

None of the management alternatives described in this EA will disproportionately place any adverse environmental, economic, social, or health impacts on minority and low-income populations. Implementation of any action alternative that includes public use and environmental education will actually provide a benefit to urban residents living in the Twin Cities Metro Area.

Climate Change Impacts: The U.S. Department of the Interior issued an order in January 2001 requiring federal agencies under its direction that have land management responsibilities to consider potential climate change impacts as part of long range planning endeavors.

The increase of carbon within the earth's atmosphere has been linked to the gradual rise in surface temperature commonly referred to as global warming. In relation to comprehensive conservation planning for national wildlife refuges, carbon sequestration constitutes the primary climate-related impact to be considered in planning. The U.S. Department of Energy's *"Carbon Sequestration Research and Development"* (U.S. DOE, 1999) defines carbon sequestration as "...the capture and secure storage of carbon that would otherwise be emitted to or remain in the atmosphere."

The land is a tremendous force in carbon sequestration. Terrestrial biomes of all sorts – grasslands, forests, wetlands, tundra, perpetual ice and desert – are effective both in preventing carbon emission and acting as a biological "scrubber"of atmospheric carbon monoxide. The Department of Energy report's conclusions noted that ecosystem protection is important to carbon sequestration and may reduce or prevent loss of carbon currently stored in the terrestrial biosphere.

Preserving natural habitat for wildlife is the heart of any long range plan for national wildlife refuges. The actions proposed in this Comprehensive Conservation Plan would preserve or restore land and water, and would thus enhance carbon sequestration. This in turn contributes positively to efforts to mitigate human-induced global climate changes.

Summary of Effects by Alternative

The following section describes the environmental consequences of adopting each refuge management alternative. Table 2 (pages 120-122) addresses the likely outcomes for specific issues and is organized by broad issue categories.

Alternative A: Public Use Emphasis

This alternative would emphasize recreational uses and environmental education while maintaining a low maintenance approach to managing habitats. Staff time and resources would be shifted to allow for more public activities in all areas of the refuge. Wetlands, grasslands or oak savannas would not be actively restored on existing refuge lands. No land for Refuge units would be acquired outside of the current boundaries. Hillside forests and goat prairies adjacent to the refuge would continue to be lost due to subdivision and housing developments.

Table 2: Summary of Environmental Consequences for Management Alternatives for the Minnesota Valley National Wildlife Refuge and Wetland Management District

Issues	Alternative A Public Use Emphasis	Alternative B Current Situation (No Action)	Alternative C Balanced Public Use and Habitat Management (Preferred Alternative)	Alternative D Habitat Management Emphasis
Habitat				
Wetlands	Decreased. No active management.	Slight increase. Mitigative mange-ment.	Increased. New water control structures.	Same as Alt. C.
Grasslands / Oak Savanna	Decreased. No active management.	Increased through restoration and active management.	Increased through planting and intensive management.	Increased through restoration of native trees, shrubs and forbs.
Floodplain Forest	Decreased. No active management.	Increased through natural regeneration.	Increased through intensive restoration (plant trees).	Increased by restoration with full complement of native trees and shrubs.
Upland Forest	Decreased. No active management.	Increased through natural regeneration.	Increased through intensive restoration (tree planting).	Increased by intensive restor-ation with native trees and shrubs.
Fish, Wildlife and Plants				
Exotic Plant Species	Loss of habitat due to lack of control measures.	Loss of habitat due to limited control measures.	Slight gain of habitat due to target species and integrated bio-logical control.	Gain of habitat due to full control of all species and integrated bio-logical control.
Nuisance Wildlife	Stable to increased populations due to reactive control and and public education.	Stable to decreased populations due to proactive control.	Same as Alt. B.	Same as Alt. B, but consider adding species to control list.
Critical Migratory Bird Nesting Areas (Bald Eagle, Herons)	Increase in disturbance. Enforce minimum legal protections.	Limited disturbance through limited access and some area closures.	Limited disturbance through minimum level of protection as stated under MnDNR guidelines.	Decreased distur-bance through maximum level of protection as stated under MnDNR guidelines.
Endangered and Threatened Species (Federal)	Stable to increased disturbance of Bald Eagle nests.	Stable. Limited closures to protect Bald Eagle nests.	Stable. Limited closures to protect Bald Eagle nests.	Reduced disturb-ance through more area closures around Bald Eagle nests.

Table 2 (Continued): Summary of Environmental Consequences for Management Alternatives for the Minnesota Valley National Wildlife Refuge and Wetland Management District

Issues	Alternative A Public Use Emphasis	Alternative B Current Situation (No Action)	Alternative C Balanced Public Use and Habitat Management (Preferred Alternative)	Alternative D Habitat Management Emphasis
Recreation				
Hunting	Increased. Allow on all Refuge units upstream of I-35W consistent with State regulations.	Stable. Allow within select units/areas (identified in hunting brochure).	Stable. Same as Alt. B except that program will be designed to improve quality of experience.	Stable to decreased hunting opportunities.
Fishing (Minnesota River, side-channels and Refuge lakes)	Increased. Open to all fishing (non-motorized boats only). Improved or new boat and shore-line access.	Stable. Bank fishing only on Minnesota River.	Increased. Improved quality of fishing and and access.	Decreased. Bank fishing with seasonal closures near sensitive wildlife habitats.
Recreational Trail System	Increased. Complete trails as proposed in 1984 Master Plan.	Same as Alt. A, plus maintain existing trails.	Increased. Partner with DNR to help complete State Trail. Possible trail development for most Refuge units.	Same as Alt. A with less emphasis on maintaining existing trails.
Secondary Recreational Uses				
Bicycling	Stable to increased. Allowed on State Trail and existing Refuge trails.	Same as Alt. A.	Stable to decreased. Limited access routes to State Trail and designated Refuge trails.	Decreased. Allowed on State Trail only.
Horseback Riding	Limited to State Trail, Fisher Lake, Rice Lake and Blue (unregulated).	Same as Alt. A.	Decreased. Allowed on State Trail and across limited access routes only.	Same as Alt. C.
Canoeing (Excluding Minnesota River, non-motorized only)	Increased. Would be allowed on all Refuge waters.	No canoeing.	Increased. More interpretive canoe trips.	Same as Alt. B.
Resource Threats				
Storm Water, Spills and Persistent Contaminants	No action.	Stable protection. Reactive actions only with minimal monitoring.	Increased protection due to proactive work with cities and routine monitoring.	Same as Alt. C.
Land Use and Development Adjacent to Refuge	No action.	Stable protection, reaction to immediate threats to Refuge resources.	Increased protection due to more work with partners and decision-makers.	Same as Alt. C.

Table 2 (Continued): Summary of Environmental Consequences for Management Alternatives for the Minnesota Valley National Wildlife Refuge and Wetland Management District

Issues	Alternative A Public Use Emphasis	Alternative B Current Situation (No Action)	Alternative C Balanced Public Use and Habitat Management (Preferred Alternative)	Alternative D Habitat Management Emphasis
Land Protection				
Land Protection: Wetland District	Decreased. No new WPA acquisitions.	Slight increase. Average 500-1,000 acres per year in fee and easements.	Increased. Acquire ~ 750 acres per year.	Increased. Acquire 25,000 acres in total.
Land Protection: Existing Refuge and Beyond	Decreased. No or limited acquisitions. Only manage lands within existing Refuge boundary.	Stable. Acquire and manage lands only within existing Refuge boundary.	Increased. Add up to 10,737 acres to Refuge.	Increased. Protect from 50,000 to to 100,000 acres.
Environmental Education				
Public Use Facilities	Increased. Add visitor education facility or facilities.	Same as Alt. A.	Same as Alt. A.	Decreased. Less effort directed toward outreach and use of Refuge.
Quality of Interpretive Media	Increased. Improved outreach media and materials.	Stable. No change in quality and quantity of outreach efforts.	Same as Alt. A.	Decreased. Less effort directed toward education.
Quality of of Exhibits	Increased. Replace and actively maintain exhibits. Create a multi-purpose room.	Slight increase. Occasional improve-ments.	Increased. Replace and actively maintain exhibits. Create a multi-purpose room.	Same as Alt. B.
Public Awareness of Refuge and Resource Protection Goals	Increased. More staff and new techniques for outreach and enforcement.	Stable. No increase in outreach or law enforcement.	Same as Alt. A.	Same as Alt. B.

Control of exotic plants or nuisance wildlife populations would be kept to a minimal and reactive level. Purple loosestrife would continue to pioneer into new areas with a resultant loss in wetland value for wildlife. However, the deer herd could be controlled through public hunting that would be expanded to new areas under this alternative.

Secondary recreational uses such as horseback riding and mountain biking would be allowed on existing trails. However, no new areas would be opened to these uses. The environmental education program could see a new visitor education facility, exhibits and interpretive materials. Additional staff and/or volunteers would be added in an effort to increase on-site public contacts throughout the Refuge.

Alternative B: The Current Situation (No Action)

Existing Refuge management and public outreach practices would be favored under this alternative. Refuge staff would continue to restore and maintain existing wetland, grassland, forest and oak savanna habitats. Land would be acquired to complete the current approved boundary of 14,000 acres. Approximately 500-1,000 acres of habitat in Waterfowl Production Areas would be added within the District each year.

Current restrictions or prohibitions remain in place on canoeing, snowmobiling, horseback riding and off-trail biking. A new visitor education facility would be constructed upriver using Trust funds. Minor improvements would occur for existing exhibits and interpretive materials.

The Current Refuge and District Program portion within Chapter 4 of the CCP contains more detail about the current situation.

Alternative C: Balanced Public Use and Habitat Management (Preferred Alternative)

The preferred alternative would promote active management of existing fish, wildlife and plant habitats and higher quality recreational experiences for visitors. Refuge staff would continue to restore and maintain existing and new wetland, grassland and floodplain forest areas. Oak savanna habitats could receive new and intensive maintenance applications. Forest restoration would include active strategies such as planting trees and protecting them from browsing damage. Integrated biological controls and harvest methods would be used to control exotic plant or nuisance wildlife species.

New Refuge lands could be acquired up to a 10,737-acre maximum (see Appendix I: Land Protection Plan). The District's Waterfowl Production Area inventory would also expand as worthy sites are identified.

Horseback riding and mountain bike use would be limited to authorized segments of the Minnesota Valley State Trail. The environmental education program would see a new visitor education facility upriver. Some improvements in existing exhibits and interpretive materials would also occur. New public outreach strategies would result in greater public understanding and advocacy for Refuge and District resources.

Alternative D: Habitat Management Emphasis

Alternative D emphasizes the active management of existing fish, wildlife and plant habitats. Available staff and discretionary funding would be applied to habitat enhancements such as prescribed burning of grasslands and oak savannas, tree plantings in converted bottomland forests and invasive plant control. The biological research and monitoring program would also receive more attention.

Refuge staff would restore and maintain existing wetland, grassland and floodplain forest areas. Oak savanna habitats would receive new and intensive maintenance applications. New Refuge lands could be acquired up to a 100,000 acre maximum (see Appendix I: Land Protection Plan). The District's Waterfowl Production Area program would expand to 25,000 acres. Integrated biological controls and harvest methods would be used to control exotic plant or nuisance wildlife species.

In contrast to the expanding habitat work, new recreational opportunities for visitors would not be pursued and environmental education and outreach programs would remain at the year 2001 level or below. Horseback riding and the use of mountain bikes would be limited to authorized segments of the Minnesota Valley State Trail. The environmental education program could see a new visitor education facility upriver but only minor improvements in existing exhibits and interpretive materials. A slight increase in public awareness of the Refuge and District is expected due to land protection efforts and the new visitor facility.

Cumulative Impact Analysis

"Cumulative impact" is the term that refers to impacts on the environment that result from the incremental impact of the proposed action when added to other past, present and reasonably foreseeable future actions, regardless of what agency (federal or nonfederal) or person undertakes such other actions. Cumulative impacts can result from individually minor but collectively significant actions taking place over a period of time. In this section, the cumulative impacts of each of the four alternatives are discussed in terms of migratory birds, wetlands and floodplain habitat, and prairie and oak savanna restoration.

Migratory Birds

The Refuge and District contains habitat important to numerous bird species including waterfowl, songbirds, marsh and wading birds, shorebirds, raptors, and upland game birds. Some of the factors relevant to migratory birds are offered in the following list; Chapter 3 of the CCP offers greater detail.

- More than 260 species of birds use Refuge and District lands during migration and up to 150 species nest there.

- In the Refuge and District, 48 birds identified as "species of concern" are rare, declining, or dependent on vulnerable habitats, including 43 that breed there.

- About 44 percent of the species of concern depend on some type of grassland habitat.

- In North America, grassland birds have exhibited steeper declines than any other avian group.

- It is important to maintain a mosaic of grassland habitats to meet the varying needs of grassland birds.

Each alternative would have a different effect on migratory birds. The cumulative benefit of Alternative 3 and 4 would be the most positive because the habitat base increases and is enhanced, and management is intensified. In the long-term, Alternative 1 would have a negative impact on migratory birds. The needs of area-sensitive species that are declining, such as Northern Harrier, Upland Sandpiper, Henslow's Sparrow and Savannah Sparrow, would not be met in the existing small Waterfowl Production Areas that average 200 acres in size or less. Population declines would likely continue in the region.

Maintaining current management and land holdings as described in Alternative 2 (Current Situation) would have a neutral to slight benefit for migratory birds. If other conservation organizations are not actively acquiring land, this alternative would have a greater long-term benefit even if land is not restored immediately because it would mean that habitat is at least being set aside for conservation purposes. If other agencies and organizations do pursue land acquisition, and if those lands adjoin Service lands, this alternative provides an even greater benefit.

Under Alternative 3 and 4, the combination of acquiring land and expanding management would contribute to improved breeding and nesting success. This alternative would position the Service to contribute to improved migratory bird population numbers, and benefits would be even greater if the Minnesota Department of Natural Resources and non-government conservation organizations also focused acquisition and management efforts on migratory birds.

Wetlands and Floodplain Habitat

All alternatives will include management of wetland and floodplain habitats. The positive cumulative impact of Alternative 3 & 4 will be the greatest because of focused wetland restoration, management and acquisition; especially throughout the District. Restoration of floodplain forest habitats on the Refuge would also be accelerated under these two alternatives.

The prairie pothole region once included about 20 million acres of small wetlands.

- Today, only about 5.3 million acres remain in 2.7 million basins within five states; drainage has been so extensive that in many areas the water table has been lowered and the hydrology of the entire region has been transformed.

- Nearly two out of three of the remaining wetlands in Minnesota are privately owned; consequently, they are vulnerable to continued drainage, development, and pollution.

- Loss of productive floodplain forest habitats on the Minnesota River and tributaries has occurred due to conversion to cropland, timber harvesting, and gravel mining.

Wetland restoration and management are high priorities on the District. Under Alternative 1, wetlands and riparian habitat would not gain increased benefit and may actually degrade as adjacent land use impacts water quality.

Conservation efforts by the Minnesota Department of Natural Resources and nongovernment conservation organizations could mitigate this impact if they acquired land adjoining the Waterfowl Production Areas and restored wetlands. Restoration efforts on wetlands and streams adjoining Service-owned lands could improve water quality and wetland functions.

Alternative 2 would benefit wetlands and riparian areas somewhat on individual Waterfowl Production Areas and Refuge units as lands are acquired over time. Although restoration may not be immediate, land uses that impact water quality, such as growing crops and grazing cattle, would likely be discontinued. These benefits would be augmented if other conservation entities acquired and restored land, but the benefits provided under Alternative 2 would not be diminished if others did not pursue land acquisition.

With land acquisition and expanded management components, Alternative 3 and 4 would provide the most benefits to wetland and floodplain forest habitat. Healthier wetland and riparian complexes in bigger blocks of land would benefit all wetland-dependent species. The positive benefits would be greater if the Minnesota Department of Natural Resources and non-government conservation organizations were also acquiring and restoring habitat, however the positive impacts would not be diminished if others did not pursue the same course.

Prairie and Oak Savanna Restoration

All alternatives would increase the amount of prairie and oak savanna but the positive cumulative impacts of alternatives 3 and 4 will be greatest because of the focused and strategic land acquisition and prairie restoration with native prairie species.

- There is perhaps no ecosystem on earth that has been so completely altered.

- Prairie and oak savanna landscapes once covered much of western and south-central Minnesota; now, less than 1 percent of the original prairie and virtually none of the oak savannas are left.

- Prairie landscapes contain hundreds of species of plants, invertebrates, and wildlife. Some prairies contain as many as 200 plant species.

- Over the past decade, virtually all plantings of upland cover on Waterfowl Production Areas have been with native grasses. In recent years, a more diverse mixture of native forbs and warm and cool season native grasses have been used.

Over time, Alternatives 2-4 would benefit prairie and oak savanna habitats as lands were acquired and restored. Benefits to prairie and oak savanna habitats would be greatest under Alternatives 3 and 4. The habitats would be restored at a faster pace than under Alternative 2. Block sizes may be greater, allowing for a higher diversity of plant species. If the Minnesota Department of Natural Resources and conservation organizations discontinued acquiring and restoring these habitats, there would be a negative impact to the species that require grasslands.

Chapter 5 – List of Preparers

Please see Appendix K

Chapter 6 – Consultation and Coordination With the Public and Others

The Minnesota Valley NWR Comprehensive Conservation Plan and Environmental Assessment has been written with the participation of Service staff, Refuge users and the local community. The CCP planning process began in October 1998 with the formation of a refuge planning team. Subsequently, the planning team hosted a series of open houses in communities along the river. Individuals from state agencies, non-profit organizations, and others were invited to join one of five small discussion groups. Each group dealt with a certain topic; refuge management and biology, environmental education and interpretation, threats and conflicts, and refuge expansion and watershed activities. The recommendations from these working groups provided valuable information for the authors of this plan. Please see Chapter 2 of the CCP for more information on the public scoping process.

Chapter 7 – Public Comments on the Draft Environmental Assessment

The Draft CCP/EA was available for public review and comment from May 8, 2002, through July 31, 2002. The Service received 32 letters and e-mail comments during the review period. However, only a few comments were directed toward information presented in the Draft EA. Nearly all reviewers limited their comments to specific objectives and strategies under the preferred alternative presented in the CCP. These verbal and written remarks received from the public contributed to several modifications in the CCP document. Please see Chapter 2 of the CCP for more details.

A comment we received that was specific to the Draft EA was that the Refuge Mitigation Trust Should not be considered the primary funding source for future land acquisition, but only one of many partnership sources. Another reviewer suggested that the land evaluation criteria should include an emphasis on calcareous fens as a desired wetland type. In addition, several writers simply endorsed the future direction of Refuge management or land protection goals presented in the preferred alternative.

Chapter 8 – References and Literature Cited

Please see Appendix H

Appendix A Exhibit 1: Goals, Objectives and Strategies by Management Alternative

Goals, Objectives and Strategies	Alt. A	Alt. B	Alt. C	Alt. D
Alternative A: Public Use Emphasis Alternative B: Current Situation Alternative C: Balanced Public Use/Habitat Management (Preferred Alternative) Alternative D: Habitat Management Emphasis				
Biological Goals				
Goal 1. Floodplain Forest: To restore, protect, and maintain natural species diversity while emphasizing priority wildlife and plants characteristic of floodplain forests within the northern tallgrass prairie ecosystem.				
1.1 Objective: By 2017, provide 4,700 acres of floodplain forest along the Minnesota River and major tributaries to benefit Bald Eagles, cavity-nesting birds such as Wood Ducks, colonial-nesting wading birds and rare plant communities.		X	X	X
Strategy: 1.1.1 Through research and investigation, determine the long-term viability of the floodplain forest community that exists on Refuge lands.		X	X	X
Strategy 1.1.2 Employ a senior wildlife biologist (GS 11/12). This position will benefit all of the biological goals set forth in this CCP.		X	X	X
Strategy 1.1.3 Continue to acquire important floodplain forests that provide valuable wildlife habitats within the Minnesota River Valley and throughout the Wetland Management District. Where possible, block sizes greater than 100 acres should be acquired.		X	X	X
Strategy 1.1.4 Protect existing Bald Eagle nests and heron and egret nesting colonies from human disturbance throughout the breeding season.	X	X	X	X
Strategy 1.1.5 Complete a forest management plan by 2005 that establishes long-term objectives for each block of floodplain forest that exists on Refuge Units.			X	X
Strategy 1.1.6 Using native species from a tree nursery and root propagation methods, continue to restore no fewer than 100 acres of floodplain forest each year until all potential floodplain forest is restored.		X	X	X
Strategy 1.1.7 Develop a root propagation nursery using local sources of tree species.			X	X

Goals, Objectives and Strategies	Alt. A	Alt. B	Alt. C	Alt. D
Strategy 1.1.8 Develop and implement a floodplain forest monitoring protocol designed to assess restoration success, vegetative changes, and wildlife response.			X	X
Goal 2. Wetlands: To restore, protect, and maintain natural species diversity while emphasizing priority fish, wildlife and plants characteristic of wetlands within the northern tallgrass prairie ecosystem.				
2.1 Objective: By 2017, provide 7,400 acres of wetlands within the floodplain of the Minnesota River and 4,600 acres of prairie pothole wetlands in the Wetland Management District to benefit priority waterfowl species, marsh, shore and wading birds and healthy aquatic ecosystems.		X	X	X
Strategy 2.1.1 Maintain the productivity of Refuge wetlands through the installation of water control structures and the active management of water levels through an annual water management plan.		X	X	X
Strategy 2.1.2 Continue to actively manage wetlands, wet meadows, and fens located on Refuge and Wetland Management District lands through periodic prescribed burning to control invasion of brush and other woody vegetation.		X	X	X
Strategy 2.1.3 Continue to seek Environmental Management Program funding and other sources of funding to improve, maintain, restore, and manage wetland habitats on Refuge.	X	X	X	X
Strategy 2.1.4 Develop monitoring protocols to determine effectiveness of wetland management actions upon vegetative diversity and use by wildlife.		X	X	X
Strategy 2.1.5 Continue to acquire important wetlands and associated habitats for both the Refuge and Wetland Management District.		X	X	X
Strategy 2.1.6 Manage and protect the Savage Fen Unit, in cooperation with the MnDNR and others, for as long as the Refuge administers the area.	X	X	X	X
Strategy 2.1.7 Inventory aquatic species (fish and macro-invertebrates) in Refuge streams, creeks and lakes using volunteers, students, and Refuge staff. Biologists from the Service s Fishery Resource Office in LaCrosse, Wisconsin, will conduct sampling surveys at least once every 5 years to detect trends in fish abundance and distribution.	X	X	X	X
Strategy 2.1.8 Restore Continental Grain berm along Eagle Creek to prevent creek degradation.	X	X	X	X

Goals, Objectives and Strategies	Alt. A	Alt. B	Alt. C	Alt. D
Strategy 2.1.9 Develop and implement a comprehensive water quality monitoring program designed to obtain baseline information and document impacts of storm water events and other adjacent land uses upon Refuge wetland flora and fauna.		X	X	X
Strategy 2.1.10 Work with partners and continue to identify and seek funding for a variety of research and monitoring projects associated with the Refuge and WMD. More specifically, support the 3-year study entitled Land Stewardship, Habitation Protection, and Avian Occurrence in the Minnesota Valley National Wildlife Refuge and Wetland Management District. Likewise, continue to support the development of a multi-faceted GIS for the Refuge and WMD.	X	X	X	X
Strategy 2.1.11 Seek operational funds to employ up to two biological technicians (GS-404-5/7) to address the District s workload.	X	X	X	X
Strategy 2.1.12 Obtain operational funds to employ a maintenance worker (WG-4749-6/7) to assist in restoring and maintaining Wetland District fee and easement lands.	X	X	X	X
2.2 Objective: Control and ultimately reduce the distribution of exotic plant species on wetlands primarily through biological control methods.	X	X	X	X
Strategy 2.2.1 Continue to monitor and release purple loosestrife beetles into Refuge wetlands where purple loosestrife exists.	X	X	X	X
Strategy 2.2.2 Control the spread of purple loosestrife using biological control methods such as purple loosestrife beetles (*Galerucella* sp.). In cooperation with others, establish a purple loosestrife field nursery to be used as a source of beetles for release on Refuge, Wetland Management District, and other suitable locations.	X	X	X	X
Strategy 2.2.3 Within staff and time limitations, seek methods to reduce and control the presence of giant reed grass (Phragmites) that exists on Refuge lands.		X	X	X
2.3 Objective: Control wildlife populations at levels consistent with available habitat to address public safety concerns and to allow effective management of wetlands.	X	X	X	X

Goals, Objectives and Strategies	Alt. A	Alt. B	Alt. C	Alt. D
Strategy 2.3.1 For aircraft safety reasons, continue to cooperate with the Metropolitan Airports Commission in the removal of Canada Geese from the Long Meadow Lake Unit.	X	X	X	X
Strategy 2.3.2 Continue to use trapping as a management tool to control beaver populations.	X	X	X	X
2.4 Objective: Maintain Round Lake at full basin water level (2001 level) to provide migration habitat for Bald Eagles, waterfowl such as Canvasbacks, and Common Loons. Maintain the capability to actively manage water levels in the future upon assurances that periodic drawdowns and reflooding would not cause undue risk to the ecosystem.	X	X	X	X
Strategy 2.4.1 Assist the U.S. Army and other agencies with studies to determine the threat, if any, of contaminants on aquatic communities.	X		X	X
Strategy 2.4.2 Develop partnership with educational institutions in the area, such as the nearby Bethel College, to monitor water quality, migratory bird use and collect baseline wildlife data.	X		X	X
Strategy 2.4.3 Maintain year-round closure of lake to fishing and boating.		X	X	X
Strategy 2.4.4 Maintain the existing partnership with the City of Arden Hills to provide trail connection through the west side of the unit to complement the City's trail system and to facilitate wildlife observation.	X	X	X	X
Goal 3. Upland Forest: To restore, protect, and maintain natural species diversity while emphasizing priority wildlife and plants characteristic of upland forests within the northern tallgrass prairie ecosystem.				
3.1 Objective: By 2017, provide 1,000 acres of upland forest along the Minnesota River, in 50-acre or larger blocks throughout the Wetland Management District, to ensure migration and nesting habitat for Bald Eagles, Red-headed Woodpeckers and songbirds.		X	X	X
Strategy 3.1.1 Through research and investigation, determine the long-term viability of the upland forest community that exists on Refuge lands.		X	X	X
Strategy 3.1.2 Continue to acquire upland forest habitats within the Minnesota River Valley and throughout the Wetland Management District. Block sizes greater than 100 acres should be a priority for acquisition.		X	X	X

Goals, Objectives and Strategies	Alt. A	Alt. B	Alt. C	Alt. D
Strategy 3.1.3 Complete a forest management plan by 2005 that sets long-term objectives for each block of hillside forest that exists on Refuge Units.			X	X
Strategy 3.1.4 Plant a shrub understory using native species from a tree nursery and/or root propagation nursery.			X	X
3.2 Objective: Control and ultimately reduce the distribution of exotic plant species on upland forests primarily through biological control methods.	X	X	X	X
Strategy 3.2.1 To the extent possible, and with the use of volunteer and youth groups, seek to control and reduce the distribution of European buckthorn in forested areas through hand cutting and treatment with chemicals.		X	X	X
3.3 Objective: Control wildlife populations at levels consistent with available habitat to address public safety concerns and to allow effective land management.	X	X	X	X
Strategy 3.3.1 In cooperation with the MnDNR and local communities, maintain whitetail deer populations at levels consistent with the carrying capacity of available habitat. Allow public hunting where feasible and sharpshooting when needed to maintain populations of 15-25 deer per square mile.	X	X	X	X
Goal 4. Grasslands and Oak Savanna: To restore, protect, and maintain natural species diversity while emphasizing priority grassland-dependent wildlife and plants characteristic of the northern tallgrass prairie ecosystem.				
4.1 Objective: By 2017, provide 800 acres of original native prairie and 8,700 acres of restored native grasses in block sizes of over 50 acres and with varying grass height, density and grass/forb ratios to benefit grassland-dependent wildlife such as Boblinks, Grasshopper Sparrows and five-lined skinks.		X	X	X
Strategy 4.1.1 Maintain the vigor and productivity of Refuge grasslands by emphasizing the use of a progressive prescribed burning regime under the Fire Management Plan. On an annual basis, burn no less than 1,500 acres located on the Refuge and District.		X	X	X
Strategy 4.1.2 Assess newly-acquired lands as to their suitability for conversion to native grassland and initiate appropriate conversion practices.		X	X	X
Strategy 4.1.3 Monitor wildlife and vegetation response using procedures developed in the Refuge s Inventory and Monitoring Plan.		X	X	X

Goals, Objectives and Strategies	Alt. A	Alt. B	Alt. C	Alt. D
Strategy 4.1.4 Initiate or continue oak savanna restoration efforts on the Louisville Swamp, Wilkie and Rapids Lake units through removal of unwanted trees and a progressive prescribed burning regime.	X	X	X	X
Strategy 4.1.5 Establish prairie and forb nurseries using local ecotype seeds for harvesting and use in restoration of native prairie.			X	X
Strategy 4.1.6 Identify hillside goat prairies on the Refuge and maintain or restore as necessary. Methods would include brush removal by volunteers and prescribed burning by trained staff.			X	X
4.2 Objective: Control spread and ultimately reduce the distribution of exotic or nuisance plant species on grasslands and oak savannas primarily through biological control methods.	X	X	X	X
Strategy 4.2.1 Control spread of invasive woody plant species and noxious weeds using accepted methods such as mechanical, chemical and biological control.	X	X	X	X
Strategy 4.2.2 Consistent with the Exotic Species Management Plan prepared for the Refuge, identify and map locations of all existing exotic species infestations.	X	X	X	X
Strategy 4.2.3 Continue to release and monitor leafy spurge beetles at sites infested with leafy spurge.	X	X	X	X
Strategy 4.2.4 Control the spread and distribution of spotted knapweed through the use of biological control methods.	X	X	X	X
Strategy 4.2.5 In cooperation with the U.S. Department of Agriculture and the Minnesota Department of Agriculture, collect leafy spurge beetles that are not needed by the Refuge for release at non-Refuge locations.	X	X	X	X
Goal 5. Land Protection: To enhance the integrity of lands within the authorized boundary of the Refuge and contribute to the protection and restoration of fish and wildlife habitats within the Minnesota River watershed.				
5.1 Objective: By 2017, achieve the appropriate conservation status necessary for permanent protection and management viability of any remaining lands within the original authorized boundary. This will also address existing and future threats to resources within the authorized Refuge boundaries.	X	X	X	X
Strategy 5.1.1 Seek Congressional appropriations and other sources of funds to purchase the Upgrala tract plus any remaining lands within the original authorized Refuge boundary.	X	X	X	X

Minnesota Valley National Wildlife Refuge and Wetland Management District

Goals, Objectives and Strategies	Alt. A	Alt. B	Alt. C	Alt. D
Strategy 5.1.2 In cooperation with the State of Minnesota, seek to transfer the 54-acre Minnesota Department of Transportation (former Northwest Airlines) tract into the Refuge.	X	X	X	X
Strategy 5.1.3 Consistent with early correspondence between the Regional Director and the Commissioner of Minnesota Department of Natural Resources, explore the possibility of exchanging Service ownership of the Savage Fen with other lands administered by the MnDNR.	X	X	X	X
Strategy 5.1.4 Continue to work cooperatively with cities, counties, developers, and others to address external threats and to avoid future impacts to Refuge flora and fauna due to development of neighboring lands.	X	X	X	X
5.2 Objective: By 2017, and in cooperation with many others, contribute to the restoration of the Minnesota River by acquiring fee or conservation easements on up to 46,000 additional acres of high quality fish and wildlife habitat within or adjacent to the Minnesota River Valley beyond the existing Refuge boundary and proceeding upstream to Mankato, Minnesota.			X	X
Strategy 5.2.1 From the amount identified above, use Trust funds to acquire no less than 4,090 acres in order to satisfy airport mitigation settlement requirements.	X	X	X	X
Strategy 5.2.2 Make a concerted effort to leverage all land acquisition funding with those of other programs such as the Wetland Restoration Program, North American Wetlands Conservation Act (NAWCA), Conservation Reserve Enhancement Program, and Reinvest in Minnesota.		X	X	X
Strategy 5.2.3 Work with the City of Bloomington to fully develop City property along the Minnesota River into good quality wildlife habitat.		X	X	X
Strategy 5.2.4 Enhance Refuge GIS capability for assessing impacts of adjacent or upstream land use on Refuge flora and fauna.	X	X	X	X
Strategy 5.2.5 Work with Friends of the Minnesota Valley to increase landowner participation in private land stewardship through the Heritage and Corporate Registry programs.	X	X	X	X
5.3 Objective: By 2017, acquire, restore, and manage an additional 10,000 acres of fee and easement lands within the Wetland Management District.			X	X

Goals, Objectives and Strategies	Alt. A	Alt. B	Alt. C	Alt. D
Strategy 5.3.1 In cooperation with the MnDNR and private conservation organizations, delineate and submit acquisition proposals for no fewer than 750 acres annually.		X	X	X
Strategy 5.3.2 In cooperation with the Natural Resource Conservation Service, identify high quality habitats where Wetland Reserve Program funds can be combined with Duck Stamp funds for the purchase of Waterfowl Production Areas.	X	X	X	X
Strategy 5.3.3 Pursue all available sources of funds for land acquisition and habitat restoration including the Migratory Bird Conservation Fund, North American Wetland Conservation Act grants and private donations. A limited amount of Refuge Mitigation funds could be made available for specific acquisitions.		X	X	X
5.4 Objective: On an annual basis, and in partnership with others, restore 1,000 acres of habitat located on private lands though the Partners for Fish and Wildlife Program.	X	X	X	X
Strategy 5.4.1 Continue to work with other agencies and organizations in the restoration and protection of wildlife habitats. Where possible, continue to broker and assist with programs of others including the Wetland Reserve Program, Conservation Reserve Enhancement Program, Conservation Reserve Program, and the Reinvest in Minnesota Program.	X	X	X	X
Strategy 5.4.2 Continue to closely work with Soil and Water Conservation Districts to assist in restoring and protecting wildlife habitats on private lands.	X	X	X	X
Strategy 5.4.3 Continue to work directly with landowners on habitat restoration projects through the use of the Service s private landowner agreements.	X	X	X	X
Strategy 5.4.4 Seek opportunities to obtain financial assistance and administrative support for field biologists within the Partners program through creative partnerships with conservation organizations and others.	X	X	X	X
5.5 Objective: Protect the cultural, historic, and prehistoric resources of federally-owned lands within the Refuge and District.	X	X	X	X
Strategy 5.5.1 Describe, identify and take into consideration all archeological and cultural values prior to implementing construction or other ground-disturbing projects. Notify the Regional Historic Preservation Officer early in project planning or upon receipt of a request for permitted activities.	X	X	X	X

Goals, Objectives and Strategies	Alt. A	Alt. B	Alt. C	Alt. D
Strategy 5.5.2 By 2006, develop a step-down plan for surveying lands to identify archeological resources and for developing a preservation program to meet the requirements of Section 14 of the Archaeological Resources Protection Act and Section 110(a)(2) of the National Historic Preservation Act.	X	X	X	X
5.6 Objective: Protect Refuge lands and resources from damaging uses adjacent to Refuge boundaries.	X	X	X	X
Strategy 5.6.1 Continue to monitor amphitheater proposals and actively participate in any public hearings, focus group discussions, and/or provide written comments to appropriate local government agencies. If constructed, retain a working relationship with amphitheater owners and local regulatory agencies to reduce impacts to Refuge users and resources.	X	X	X	X
Goal 6. Public Use: To provide high quality wildlife-dependent recreational and environmental education opportunities to a diverse audience. These activities will promote understanding, appreciation and support for Minnesota Valley National Wildlife Refuge and the Wetland Mangement District as well as the entire National Wildlife Refuge System.				
6.1 Objective: Provide no less than 14,000 high quality hunting experiences for area residents per year. Seventy-five percent of hunters will report no conflicts with other users, a reasonable harvest opportunity and satisfaction with the overall experience.	X		X	
Strategy 6.1.1 By 2005 and in cooperation with the MnDNR, develop a plan to improve waterfowl hunting on Rice Lake of the Wilkie Unit. The plan will explore alternatives such as hunter education and the use of limited permits to improve the quality of hunting at this location.	X		X	
Strategy 6.1.2 By 2005, through revision of the Refuge Hunting Plan, examine opportunities to expand bow hunting for deer on the Refuge to assist in maintaining deer densities between 15-25 deer per square mile. Coordinate efforts with the MnDNR and cities adjacent to the Minnesota River Valley.	X	X	X	X
Strategy 6.1.3 Maintain disabled hunting opportunities in cooperation with Capable Partners or another suitable organization. Expand disabled hunting opportunities to include turkey and deer in designated areas on the Refuge.	X	X	X	
Strategy 6.1.4 Continue to improve the Refuge s youth waterfowl hunting program. Provide this opportunity to no fewer than 25 young people each year and seek to enroll disabled and disadvantaged youth plus youth of single-parent households located in urban areas.	X	X	X	

Goals, Objectives and Strategies	Alt. A	Alt. B	Alt. C	Alt. D
Strategy 6.1.5 Enhance public understanding of Refuge hunting opportunities by increasing the quality of maps, signs and wording within brochures and on the Refuge web page.	X	X	X	X
Strategy 6.1.6 Increase the visibility of Refuge law enforcement and hunter adherence to federal and state regulations to ensure high quality, ethical hunting.	X	X	X	X
Strategy 6.1.7 At least one parking lot will be developed on each Waterfowl Production Area to allow for hunting, fishing, and other wildlife-dependent activities.	X	X	X	X
Strategy 6.1.8 Where appropriate, a Waterfowl Production Area entrance sign will be erected to recognize contributions from private conservation organizations and agencies.	X	X	X	X
Strategy 6.1.9 Obtain operational funding amounting to approximately $100,000 a year to employ a full-time law enforcement officer to enhance the Refuge s law enforcement and public use programs.	X		X	
Strategy 6.1.10 Each Waterfowl Production Area will be clearly posted to avoid any potential landowner/visitor conflicts.	X	X	X	X
6.2 Objective: By 2005, provide for 6,000 high quality fishing visits per year to the Refuge by Twin Cities residents. Seventy-five percent of anglers will report no conflicts with other users and will recollect awareness that they were fishing on a national wildlife refuge.	X		X	
Strategy 6.2.1 Promote catch and release fishing opportunities on Refuge waters through the development and maintenance of good quality maps, signs, multi-lingual brochures, and the Refuge sweb page. Ensure that the fishing public clearly understands the fish consumption advisories for the Lower Minnesota River through signs and brochures.	X		X	
Strategy 6.2.2 In cooperation with the MnDNR and the City of Bloomington, maintain existing boat ramp and parking facilities located at Lyndale Avenue. Likewise, cooperate with the City of Shakopee, the MnDNR, and others to develop an additional boat ramp near State Highway 101.	X	X	X	
Strategy 6.2.3 In cooperation with the MnDNR and Federal fish hatcheries, optimize Refuge fishing opportunities for youth and the disabled by annually stocking, in order of	X	X	X	X

Goals, Objectives and Strategies	Alt. A	Alt. B	Alt. C	Alt. D
priority, Youth Fishing Pond, Cedar Pond, and Hogback Ridge Pond. Maintain the two existing accessible fishing piers at these locations.				
Strategy 6.2.4 In cooperation with other partners, continue to promote fishing opportunities for disadvantaged persons and others through activities such as Youth Fishing Day.	X	X	X	X
6.3 Objective: By 2005, provide for 180,000 wildlife observation visits per year to the Refuge and Waterfowl Production Areas. Ninety percent of all visitors will report a memorable wildlife observation and that it occurred on land managed by the U.S. Fish and Wildlife Service.	X		X	
Strategy 6.3.1 Cooperate in the development of the Audubon-sponsored Minnesota Valley Birding Trail. Identify locations on Refuge units that would serve as wildlife observation stops for this trail.	X	X	X	X
Strategy 6.3.2 With Refuge staff and/or volunteers, conduct no fewer than six birdwatching/wildlife observation programs for the public each year. In addition, conduct no fewer than two birdwatching/wildlife observation tours for disabled visitors per year. A portion of these wildlife observation tours will be conducted from canoes or other suitable water craft.	X	X	X	X
Strategy 6.3.3 Explore the possibility of developing a wildlife observation tour of the Minnesota River Valley using a van or motorized tram.	X		X	
Strategy 6.3.4 Modify the Refuge web site to include current and accurate information about wildlife observations and opportunities available to the public. Link Refuge web site to other important wildlife observation web sites.	X	X	X	
Strategy 6.3.5 Maps and information describing Waterfowl Production Areas and their appropriate uses will be continuously updated on the Refuge s web site.	X	X	X	X
Strategy 6.3.6 Establish state-of-the-art bird feeding stations at existing and future Refuge visitor centers. Manage these stations as dynamic exhibits that promote wildlife observation opportunities to the public.	X	X	X	X
Strategy 6.3.7 Maintain strong partnership with the Minnesota River Valley Audubon Chapter and the Native Plant Society and continue to provide them monthly meeting space. Seek ways to coordinate organized wildlife and plant observation activities with those of the Refuge.	X	X	X	X

Appendix A Exhibit 2 / Goals, Objectives and Strategies by Management Alternative

Goals, Objectives and Strategies	Alt. A	Alt. B	Alt. C	Alt. D
Strategy 6.3.8 Enhance wildlife observation opportunities on Refuge wetlands by designing, constructing and installing elevated observation decks at several locations. at a minimum, observation decks will be installed at Fisher lake, Rapids Lake, and Long meadow Lake at locations that would enhance visitor opportunities to view waterfowl and waterbirds.	X		X	
6.4 Objective: On an annual basis, provide for 3,000 high quality wildlife photography visits to the Minnesota River Valley and adjacent areas.	X	X	X	X
Strategy 6.4.1 Provide the public with no fewer than two portable photography blinds to be used at specific sites throughout the Refuge. In addition, allow the public to use existing hunting blinds during off-season for additional wildlife photography sites.	X		X	
Strategy 6.4.2 In cooperation with the Minnesota Nature Photography Club and others, enhance and promote the annual Refuge photography contest and display winning photos in Refuge Visitor Center for a 45-day period each year.	X	X	X	X
Strategy 6.4.3 Maintain strong partnership with the Minnesota Nature Photography Club and continue to provide monthly meeting space for this organization.	X	X	X	X
6.5 Objective: By 2004, provide for 30,000 high quality wildlife interpretive visits per year to the Refuge and Waterfowl Production Areas. Fifty percent of visitors will independently report that wildlife comes first on System lands and understand the need for seasonal closures on sensitive wildlife habitats.	X	X	X	
Strategy 6.5.1 By 2004, review, revise, and upgrade the Refuge s Interpretive Plan to reflect Refuge contribution to local and national conservation efforts. The plan will identify a Refuge theme that will be promoted in all interpretive products.	X		X	
Strategy 6.5.2 Upgrade and/or replace Refuge Visitor Center exhibits consistent with the Refuge theme. New exhibits need to be dynamic, affordable, and easy to repair and replace if needed.	X		X	

Goals, Objectives and Strategies	Alt. A	Alt. B	Alt. C	Alt. D
Strategy 6.5.3 Upgrade and replace all interpretive and information panels that exist on Refuge kiosks consistent with the Refuge theme. The panels and kiosks will conform to U.S. Fish & Wildlife Service, Region 3, policy and will be environmentally sensitive in their design and placement.	X	X	X	
Strategy 6.5.4 Develop appropriate signs and materials which interpret the cultural and historic sites located on the Refuge and their relationship with historic wildlife populations. Six kiosks that serve this purpose have been identified in the current Refuge Sign Plan.	X	X	X	X
Strategy 6.5.5 In cooperation with Refuge volunteers and others, conduct no fewer than 125 high quality interpretive programs annually. Keep interpretive programming fresh by continually upgrading, improving, and/or replacing individual programs.	X		X	
Strategy 6.5.6 In cooperation with the Friends of the Minnesota Valley, upgrade the interpretive and educational materials offered for sale in the Blufftop Bookshop.	X		X	
Strategy 6.5.7 Upgrade audio visual equipment in the Visitor Center auditorium, update the content of the orientation slide show and offer a variety of wildlife-related videos for the visiting public.	X		X	
Strategy 6.5.8 Write and distribute no fewer than 24 news releases each year that increase the public s understanding and knowledge of the Refuge and its programs.	X		X	
Strategy 6.5.9 In cooperation with many partners, sponsor no fewer than 10 special events annually that engage the public in Refuge activities and increase people s knowledge and understanding of wildlife conservation and associated issues.	X	X	X	
6.6 Objective: By 2004, provide environmental education programing to no less than 12,000 students per year followed by 2 percent annual growth until 2017. Eighty percent of students will report an increased desire to protect fish and wildlife habitats as a result of the programs.	X		X	
Strategy 6.6.1 The Refuge s environmental education curriculum will be thoroughly reviewed by 2003 and every 4 years thereafter with the assistance of local educators. Ensure curriculum is fresh and dynamic and meets the needs of students in preschool on up to high school seniors.	X	X	X	X

Goals, Objectives and Strategies	Alt. A	Alt. B	Alt. C	Alt. D
Strategy 6.6.2 Effectively promote the environmental program through a number of mediums including an annual syllabus, maintaining current information on the Refuge s web page, and periodic distribution of CDs for use on computers.	X	X	X	X
Strategy 6.6.3 Refine and expand the use of Partnership Agreements with area schools in order to clearly articulate program goals and objectives and to build strong educational partnerships.	X	X	X	X
Strategy 6.6.4 Emphasize the delivery of environmental education services to inner-city schools with both on-site and off-site programing. Secure funding through partnerships for busing for those schools that do not have the ability to assume those costs on their own.	X	X	X	X
Strategy 6.6.5 Develop and strengthen internships/work study opportunities through partnerships with academic institutions. In partnership with local universities, hire interns in the natural resource field using funds provided to the Refuge annually through the Jack Lynch Endowment. Where possible, leverage these funds with those provided by the universities.	X	X	X	X
Strategy 6.6.6 Following completion of a new environmental education facility, expand environmental education programing to suburban and rural schools and incorporate the use of waterfowl production areas in curriculum.	X		X	
Strategy 6.6.7 Administer the Regional Resource Center as an integral component of the Refuge s environmental education program by providing appropriate educational and interpretive materials to area schools.	X	X	X	X
6.7 Objective: By 2003, working with the MnDNR, the City of Bloomington, mountain biking organizations and others, eliminate inappropriate biking on Refuge lands and concentrate this activity on authorized and designated trails only.	X	X	X	X
Strategy 6.7.1 If possible, and in cooperation with the City of Bloomington, eliminate mountain biking on the Bloomington Bluffs between Indian Mounds School and I-35W. In addition, develop and implement a plan to address the environmental degradation that currently exists throughout this area.	X	X	X	X

Goals, Objectives and Strategies	Alt. A	Alt. B	Alt. C	Alt. D
Strategy 6.7.2 In cooperation with others, monitor and, if needed, strictly enforce appropriate trail usage on Refuge lands.	X	X	X	X
6.8 Objective: By 2003, eliminate horseback riding on all Refuge and District lands and trails except on the State Trail.	X	X	X	X
Strategy 6.8.1 Following appropriate public notice, and the installation of signs, restrict horseback riding to the State Trail within the Louisville Swamp Unit.	X	X	X	X
Strategy 6.8.2 Consistent with the Refuge web site and its brochures, ensure that good quality information about horseback usage on Refuge/State Trail lands is provided to the public.	X	X	X	X
Strategy 6.8.3 In cooperation with the MnDNR and the horseback riding community, monitor and, if needed, strictly enforce appropriate trail usage of the Louisville Swamp Unit.	X	X	X	X
6.9 Objective: Provide a highly visible and dynamic volunteer and intern work force to assist in all aspects of Refuge and District operations including environmental education, habitat improvement and visitor facility maintenance.	X	X	X	X
Strategy 6.9.1 Seek opportunities to increase coordination between Refuge volunteers and Friends of the Minnesota Valley.	X	X	X	X
Strategy 6.9.2 Enhance communication with Refuge volunteers through various forums including periodic newsletters, a volunteer hotline, the Refuge s web site, and recognition picnics, dinners and socials.	X	X	X	X
Strategy 6.9.3 Renew efforts to provide high quality training to Refuge volunteers so they are able to effectively and efficiently complete projects and responsibilities.	X	X	X	
Strategy 6.9.4 Expand efforts to provide volunteer opportunities to members of the disabled public.	X	X	X	X
Strategy 6.9.5 Continue to provide Refuge projects for kids at risk through a variety of programs including the Twin Cities Tree Trust, Skills for Tomorrow, and community programs like Sentenced to Serve.	X	X	X	

Goals, Objectives and Strategies	Alt. A	Alt. B	Alt. C	Alt. D
Strategy 6.9.6 Seek to expand volunteer opportunities for retired citizens and explore the possibility of developing trailer pads and a septic system for seasonal retiree volunteers with recreational vehicles.	X		X	
Strategy 6.9.7 Employ interns as needed through the use of the Jack Lynch Endowment Fund. Leverage the use of these funds by entering into agreements with universities and colleges.	X	X	X	X
6.10 Objective: By 2005, develop new and maintain existing facilities to promote public advocacy and use of the Refuge and Waterfowl Production Areas. Ninety percent of visitors will report satisfaction with the safety, comfort and functionality of these facilities and express a desire for a return visit.	X	X	X	
Strategy 6.10.1 By 2004, submit a major Visitor Center upgrading package that addresses current outstanding maintenance needs and that will serve to keep this facility in excellent condition for the next 10 years.	X	X	X	
Strategy 6.10.2 By 2004, all Refuge facilities will be reviewed to determine what measures need to be taken to make them more accessible to disabled persons. Following this review, an implementation plan will be developed and funding will be sought to upgrade these facilities.	X	X	X	X
Strategy 6.10.3 By 2004, begin the conversion of the historic Rapids Lake home into an environmental education and interpretive site. As part of this effort, design and build trails, interpretive kiosks, and parking lots in support of this project. Upon completion, allow this site to be used by local governments, non-profit organizations and others for meetings and natural resource-related workshops and conferences.	X	X	X	
Strategy 6.10.4 Obtain or construct intern housing on or near the Rapids Lake Unit to meet expanded responsibilities for wildlife interpretation and environmental education as well as to attract candidates of diverse backgrounds, cultures, and experiences.	X	X	X	X
Strategy 6.10.5 Stabilize the historic buildings on the Jabs and Ehmiller farm sites to ensure their longevity and their historic interpretive value.	X	X	X	X
Strategy 6.10.6 Obtain operational funding to employ a maintenance worker (WG- 4749-6/7) to enhance the Refuge s capability to address its maintenance needs.	X	X	X	X

Goals, Objectives and Strategies	Alt. A	Alt. B	Alt. C	Alt. D
Strategy 6.10.7 Establish a hard surfaced trail open to hiking and bicycling between the Refuge Visitor Center and the Bass Ponds.	X		X	
Strategy 6.10.8 In cooperation with the cities of Chaska and Carver, develop a plan for the Chaska Unit and nearby city lands that addresses wildlife interpretive trails, public parking, and related interpretive facilities and programming.	X	X	X	X
Strategy 6.10.9 Seek a sufficient increase in operational funds to maintain, to a high standard, the existing Refuge Visitor Center, parking lots, kiosks, and signing.	X	X	X	X
Strategy 6.10.10 Seek annual funding to enter into contracts for routine mowing, snow plowing, and custodial services for the Refuge s visitor centes, parkings lots, and nature trails.	X	X	X	X
Strategy 6.10.11 Using Trust funds, employ a supervisory park ranger (GS-025-11/12) who will initiate early planning for new environmental education center(s) and associated facilities. Following completion of the center, this employee will assume responsibility for operations of these facilities.	X	X	X	X
Strategy 6.10.12 Using Trust funds, employ up to two park rangers (GS-025-5/7/9) and one maintenance worker (WG-4749-6/7/8) to assist in planning and conducting environmental education programming and in the management of new Refuge units.	X	X	X	X
Strategy 6.10.13 Seek construction funding to replace the existing Shakopee shop facility with a combination cold storage/heated staff building. The new building would also contain a small office suitable for two staff. The commercial lot owned by the Service near the Savage Fen would be a likely location for this facility.	X	X	X	X
Strategy 6.10.14 Seek construction funding to replace the existing Rapids Lake maintenance facility. The new facility would contain office space suitable for three Refuge maintenance staff and three District employees.	X	X	X	X
Strategy 6.10.15 Enhance the Refuge s capability to reduce the amount of vandalism and arson that occurs on Refuge facilities. Seek funding for installation and use of remote sensors designed to detect damage to facilities and apprehend those responsible for such activities.	X	X	X	X

Goals, Objectives and Strategies	Alt. A	Alt. B	Alt. C	Alt. D
6.11 Objective: To work in partnership with the MnDNR, cities, and other organizations to finish the Minnesota Valley State Trail and to provide appropriate public access to the trail from Refuge lands.	X	X	X	X
Strategy 6.11.1 In cooperation with the MnDNR, identify the State Trail corridor across the Wilkie Unit, which will connect this part of the Refuge with the City of Shakopee.	X	X	X	X
Strategy 6.11.2 In cooperation with the MnDNR, identify the State Trail corridor across the Long Meadow Lake Unit between Old Cedar Avenue and Lyndale Avenue. Seek sources of funding to construct access across at least two large gullies that occur along this section of the trail.	X	X	X	X
Strategy 6.11.3 Working with partners, seek sources of funding (TEA-21, etc.) for the replacement of the Old Cedar Avenue Bridge with a pedestrian bridge that will connect Old Cedar Avenue with the State Trail.	X	X	X	X
Strategy 6.11.4 Working with partners, acquire in fee or easement remaining lands on the Bloomington Ferry Unit that will allow the completion of the State Trail between I-35W and the Bloomington Ferry Bridge. Work with the City of Bloomington and the MnDNR to specifically identify the corridor on this section of the State Trail.	X	X	X	X
Strategy 6.11.5 In cooperation with the City of Eden Prairie, develop a hiking and bicycling trail on the north side of the Minnesota River connecting River View Road with the Bloomington Ferry Bridge.	X	X	X	X
Strategy 6.11.6 Following Service acquisition of the Upgrala Unit, develop a hiking and bicycling trail connecting River View Road with the City of Shakopee trail facilities located near U.S. Highway 101. This work will be completed in cooperation with the cities of Eden Prairie and Shakopee.	X	X	X	X
Strategy 6.11.7 As soon as practicable and in cooperation with all appropriate parties, develop a brochure that specifically identifies all trails within the Lower Minnesota River Valley and their allowed uses. This information will also be made available on the Refuge s web site.	X	X	X	X

Appendix B: Glossary

Appendix B: Glossary

Alternative	A set of objectives and strategies needed to achieve refuge goals and the desired future condition.
Biological Diversity	The variety of life forms and its processes, including the variety of living organisms, the genetic differences among them, and the communities and ecosystems in which they occur.
Compatible Use	A wildlife-dependent recreational use, or any other use on a refuge that will not materially interfere with or detract from the fulfillment of the mission of the Service or the purposes of the refuge.
Comprehensive Conservation Plan	A document that describes the desired future conditions of the refuge, and specifies management actions to achieve refuge goals and the mission of the National Wildlife Refuge System.
Ecosystem	A dynamic and interrelated complex of plant and animal communities and their associated non-living environment.
Ecosystem Approach	A strategy or plan to protect and restore the natural function, structure, and species composition of an ecosystem, recognizing that all components are interrelated.
Ecosystem Management	Management of an ecosystem that includes all ecological, social and economic components that make up the whole of the system.
Endangered Species	Any species of plant or animal defined through the Endangered Species Act as being in danger of extinction throughout all or a significant portion of its range, and published in the <u>Federal Register</u>.
Environmental Assessment	A systematic analysis to determine if proposed actions would result in a significant effect on the quality of the environment.
Extirpation	The local extinction of a species that is no longer found in a locality or country, but exists elsewhere in the world.
Goals	Descriptive statements of desired future conditions.
Interjurisdictional Fish	Fish that occur in waters under the jurisdiction of one or more states, for which there is an interstate fishery management plan or which migrates between the waters under the jurisdiction of two or more states bordering on the Great Lakes.

Issue	Any unsettled matter that requires a management decision. For example, a resource management problem, concern, a threat to natural resources, a conflict in uses, or in the presence of an undesirable resource condition.
National Wildlife Refuge System	All lands, waters, and interests therein administered by the U.S. Fish and Wildlife Service as wildlife refuges, wildlife ranges, wildlife management areas, waterfowl production areas, and other areas for the protection and conservation of fish, wildlife and plant resources.
Objectives	Actions to be accomplished to achieve a desired outcome.
Preferred Alternative	The Service's selected alternative identified in the Draft Comprehensive Conservation Plan.
Scoping	A process for determining the scope of issues to be addressed by a comprehensive conservation plan and for identifying the significant issues. Involved in the scoping process are federal, state and local agencies; private organizations; and individuals.
Species	A distinctive kind of plant or animal having distinguishable characteristics, and that can interbreed and produce young. A category of biological classification.
Strategies	A general approach or specific actions to achieve objectives.
Wildlife-dependent Recreational Use	A use of refuge that involves hunting, fishing, wildlife observation and photography, or environmental education and interpretation, as identified in the National Wildlife Refuge System Improvement Act of 1997.
Threatened Species	Those plant or animal species likely to become endangered species throughout all of or a significant portion of their range within the foreseeable future. A plant or animal identified and defined in accordance with the 1973 Endangered Species Act and published in the <u>Federal Register</u>.
Vegetation	Plants in general, or the sum total of the plant life in an area.
Vegetation Type	A category of land based on potential or existing dominant plan species of a particular area.
Watershed	The entire land area that collects and drains water into a stream or stream system.

Wetland	Areas such as lakes, marshes, and streams that are inundated by surface or ground water for a long enough period of time each year to support, and that do support under natural conditions, plants and animals that require saturated or seasonally saturated soils.
Wildlife Diversity	A measure of the number of wildlife species in an area and their relative abundance.

Appendix C: Priority Refuge and District Operational and Maintenance Needs

Appendix C: Priority Refuge and District Operational and Maintenance Needs

The CCP directs an ambitious course for the future management of Minnesota Valley National Wildlife Refuge and Wetland Management District. The following provides a brief description of the second-highest priority Refuge and District projects. The highest priority, or Tier 1, projects are described in Chapter 5 of the plan. Each project description also includes the number of a corresponding strategy; linking it to the Goals/Objectives/Strategies section of Chapter 4.

Most of these projects are listed in the Refuge Operating Needs System (RONS); the Service's national database of unfunded operational activities. The RONS was established in 1990 as a planning, budgeting, and communication tool to enhance identification of funding and staffing needs for the National Wildlife Refuge System. RONS projects describe the need for new or expanded activities in order to implement plans, attain goals, or satisfy legal mandates. Data within RONS are used regularly in budget justifications presented to the Department of the Interior, the Office of Management and Budget, and Congress.

The Maintenance Management System (MMS) is another database used by the Service to document needed equipment and construction projects. The MMS is structured around property items while RONS focuses on management activities. All large-scale (typically over $500,000) construction projects are housed in MMS.

Replace Shakopee and Rapids Lake Maintenance Facilities. The Refuge will seek funds for upgrading and replacing the existing maintenance facilities at Shakopee and the Rapids Lake Unit. The Shakopee facility will consist of a single building containing a heated bay, cold storage, and a small office. The Rapids Lake maintenance facility will consist of no less than four heated stalls plus a heated carpentry shop. This facility will also be capable of housing all Refuge equipment in cold storage. **Strategies 6.10.14 & 6.10.15.** Estimated cost: $1,200,000

Continue Partners for Fish and Wildlife Program Activities. The continuance of a progressive and opportunist Partners for Fish and Wildlife Program near the Refuge and throughout the District is of extreme importance. Through this program, the Refuge builds good will throughout the community and contributes to high quality habitat restoration activities on private lands. Appropriated habitat restoration funds are frequently matched by contributions from a very supportive private conservation community. **Strategy 5.4.4.** Estimated cost: $200,000 annually.

Establish Prairie Grass, Forb, and Root Propagation Nurseries. In support of a Regional effort to utilize local eco-type seeds, the Refuge will establish grass, forb, and tree propagation facilities and nurseries. This facility will assist in developing a local seed source for use across the Refuge and throughout the District. Equipment for harvesting and handling locally produced seeds will also be acquired. **Strategy 4.1.5.** Estimated cost: $400,000.

Review and Revise Refuge's Interpretive Plan. As soon as practicable, the Refuge will seek operation funding to review and review its interpretive plan. The revised plan will form the basis for new environmental education and wildlife interpretive programming.

It will also for the basis for upgrading and replacement of current Visitor Center exhibits and interpretive kiosks. Strategy **6.5.1.** Estimated cost: $100,000.

Upgrade and Improve Exhibits in the Visitor Center. Following the review of the Refuge Interpretive Plan, exhibits, displays, audio visual equipment, and productions will be upgraded. As part of this project, information about the Refuge and the Refuge system will be developed and upgraded regularly. Minnesota Valley NWR is an urban refuge located within an hours drive of three million people. Strategy 6.5.2. Estimated cost: $1,000,000.

Seek Funding for Completion of State Trail Across Refuge's Long Meadow Lake Unit. In cooperation with MnDNR and others, the Refuge will seek funding and materials to complete the section of the Minnesota Valley State Trail that lies between Old Cedar and Lyndale Avenues. Strategy **6.11.2.** Estimated cost: Unknown.

Seek Funding for Replacement of Old Cedar Bridge. In cooperation with the City of Bloomington, Minnesota Department of Transportation, MnDNR, the biking community, and others, the Refuge will seek funding for the replacement of the Old Cedar Avenue Bridge with a new pedestrian/bicycling bridge. **Strategy 6.11.3.** Estimated cost: Unknown.

Prepare Restoration Plan and Seek Funding to Repair and Stabilize Bloomington Bluffs. In cooperation with the City of Bloomington, the Friends of Minnesota Valley, Lower Minnesota River Watershed District, Refuge neighbors, and the biking community, the Refuge will complete a bluff restoration plan that, upon implementation, will repair and stabilize the erosion and gullying that occurs along the Bloomington Bluff. The partners will seek funding for costs associated with this project once the plan is completed. **Strategy 6.7.2.** Estimated cost: Unknown.

Develop Hiking and Biking Trails on Bloomington Ferry and Upgrala Units. In cooperation with the cities of Eden Prairie and Shakopee, Refuge neighbors, and Murphy's Landing, develop a hiking and biking trail that connects River View Road with the City of Shakopee trails near State Highway 101. Also, develop a hiking and biking trail that connects the Upgrala Unit with the Bloomington Ferry Unit. In addition, also cooperate in the development of a river ferry crossing that connects Murphy's Landing with the Upgrala Unit. **Strategies 6.11.5 & 6.11.6.** Estimated cost: Unknown

Restore Floodplain Forest. Restore 150 acres of flood plain forest in the Minnesota River bottoms. This land was previously row cropped and needs to be planted with species native to the river bottoms. The planting will benefit many species of wildlife, especially migrant songbirds that depend on large tracts of contiguous forest. Other species such as migratory waterfowl, especially wood ducks, bald eagles, herons and several species of concern will benefit from the plants. The Refuge will work in partnership with the Minnesota Waterfowl Association as well as several other local conservation groups to secure matching funds. **Strategy 1.1.6.** Estimated cost: Unknown

Provide Bus Transportation Funds For Inner City Schools. This project will provide funds to bus children from inner city schools to the Refuge for environmental education programming. Among other benefits, this project will assist the Refuge and the Service in reaching out to diverse audiences who may have an interest in natural resource issues. **Strategy 6.6.4.** Estimated cost: $75,000 annually.

Improve Refuge Access to Persons with Disabilities. By 2003, all Refuge facilities and programs will be reviewed to determine what measures need to be taken to make them more accessible to disabled persons. Following this review, a plan will be developed and funding will be sought to make these improvements to Refuge facilities and programs. **Strategy 6.10.2.** Estimated cost: Unknown.

Upgrade Visitor Center Parking Lots and Install Water Garden: As soon as practical, the Visitor Center parking lots will be upgraded to address some long-term drainage prolems that have existed since construction. In addition, the lots will be modified to direct storm waters into the unpaved portions of the area where a water garden will be constructed. This water garden will demonstrate how parking lots can be designed to reduce pollutants entering downstream wetlands, lakes and streams, including Long Meadow Lake. **Strategy 5.1.4** Estimated cost: unknown.

Public Use Facility Upgrade: Identify funding for the upgrade of all Refuge parking lots, kiosks, trails and boardwalks. Within each parking lot, the gates, kiosks, brochure boxes, and post and rail will be repaired, replaced and otherwise upgraded to a high standard. In addition, these facilities will be modified to ensure they are accesible to disableded people. **Strategies 6.10.2 and 6.10.10.** Estimated cost: $250,000.

Appendix D: List of Compatibility Determinations

Appendix D: Compatibility Determinations

The following compatibility determinations were presented for public review in the draft CCP, which was published in July 2002. The final, signature copies are available at the Refuge Headquarters.

- Interpretation and Environmental Education
- Hunting of Resident Game and Furbearers
- Wildlife Observation and Photography
- Recreational Fishing
- Permit Archeological Investigations
- Collection of Edible Wild Plant Foods for Personal Use
- Cooperative Farming for Cover Enhancement
- Disability Access to Refuge and Wetland District
- Establishing Foods Plots and Placing Feeder Cribs for Resident Wildlife
- Controlled Grazing on the Refuge, WPA Areas and Conservation Easements
- Haying
- Irrigation
- Installation of Bluebird Boxes, other Nest Boxes or Nesting Structures by Public or Groups
- One-time Fruits of the Soil Harvest
- Placement of New, Small Parking Areas on Waterfowl Production Areas
- Access to State Trail Through the Refuge Via Snowmobile and Horseback
- Reocurring Special Events
- State Trail
- Short-term Upland Disturbance for Highway or Other Public Interest Projects with No ROW Expansion and Full Restoration
- Wood Cutting / Timber Harvest
- Trapping of Furbearers
- Placement of Wetland Accesses/Ramps in Support of Priority Public Uses
- Use of Refuge and WPAs for Fire Department Training: Burning Structures

Appendix E: Species List

Appendix E: Species List

Mammals

Common name	Scientific Name	Oak Savanna/ Dry Prairie Upland	Floodplain Forest & Low Prairie or Meadow	Marsh &Open Water
			Habitat Types	
Opossum				
Virginia Oposum	*Didelphis virginiana*	r	r	
Shrews				
Masked shrew	*Sorex cinereus*		u	
Arctic Shrew	*Sorex arcticus*		r	
Pigmy Shrew	*Microsorex hoyi*		r	
Shorttail Shrew	*Blarina brevicauda*	r	c	u
Moles				
Eastern Mole	*Scalopus aquaticus*	u	u	
Starnose Mole	*Condylura cristata*		r	
Bats				
Little Brown Myotis	*Myotis lucifugus*		c	
Keen Myotis	*Myotis keenii*		r	
Silver-haired Bat	*Lasionycteris noctivagans*		r	
Eastern Pipistrel	*Pipistrellus subflavus*		r	
Big Brown Bat	*Eptesicus fuscus*		c	
Red Bat	*Lasiurus borealis*		c	c
Hoary Bat	*Lasiurus cinereus*		c	
Rabbits				
Eastern cottontail	*Sylvilagus floridanus*	c	a	u
Whitetail Jackrabbit	*Lepus townsendii*	u		
Rodents				
Woodchuck	*Marmota monax*	a	c	
Richardson Ground Squirrel	*Citellus richardsoni*		u	
Thirteen-lined Ground Squirrel	*Citellus tridecemlineatus*	c	u	
Franklin Ground Squirrel	*Citellus franklinii*	u	u	
Eastern Chipmunk	*Tamias striatus*	a	c	
Eastern Gray Squirrel	*Sciurus carolinensis*	c	c	
Eastern Fox Squirrel	*Sciurus niger*		c	
Red Squirrel	*Tamiasciurus hudsonicus*		c	
Southern Flying Squirrel	*Glaucomys volns*		u	

Common name	Scientific Name	Habitat Types		
		Oak Savanna/ Dry Prairie Upland	Floodplain Forest & Low Prairie or Meadow	Marsh &Open Water

Rodents (continued)

Common name	Scientific Name	Oak Savanna/ Dry Prairie Upland	Floodplain Forest & Low Prairie or Meadow	Marsh &Open Water
Plains Pocket Gopher	*Geomys bursarius*	a		
Plains Pocket Mouse	*Perognathus flavescens*	u		
Beaver	*Castor canadensis*			c
Western Harvest Mouse	*Reithrodontomys megalotis*	r		
Deer Mouse	*Peromyscus maniculatus*	u		
White-footed Mouse	*Peromyscus leucopus*	c	c	
Gapper's Red-backed Vole	*Clethrionomys gapperi*		u	
Meadow Vole	*Microtus pennsylvanicus*		u	
Muskrat	*Ondatra zibethica*			a
Norway Rat	*Rattus norvegicus*	u		
House Mouse	*Mus musculus*	u		
Meadow Jumping Mouse	*Zapus hudsonicus*	r	c	

Coyote/Fox

Common name	Scientific Name	Oak Savanna/ Dry Prairie Upland	Floodplain Forest & Low Prairie or Meadow	Marsh &Open Water
Coyote	*Canis latrans*	r		
Red Fox	*Vuples fulva*	c	u	
Gray Fox	*Urocyon cinereoargenteus*	u		

Raccoon

Common name	Scientific Name	Oak Savanna/ Dry Prairie Upland	Floodplain Forest & Low Prairie or Meadow	Marsh &Open Water
Raccoon	*Procyon lotor*		c	c

Weasel/Skunk/Otter

Common name	Scientific Name	Oak Savanna/ Dry Prairie Upland	Floodplain Forest & Low Prairie or Meadow	Marsh &Open Water
Ermine/ Shorttail Weasel	*Mustela ermina*		u	
Least Weasel	*Mustela rixosa*	u		
Longtail Weasel	*Mustela frenata*		u	
Mink	*Mustela vison*			u
Badger	*Taxidea taxus*	r		
Spotted Skunk	*Spilogale putoris*	u	u	
Striped Skunk	*Mephitis mephitis*	c	c	
River Otter	*Lutra canadensis*			r

Deer

Common name	Scientific Name	Oak Savanna/ Dry Prairie Upland	Floodplain Forest & Low Prairie or Meadow	Marsh &Open Water
Whitetail Deer	*Odocoileus virginianus*	c	a	c

Reptile and Amphibians

Common name	Scientific Name	Oak Savanna/ Dry Prairie Upland	Floodplain Forest & Low Prairie or Meadow	Marsh &Open Water
			Habitat Types	
Turtles				
Snapping Turtle	*Chelydra serpentina*		c	c
Map Turtle	*Graptemys geographica*			r
False Map Turtle	*Graptemys pseudogeographica*			c
Painted Turtle	*Chrysemys picta*	u	c	c
Blanding's Turtle	*Emydoidea blandingi*		r	r
Smooth Softshell	*Trionyx muticus*			c
Spiny Softshell	*Trionyx spiniferus*			u
Lizards				
Prairie Skink	*Eumeces septentrionalis*		u	
Snakes				
Northern Water Snake	*Nerodia sipedon*		c	c
Brown (DeKay's) Snake	*Storeria dekayi*		u	u
Redbelly Snake	*Storeria occiptomaculata*		u	
Common Garter Snake	*Thamnophis sirtalis*	c	a	a
Plains Garter Snake	*Thamnophis radix*	c	c	c
Western Hognose Snake	*Heterodon nasicus*	c	u	
Racer	*Coluber constrictor*	u		
Smooth Green Snake	*Opheodrys vernalis*		u	
Fox Snake	*Elaphe vulpina*	u	c	c
Gopher Snake	*Pituophis melanoleucus*	c	u	
Milk Snake	*Lampropeltis triangulum*		u	
Salamanders				
Mudpuppy	*Necturus maculosus*			u
Eastern Newt	*Notophthalmus viridescens*		u	u
Blue-spotted Salamander	*Ambystoma laterale*		r	
Tiger Salamander	*Ambystoma trigrinum*		c	

Common name	Scientific Name	Habitat Types		
		Oak Savanna/ Dry Prairie Uplands	Floodplain Forest & Low Prairie or Meadow	Marsh &Open Water
Toads				
American Toad	*Bufo americanus*	c	c	c
Frogs				
Spring Peeper	*Hyla crucifer*		c	c
Gray Tree Frog	*Hyla versicolor*		c	
Striped Chorus Frog	*Pseudacris triseriata*		c	c
Green Frog	*Rana clamitans*			c
Wood Frog	*Rana sylvatica*		c	
Northern Leopard Frog	*Rana pipiens*	u	a	a

Birds

Legend: Symbols are used as follows:
- Sp – March-May
- S – June-August
- F – September-November
- W – December - February
- * – indicates nesting occurs on the Refuge

a – abundant: a common species that is very numerous.
c – common: certain to be seen or heard in suitable habitat, not in large numbers.
u – uncommon: present but not always seen.
o – occasional: seen only a few times during the season.
r – rare: seen every 2 to 5 years.
x – accidental: seen only once or twice.

Species	Sp	S	F	W
Loons				
Common loon	o		o	
Grebes				
Pied-billed Grebe*	c	c	c	
Horned Grebe	u		r	
Red-necked Grebe	r		r	
Pelicans				
American White Pelican	u		u	r
Cormorants				
Double-crested Cormorant	c	c	c	r
Herons & Bitterns				
American Bittern*	o	o	o	
Least Bittern*	u	u	u	
Great Blue Heron*	c	c	c	r
Great Egret*	c	c	c	
Green Heron*	u	u	u	
Black-crowned Night Heron*	u	u	u	
Vultures				
Turkey Vulture	u	u	u	
Swans, Geese & Ducks				
Greater White-fronted Goose	r		r	
Snow Goose	o		o	
Canada Goose*	c	c	c	c
Tundra Swan	u		u	r
Wood Duck*	c	u	c	r
Gadwall	c	u	o	
American Wigeon	c		c	
American Black Duck	u		u	u
Mallard*	a	a	a	a
Blue-winged Teal	c	u	c	
Northern Shoveler	c	o	c	

Species	Sp	S	F	W
Swans, Geese & Ducks continued				
Northern Pintail	o		u	r
Green-winged Teal	u		u	r
Canvasback	u		u	r
Redhead	u	r	o	r
Ring-necked Duck	c		u	r
Greater Scaup	r		r	
Lesser Scaup	c		u	r
Bufflehead	c		c	
Common Goldeneye	c		c	c
Hooded Merganser*	c	o	u	
Common Merganser	c		c	c
Red-breasted Merganser	o		o	
Ruddy Duck*	u	r	u	
Hawks & Eagles				
Osprey	o		o	
Bald Eagle*	c	u	c	u
Northern H arrier	o		o	
Sharp-shinned Hawk	u		u	o
Cooper's Hawk*	u	o	u	o
Northern Goshawk			r	r
Red-shouldered Hawk*	r		r	
Broad-winged Hawk	o	r	o	
Red-tailed Hawk*	c	c	c	u
Rough-legged Hawk	o		o	o
Falcons				
American Kestrel*	c	c	c	u
Peregrine Falcon*	u	u	u	u
Upland Game Birds				
Ring-necked Pheasant*	c	c	c	c
Wild Turkey*	u	u	u	u
Rails & Coots				
Virginia Rail*	u	u	u	
Sora*	c	u	u	
Common Moorhen	r	r	r	
American Coot*	a	a	a	r
Cranes				
Sandhill Crane	r			

Species	Sp	S	F	W
Shorebirds				
Black-bellied Plover	r		r	
Semipalmated Plover	r		r	
Killdeer*	c	c	c	
American Avocet	r		r	
Greater Yellowlegs	u		o	
Lesser Yellowlegs	u	r	o	
Solitary Sandpiper	c		u	
Spotted Sandpiper*	c	u	u	
Semipalmated Sandpiper	o		o	
Least Sandpiper	u	r	u	
Pectoral Sandpiper	o		o	
Dunlin	r		r	
Stilt Sandpiper	o		o	
Short-billed Dowitcher	r			
Common Snipe*	o	r	o	r
American Woodcock*	u	r	o	
Wilson's Phalarope	r		r	
Gulls & Terns				
Franklin's Gull	r		o	
Bonaparte's Gull	o		o	
Ring-billed Gull	a	u	a	o
Herring Gull	u		u	u
Thayer's Gull			o	o
Iceland Gull			o	o
Lesser Black-backed Gull			r	
Glaucous Gull	o			o
Caspian Tern	o	r	o	
Forster's Tern*	u	u	u	
Black Tern*	u	u	u	
Doves				
Rock Dove*	u	u	u	u
Mourning Dove*	c	c	c	o
Cuckoos & Roadrunners				
Black-billed Cuckoo*	o	o	o	
Yellow-billed Cuckoo	o	o	o	

Species	Sp	S	F	W
Owls				
Eastern Screech-Owl*	r	r	r	r
Great Horned Owl*	u	u	u	u
Snowy Owl				r
Barred Owl	u	u	u	u
Long-eared Owl				o
Short-eared Owl			r	r
Northern Saw-whet Owl				r
Nighthawks & Nightjars				
Common Nighthawk*	u	u	u	
Whip-poor-will	r		r	
Swifts				
Chimney Swift*	c	c	c	
Hummingbirds				
Ruby-throated Hummingbird*	u	u	u	
Kingfishers				
Belted Kingfisher*	u	u	u	r
Woodpeckers				
Red-headed Woodpecker*	u	u	u	
Red-bellied Woodpecker*	c	u	u	u
Yellow-bellied Sapsucker*	u	o	u	
Downy Woodpecker*	c	c	c	c
Hairy Woodpecker*	c	c	c	c
Northern Flicker*	c	c	c	r
Pileated Woodpecker*	u	u	u	u
Flycatchers				
Olive-sided Flycatcher	o		o	
Eastern Wood-Pewee	u	u	u	
Yellow-bellied Flycatcher	r		r	
Alder Flycatcher	r		r	
Willow Flycatcher	u	u	u	
Least Flycatcher	c	u	u	
Eastern Phoebe*	u	u	u	
Great Crested Flycatcher*	u	u	u	
Eastern Kingbird*	u	u	u	
Shrikes				
Northern Shrike	o		o	u

Species	Sp	S	F	W
Vireos				
Bell's Vireo*	r	r	r	
Yellow-throated Vireo*	u	u	u	
Blue-headed Vireo	u		u	
Warbling Vireo	c	c	c	
Philadelphia Vireo	r		r	
Red-eyed Vireo	c	c	c	
Jays & Crows				
Blue Jay*	c	c	c	c
American Crow*	a	a	a	a
Larks				
Horned Lark		o		
Swallows				
Purple Martin*	o	o	o	
Tree Swallow*	c	c	c	
Northern Rough-winged Swallow*	c	u	u	
Bank Swallow*	u	u	u	
Cliff Swallow*	u	u	u	
Barn Swallow*	c	c	c	
Chickadees & Titmice				
Black-capped Chickadee*	a	a	a	a
Nuthatches				
Red-breasted Nuthatch	o	r	o	o
White-breasted Nuthatch*	c	c	c	c
Creepers				
Brown Creeper	u		u	u
Wrens				
House Wren*	c	c	u	
Winter Wren	o		o	
Sedge Wren*	u	u	u	
Marsh Wren*	u	u	u	
Kinglets & Gnatcatchers				
Golden-crowned Kinglet	u		u	u
Ruby-crowned Kinglet	c		u	
Blue-gray Gnatcatcher*	u	u	u	

Species	Sp	S	F	W
Thrushes				
Eastern Bluebird*	u	u	u	
Veery	o		o	
Gray-cheeked Thrush	o		o	
Swainson's Thrush	u		u	
Hermit Thrush	u		u	o
Wood Thrush	o	o	o	
American Robin*	a	a	a	u
Mockingbirds & Thrashers				
Gray Catbird*	c	c	c	
Brown Thrasher*	u	u	u	
Starlings				
European Starling*	c	c	c	c
Waxwings				
Cedar Waxwing*	u	u	u	o
Warblers				
Blue-winged Warbler	r	r	r	
Golden-winged Warbler	r	r	r	
Tennessee Warbler	c		c	
Orange-crowned Warbler	u		u	
Nashville Warbler	c		c	
Northern Parula	o		o	
Yellow Warbler*	c	c	c	
Chestnut-sided Warbler	u	r	u	
Magnolia Warbler	u		u	
Cape May Warbler	o		o	
Black-throated Blue Warbler	r		r	
Yellow-rumped Warbler	a		a	r
Black-throated Green Warbler	u		u	
Blackburnian Warbler	u		u	
Pine Warbler	r		r	
Palm Warbler	c		c	
Bay-breasted Warbler	o		o	
Blackpoll Warbler	u		u	
Cerulean Warbler	r	r	r	
Black-and-white Warbler	u		u	
American Redstart*	c	c	c	
Prothonotary Warbler*	o	o	o	
Ovenbird	u	o	u	
Northern Waterthrush	u		u	

Species	Sp	S	F	W
Warblers (continued)				
Connecticut Warbler	r		r	
Mourning Warbler	o		o	
Common Yellowthroat*	c	c	c	
Wilson's Warbler	u		u	
Canada Warbler	o		o	
Yellow-breasted Chat	r	r	r	
Tanagers				
Scarlet Tanager*	u	r	u	
Sparrows, Buntings & Grosbeaks				
Eastern Towhee	o	o	o	
American Tree Sparrow	c		c	c
Chipping Sparrow*	c	c	c	
Clay-colored Sparrow*	c	u	c	
Field Sparrow*	c	u	c	r
Vesper Sparrow*	o	o	o	
Lark Sparrow	o	o	o	
Savannah Sparrow*	u	u	u	
Grasshopper Sparrow*	o	o	o	
Le Conte's Sparrow	r		r	
Fox Sparrow	u		u	
Song Sparrow*	c	c	c	r
Lincoln's Sparrow	u		u	
Swamp Sparrow*	u	u	u	
White-throated Sparrow	c		c	r
Harris's Sparrow	o			
White-crowned Sparrow	u		u	
Dark-eyed Junco	c		c	c
Cardinals & Allies				
Northern Cardinal*	c	c	c	c
Rose-breasted Grosbeak*	c	c	c	
Indigo Bunting*	c	c	c	
Dickcissel*	o	o	o	
Blackbirds & Orioles				
Bobolink	u	u	u	
Red-winged Blackbird*	a	a	a	u
Eastern Meadowlark	u	u	u	
Western Meadowlark	r	r	r	
Yellow-headed Blackbird*	u	u	u	

Species	Sp	S	F	W
Blackbirds & Orioles (continued)				
Rusty Blackbird	o		o	r
Brewer's Blackbird	o		o	
Common Grackle*	a	a	a	o
Brown-headed Cowbird*	a	a	c	o
Orchard Oriole	r	r	r	
Baltimore Oriole*	u	u	u	
Finches				
Purple Finch	o		o	o
House Finch*	a	a	a	c
Red Crossbill				r
White-winged Crossbill				r
Common Redpoll	r		r	o
Pine Siskin	o		o	o
American Goldfinch*	c	c	c	c
Old World Sparrows				
House Sparrow*	a	a	a	a
Accidentals to the Refuge				
Eared Grebe	x	x		
Western Grebe	x			
Snowy Egret		x		
Little Blue Heron	x			
Cattle Egret	x			
Yellow-crowned Night Heron	x			
Tricolored Heron	x			
White-faced Ibis	x			
Whooper Swan	x	x	x	x
Mute Swan	x	x	x	x
Trumpeter Swan	x		x	
Cinnamon Teal	x			
Harlequin Duck				x
Surf Scoter	x			
White-winged Scoter	x		x	
Long-tailed Duck	x			x
Mississippi Kite	x			
Golden Eagle	x			
Merlin	x			
Prairie Falcon			x	

Species	Sp	S	F	W
Accidentals to the Refuge (continued)				
Gray Partridge	x	x	x	x
Ruffed Grouse	x	x	x	x
Northern Bobwhite	x	x	x	x
King Rail		x		
American Golden-Plover	x		x	
Piping Plover	x		x	
Willet	x		x	
Upland Sandpiper	x	x	x	
Hudsonian Godwit	x		x	
Marbled Godwit		x		
Ruddy Turnstone	x		x	
Sanderling	x		x	
White-rumped Sandpiper	x	x		
Baird's Sandpiper	x		x	
Buff-breasted Sandpiper	x		x	
Long-billed Dowitcher	x		x	
Black-necked Stilt	x			
Red-necked Phalarope	x		x	
Glaucous-winged Gull			x	
Great Black-backed Gull				x
Black-legged Kittiwake				x
Common Tern	x		x	
Great Gray Owl				x
Western Kingbird	x	x	x	
Loggerhead Shrike	x	x	x	
White-eyed Vireo	x			
Tufted Titmouse	x	x	x	x
Carolina Wren	x		x	
Rock Wren	x			
Bohemian Waxwing	x		x	x
Louisiana Waterthrush	x			
Hooded Warbler	x			
Summer Tanager	x			
Henslow's Sparrow			x	
Nelson's Sharp-tailed Sparrow		x		
Lapland Longspur	x		x	
Snow Bunting				x
Hoary Redpoll				x
Evening Grosbeak				x

Appendix F: Compliance Requirements

Appendix F: Compliance Requirements

Rivers and Harbor Act (1899) (33 U.S.C. 403): Section 10 of this Act requires the authorization by the U.S. Army Corps of Engineers prior to any work in, on, over, or under a navigable water of the United States.

Antiquities Act (1906): Authorizes the scientific investigation of antiquities on Federal land and provides penalties for unauthorized removal of objects taken or collected without a permit.

Migratory Bird Treaty Act (1918): Designates the protection of migratory birds as a Federal responsibility. This Act enables the setting of seasons, and other regulations including the closing of areas, Federal or non-Federal, to the hunting of migratory birds.

Migratory Bird Conservation Act (1929): Establishes procedures for acquisition by purchase, rental, or gift of areas approved by the Migratory Bird Conservation Commission.

Fish and Wildlife Coordination Act (1934), as amended: Requires that the Fish and Wildlife Service and State fish and wildlife agencies be consulted whenever water is to be impounded, diverted or modified under a Federal permit or license. The Service and State agency recommend measures to prevent the loss of biological resources, or to mitigate or compensate for the damage. The project proponent must take biological resource values into account and adopt justifiable protection measures to obtain maximum overall project benefits. A 1958 amendment added provisions to recognize the vital contribution of wildlife resources to the Nation and to require equal consideration and coordination of wildlife conservation with other water resources development programs. It also authorized the Secretary of Interior to provide public fishing areas and accept donations of lands and funds.

Migratory Bird Hunting and Conservation Stamp Act (1934): Authorized the opening of part of a refuge to waterfowl hunting.

Historic Sites, Buildings and Antiquities Act (1935), as amended: Declares it a national policy to preserve historic sites and objects of national significance, including those located on refuges. Provides procedures for designation, acquisition, administration, and protection of such sites.

Refuge Revenue Sharing Act (1935), as amended: Requires revenue sharing provisions to all fee-title ownerships that are administered solely or primarily by the Secretary through the Service.

Transfer of Certain Real Property for Wildlife Conservation Purposes Act (1948): Provides that upon a determination by the Administrator of the General Services Administration, real property no longer needed by a Federal agency can be transferred without reimbursement to the Secretary of Interior if the land has particular value for migratory birds, or to a State agency for other wildlife conservation purposes.

Federal Records Act (1950): Directs the preservation of evidence of the government's organization, functions, policies, decisions, operations, and activities, as well as basic historical and other information.

Fish and Wildlife Act (1956): Established a comprehensive national fish and wildlife policy and broadened the authority for acquisition and development of refuges.

Refuge Recreation Act (1962): Allows the use of refuges for recreation when such uses are compatible with the refuge's primary purposes and when sufficient funds are available to manage the uses.

Wilderness Act (1964), as amended: Directed the Secretary of Interior, within 10 years, to review every roadless area of 5,000 or more acres and every roadless island (regardless of size) within National Wildlife Refuge and National Park Systems and to recommend to the President the suitability of each such area or island for inclusion in the National Wilderness Preservation System, with final decisions made by Congress. The Secretary of Agriculture was directed to study and recommend suitable areas in the National Forest System.

Land and Water Conservation Fund Act (1965): Uses the receipts from the sale of surplus Federal land, outer continental shelf oil and gas sales, and other sources for land acquisition under several authorities.

National Wildlife Refuge System Administration Act (1966), as amended by the National Wildlife Refuge System Improvement Act (1997)16 U.S.C. 668dd668ee. (Refuge Administration Act): Defines the National Wildlife Refuge System and authorizes the Secretary to permit any use of a refuge provided such use is compatible with the major purposes for which the refuge was established. The Refuge Improvement Act clearly defines a unifying mission for the Refuge System; establishes the legitimacy and appropriateness of the six priority public uses (hunting, fishing, wildlife observation and photography, or environmental education and interpretation); establishes a formal process for determining compatibility; established the responsibilities of the Secretary of Interior for managing and protecting the System; and requires a Comprehensive Conservation Plan for each refuge by the year 2012. This Act amended portions of the Refuge Recreation Act and National Wildlife Refuge System Administration Act of 1966.

National Historic Preservation Act (1966), as amended: Establishes as policy that the Federal Government is to provide leadership in the preservation of the nation's prehistoric and historic resources.

Architectural Barriers Act (1968): Requires federally owned, leased, or funded buildings and facilities to be accessible to persons with disabilities.

National Environmental Policy Act (1969): Requires the disclosure of the environmental impacts of any major Federal action significantly affecting the quality of the human environment.

Uniform Relocation and Assistance and Real Property Acquisition Policies Act (1970), as amended: Provides for uniform and equitable treatment of persons who sell their homes, businesses, or farms to the Service. The Act requires that any purchase offer be no less than the fair market value of the property.

Endangered Species Act (1973): Requires all Federal agencies to carry out programs for the conservation of endangered and threatened species.

Rehabilitation Act (1973): Requires programmatic accessibility in addition to physical accessibility for all facilities and programs funded by the Federal government to ensure that anybody can participate in any program.

Archaeological and Historic Preservation Act (1974): Directs the preservation of historic and archaeological data in Federal construction projects.

Clean Water Act (1977): Requires consultation with the Corps of Engineers (404 permits) for major wetland modifications.

Surface Mining Control and Reclamation Act (1977) as amended (Public Law 95-87) (SMCRA): Regulates surface mining activities and reclamation of coal-mined lands. Further regulates the coal industry by designating certain areas as unsuitable for coal mining operations.

Executive Order 11988 (1977): Each Federal agency shall provide leadership and take action to reduce the risk of flood loss and minimize the impact of floods on human safety, and preserve the natural and beneficial values served by the floodplains.

Executive Order 11990: Executive Order 11990 directs Federal agencies to (1) minimize destruction, loss, or degradation of wetlands and (2) preserve and enhance the natural and beneficial values of wetlands when a practical alternative exists.

Executive Order 12372 (Intergovernmental Review of Federal Programs): Directs the Service to send copies of the Environmental Assessment to State Planning Agencies for review.

American Indian Religious Freedom Act (1978): Directs agencies to consult with native traditional religious leaders to determine appropriate policy changes necessary to protect and preserve Native American religious cultural rights and practices.

Fish and Wildlife Improvement Act (1978): Improves the administration of fish and wildlife programs and amends several earlier laws including the Refuge Recreation Act, the National Wildlife Refuge System Administration Act, and the Fish and Wildlife Act of 1956. It authorizes the Secretary to accept gifts and bequests of real and personal property on behalf of the United States. It also authorizes the use of volunteers on Service projects and appropriations to carry out a volunteer program.

Archaeological Resources Protection Act (1979), as amended: Protects materials of archaeological interest from unauthorized removal or destruction and requires Federal managers to develop plans and schedules to locate archaeological resources.

Federal Farmland Protection Policy Act (1981), as amended: Minimizes the extent to which Federal programs contribute to the unnecessary and irreversible conversion of farmland to nonagricultural uses.

Emergency Wetlands Resources Act (1986): Promotes the conservation of migratory waterfowl and offsets or prevents the serious loss of wetlands by the acquisition of wetlands and other essential habitats.

Federal Noxious Weed Act (1990): Requires the use of integrated management systems to control or contain undesirable plant species, and an interdisciplinary approach with the cooperation of other Federal and State agencies.

Native American Graves Protection and Repatriation Act (1990): Requires Federal agencies and museums to inventory, determine ownership of, and repatriate cultural items under their control or possession.

Americans With Disabilities Act (1992): Prohibits discrimination in public accommodations and services.

Executive Order 12898 (1994): Establishes environmental justice as a Federal government priority and directs all Federal agencies to make environmental justice part of their mission. Environmental justice calls for fair distribution of environmental hazards.

Executive Order 12996 Management and General Public Use of the National Wildlife Refuge System (1996): Defines the mission, purpose, and priority public uses of the National Wildlife Refuge System. It also presents four principles to guide management of the System.

Executive Order 13007 Indian Sacred Sites (1996): Directs Federal land management agencies to accommodate access to and ceremonial use of Indian sacred sites by Indian religious practitioners, avoid adversely affecting the physical integrity of such sacred sites, and where appropriate, maintain the confidentiality of sacred sites.

National Wildlife Refuge System Improvement Act (1997): Considered the "Organic Act of the National Wildlife Refuge System. Defines the mission of the System, designates priority wildlife-dependent public uses, and calls for comprehensive refuge planning.

National Wildlife Refuge System Volunteer and Community Partnership Enhancement Act (1998): Amends the Fish and Wildlife Act of 1956 to promote volunteer programs and community partnerships for the benefit of national wildlife refuges, and for other purposes.

National Trails System Act: Assigns responsibility to the Secretary of Interior and thus the Service to protect the historic and recreational values of congressionally designated National Historic Trail sites.

Appendix G: Mailing List

Appendix G: Mailing List

The following is an initial list of government offices, private organizations, and individuals who will receive notice of the availablity of this CCP. We continue to add to this list and expect to mail several thousand notices or summary CCPs.

Elected Officials

Sen. Mark Dayton
Sen. Norm Coleman

Rep. Jim Ramstad
Rep. John Kline
Rep. Mark Kennedy
Rep. Betty McCollum
Rep. Martin Sabo
Rep. Collin Peterson
Rep. Gil Gutknecht

Gov. Tim Pawlenty

Local Government

City of Bloomington
City of Arden Hills
City of Eden Prairie
City of Eagan
City of Burnsville
City of Savage
City of Shakopee
City of Chanhassen
City of Chaska
City of Carver
City of Jordon

Hennepin County
Dakota County
Carver County
Scott County
Sibley County
Le Sueur County
Rice County
Waseca County
Steel County
Blue Earth County
Nicollet County
Ramsey County

Washington County
Chisago County

Hennepin County Park District
Metropolitan Airports Commission

Hennepin County Soil and Water Conservation District
Dakota County Soil and Water Conservation District
Carver County Soil and Water Conservation District
Scott County Soil and Water Conservation District
Sibley County Soil and Water Conservation District
Le Sueur County Soil and Water Conservation District
Rice County Soil and Water Conservation District
Waseca County Soil and Water Conservation District
Steel County Soil and Water Conservation District
Blue Earth County Soil and Water Conservation District
Nicollet County Soil and Water Conservation District
Ramsey County Soil and Water Conservation District
Washington County Soil and Water Conservation District
Chisago County Soil and Water Conservation District

Cannon Valley Watershed Partnership
Minnesota River Basin Joint Powers Board
Lower Minnesota River Watershed District
Nine Mile Creek Watershed District
Riley-Purgatory-Bluff Creek Watershed District
Richfield/Bloomington Watershed Management Organization
Spring Lake/Prior Lake Watershed District

Businesses

Xcel Energy
Ceridian Corporation
Cyprus Semiconductor
Seagate Corporation
Reliant Energy

Federal Agencies

USDA, Natural Resource Conservation Service
USFWS, Albuquerque, New Mexico; Anchorage, Alaska; Atlanta, Georgia; Denver,
Colorado; Fort Snelling, Minnesota; Hadley, Massachusetts; Portland, Oregon
Federal Aviation Administration

State Agencies

Minnesota Environmental Quality Board
Minnesota Pollution Control Agency
Minnesota Department of Natural Resources

State Historic Preservation Officer, St. Paul, Minnesota
Minnesota Environmental Education Association

Colleges and Universities

University of Minnesota / Water Resources Center
Mankato State University
Normandale Community College
Gustavus Adolphus College

Organizations

Friends of Minnesota Valley National Wildlife Refuge
The Nature Conservancy
Minnesota Deer Hunters Association
Minnesota Waterfowl Association
Pheasants Forever
Ducks Unlimited
National Audubon Society
Minnesota River Valley Audubon Chapter
Wildlife Management Institute
PEER Refuge Keeper
The Wilderness Society, Washington, D.C.
National Wildlife Federation
Sierra Club, Midwest Office, Madison, Wisconsin
The National Wildlife Refuge Association, Washington, D.C.
The Conservation Fund, Arlington, Virginia
Native Plant Society
Minnesota Nature Photography
Trust for Public Lands
Minnesota Land Trust
Minnesota Off Road Cyclists
International Mountain Biking Association

Individuals who have requested a copy of the draft CCP

Tribes

Upper Sioux Community of Minnesota
Iowa Tribe of Kansas and Nebraska
Lower Sioux Mdewakanton Indian Community
Omaha Tribe of Nebraska
Otoe-Missouria Tribe
Shakopee Mdewakanton Sioux Community
Ho-Chunk Nation of Wisconsin
Iowa Tribe of Oklahoma
Sac and Fox Tribe of the Mississippi in Iowa
Winnebago Tribe of Nebraska
Minnesota Mdewakanton Sioux
Wyandotte Nation

Media

Outdoor News
St. Paul Pioneer Press
StarTribune
Sun Current Newspapers
WCCO Radio
WCCO Television
KSTP Radio
KSTP Television
KNOW Minnesota Public Radio
Minnesota Public Television

Appendix H: Bibliography

Appendix H: Bibliography

Godfrey, A. 1999. Cultural Resource Management Plan for Cultural Resources within the Minnesota Valley National Wildlife Refuge. U.S. West Research, Inc. Salt Lake City, Utah (Three volumes).

Minnesota Department of Natural Resources and Minnesota River Basin Joint Powers Board. 1998. Minnesota River Watershed Comprehensive Recreational Guidance Document & Trail Corridor Concept Plan. St. Paul, Minnesota. 52 p.

Minnesota Department of Natural Resources. 1997. Metro Greenprint: Planning for nature in the face of urban growth. Greenways and Natural Areas Collaborative. St. Paul, Minnesota. 48 p.

Minnesota Pollution Control Agency. 1994. Working Together: A Plan to Restore the Minnesota River. Minnesota River Citizen's Advisory Committee Final Report. St. Paul, Minnesota. 58 p.

U.S. Department of Energy. 1999. Carbon Sequestration Research and Development. Washington, D.C.

U.S. Fish and Wildlife Service. 1984. Comprehensive Plan, Minnesota Valley National Wildlife Refuge, Recreation Area and State Trail. U.S. Dept. of the Interior. 187 p.

Appendix I: Land Protection Plan

Contents

Appendix I: Land Protection Plan

I. Introduction

The poor water quality of the Minnesota River has received a great deal of attention in recent years from conservation agencies, non-profit groups and the media. Runoff from agricultural operations in the watershed and storm water events from adjacent developments contribute significant amounts of sediments and chemicals into the river. However, commercial and residential development continues to be the most imminent threat to wildlife habitats in the valley.

The Twin Cities of Minneapolis and St. Paul anchor a growing metropolitan area that is home to 2.2 million people. The counties surrounding the Twin Cities metro area are experiencing some of the fastest rates of suburban sprawl in the nation. Developments continue to march up the Minnesota Valley at a steady rate. Although housing and industrial developments are somewhat restricted by frequent flooding adjacent to the river, sensitive river bluff habitats continue to be lost.

Background

In 1991, the Service proposed a 6,445-acre addition to Minnesota Valley NWR. The primary purpose of the expansion proposal was to provide a contiguous corridor of habitat from Fort Snelling upstream to LeSueur, Minnesota, a distance of 60 river miles. During public meetings concerning this proposal, the Service received recommendations to evaluate the feasibility of including important habitats further upstream along the Minnesota River, possibly as far as New Ulm, Minnesota. At the same time, an inter-agency planning team commissioned by the Governor of Minnesota began work on the broader task of making recommendations for protection of habitat and improving water quality throughout the entire Minnesota River watershed. Beginning in October, 1994, the Service decided to suspend further work on a Refuge expansion assessment pending the outcome of this study and further development of public support for restoration and protection of existing habitats of the Minnesota River.

Minnesota River Study Recommendations

Concurrent with the Service's initiative to expand the Refuge in the early 1990's, a citizens advisory group was convened by the Minnesota Pollution Control Agency to develop recommendations for the restoration of the Minnesota River. In December 1994, their final product, known as *Working Together: A Plan to Restore the Minnesota River,* was released to the public. Along with other recommendations, this plan identified the need to restore and protect up to 200,000 acres of Minnesota River floodplain habitat between Fort Snelling and Big Stone National Wildlife Refuge. The plan also identified the need to restore riparian and wetland habitat in the watershed of the Minnesota River and its associated tributaries.

In 1998, the Refuge began the process of preparing a Comprehensive Conservation Plan. Public comment obtained during initial open houses and focus group meetings again confirmed a high level of interest in refuge expansion. The CCP planning team decided to explore a larger role for the Refuge in the Minnesota River Valley.

The decision to move forward with this proposal also coincides with a unique opportunity brought about by unfortunate circumstance. In 2000, the Service reached a compensation agreement with the Metropolitan Airport Commission (MAC) for damages to the Refuge resulting from the future construction of a north-south runway at the nearby Minneapolis/St. Paul International Airport. When the new runway is completed, it is expected that planes will be directed over the Refuge about once every other minute. The noise level will significantly detract from the value of the existing facilities for environmental education, recreation and overall public enjoyment. In the terms of the agreement, approximately $26 million in mitigation funds was obtained from the MAC for losses to existing Refuge lands and programs as the result of the airport expansion. A portion of these funds will be used for land acquisition but only for lands outside the Refuge's original acquisition boundary.

The Minnesota Valley National Wildlife Refuge Trust was established in September 2000 as a 501(c)(3) to administer the mitigation fund. The Board of Directors includes a representative of the following organizations: Friends of the Minnesota Valley, Minnesota Department of Natural Resources, National Audubon Society, Minnesota Waterfowl Association, and the Minnesota River Basin Joint Powers Board.

Establishing Authority

Lands acquired by the Service for the Refuge and Wetland District would be purchased under the authority of the Minnesota Valley National Wildlife Refuge Act *(P.L. 94-466, as amended)*, the Migratory Bird Conservation Act and the Emergency Wetland Resources Act of 1986.

II. Affected Environment

The study area is the lower one-half of the Minnesota River Valley and encompasses a portion of seven counties including Blue Earth, Brown, Carver, Dakota, Hennepin, Le Sueur and Nicollet. The study area contains portions of four of 13 watersheds flowing into the Minnesota River. This a relatively flat section of the river and drops approximately 90 feet in elevation from Mankato to its confluence with the Mississippi River in St. Paul. Although the Minnesota is generally not used for navigational purposes, the lower fifteen miles from Savage downstream to the mouth have been dredged to provide a nine-foot-deep channel for commercial barge navigation. The Rush River and High Island Creek, two moderate tributaries, empty into the lower Minnesota River watershed in addition to several smaller first and second order streams.

The University of Minnesota's Department of Soil, Water and Climate delineates the western half of the lower Minnesota watershed as fairly flat with surface deposits composed mainly of wetter clays and silts. Landscapes here are primarily flat (0-2 percent slopes), extensively ditched and poorly drained or tile drained. A geomorophological shift occurs in the eastern half of the watershed as landscapes are composed mainly of morainal complexes. The western half of this section of the watershed is classified as being composed of Less Steep Moraine. Agricultural lands within this area are dominated by moderately steep (2-12 percent) well drained soils, although one fourth of the land is flat sloped (0-2 percent) and tile drained. Fifty percent of the cropped lands have a high potential for water erosion. The eastern quarter of the watershed is found within Steep Wetter Moraine. This region includes the rapidly expanding suburban areas of the Twin Cities. Much of the land next to streams is very steep, with a large potential for sediment delivery to streams. Soil textures in this region range from sandy loam to loam, and landscapes are primarily well drained with a high water erosion potential.

Pre-settlement vegetation was comprised of a wide variety of tree and plant species, intermixed in a riparian/floodplain system. Upland vegetation typically ranged from wet prairie meadows to oak savanna to mixed stands of oak and maple. The area's lowlands consisted mainly of peat bogs interspersed with lakes. The seasonal flood regime of the Minnesota River was the dominant factor shaping the habitat of the region.

Major vegetation community types found within the study area include floodplain forest, upland forest, oak savanna and native prairie. The floodplain forests, which can flood in the spring or after a heavy rainfall, are dominated by water tolerant tree species such as silver maple, cottonwood and black willow. The upland forests consist of oak forest in well drained areas and maple-basswood forests in wetter sites such as ravines and moist terrace slopes. Existing oak savannas are primarily grazed pastures with scattered bur and northern pin oak trees. Remnant prairies, with a mix of warm season grasses and forbs, are generally found at sites along the river bluff (goat prairies) or are maintained on state and county park lands.

Fish, wildlife and plant communities of the Minnesota River basin have already been described in this EA. The Minnesota River drainage basin represents 19 percent of the land mass of Minnesota and is a key component of the Prairie Pothole Region which produces 20 percent of the continental population of waterfowl. The Minnesota Department of Natural Resources Natural Heritage and Nongame Program documents 31 occurrences of rare and unique plant and animal communities in the northern portion of the proposed study area (upstream to Le Sueur).

Several Minnesota State Parks and Recreational Areas and a few county and city parks are found along the river corridor within the study area. Fort Snelling State Park is located at the confluence of the Mississippi and Minnesota Rivers adjacent to the existing Refuge at Minneapolis. The Minnesota Valley Trail links Fort Snelling with units of the Refuge, a few waysides and other scattered public lands for nearly 50 river miles. Minneopa State Park is located about 5 miles upstream from Mankato. Flandrau State Park, at the confluence of the Big Cottonwood River, is near the western boundary of the study area.

Social and Economic Context

The seven-county Twin Cities Metropolitan Area serves as a major hub for agriculture, transportation, industry, finance, trade, and technology. Several renowned universities, including the University of Minnesota, make significant contributions to education, science, and medical research. The Guthrie Theater and the world-class Minneapolis

Institute of Art reflect the local interest in the arts. The world famous Mall of America in Bloomington is located directly upstream from the refuge headquarters. Year-round outdoor recreation is very important to the citizens of the area and many enjoy activities such as boating, fishing, swimming, skating, skiing, and snowmobiling. These residents are concerned about the quality of their environment as reflected by the presence of over 30 environmental education and interpretive centers. Over the past decade, this vibrant economy has seen unprecedented growth which has lead to significant suburban sprawl. New or modernized infrastructure that support this growth includes roads, bridges, utilities, and airports. To a large degree, all of this places added developmental pressure on any remaining open space in this portion of Minnesota.

The landscape changes gradually as you travel up the Minnesota River Valley from the metro area. The valley stretches as a ribbon of green interrupted by small to medium-sized towns, villages and cities clinging to the river. Communities upriver from Chaska, including Le Sueur, Saint Peter and New Ulm are tied closely to the agricultural industry of the surrounding watershed. Primary agricultural products of the area include milk, soybeans, corn, and wheat. Mankato and North Mankato, adjacent cities with over 40,000 residents combined, have grown significantly in the past 20 years and include a diversified economy. Growth has occurred in several smaller cities as well including Jordan and Belle Plaine. Many residents of the lower part of the river valley commute to work in the Twin Cities metro area.

III. Land Protection Alternatives

The Environmental Assessment includes a proposal to contribute toward the protection of the natural values and function of the Minnesota River Valley upstream from the existing Refuge boundary. Table 1 summarizes land protection recommendations under each alternative. Alternative C has been selected as the preferred alternative and is the basis for the Comprehensive Conservation Plan.

We envision using a variety of land protection tools throughout the valley to meet site-specific objectives. Fee title acquisition from willing sellers would be the preferred option for the more sensitive habitats adjacent to the river. However, existing conservation measures by the State of Minnesota and non-profit groups would be instrumental in meeting the larger scale restoration goals. For instance, a portion of the agricultural lands within the floodplain are temporarily enrolled in the Conservation Reserve Program. Many landowners would be interested in securing permanent easements through the State's Reinvest in Minnesota program or the Conservation Reserve Enhancement Program (CREP). However, funding remains limited for all programs and new enrollments in CREP ended in September 2002. Landowners retain the access rights, and the responsibility to pay property taxes, on lands encumbered by these conservation easements. Some landowners may be interested in selling all rights and responsibilities on some parcels. The Service could purchase the remainder of land rights from willing sellers on some of these lands and provide for public access and more flexibility in habitat restoration.

In addition, for landowners not interested in selling land or rights, technical assistance for sensitive habitat management is available through the Minnesota Valley Heritage

Table 1: Summary of Land Protection by Environmental Assessment Alternative on the Minnesota Valley National Wildlife Refuge and Wetland District

	Alternative A Public Use Emphasis	Alternative B Current Situation (No Action)	Alternative C Balanced Public Use and Habitat Management (Preferred Alternative)	Alternative D Habitat Management Emphasis
Existing Refuge and Beyond	No or limited acquisition. Only manage lands within existing Refuge boundary.	Acquire and manage lands only within existing Refuge boundary (14,000 acres total).	Acquire and/or protect an additional 10,737 acres .	Acquire and/or protect 50,000-100,000 acres. Maximum acreage is based on 1994 Citizens' Advisory Committee rec-omendations.
Wetland Management District	No new WPA acquisitions.	Acquire an average of 500-1,000 acres per year in fee and ease-ments.	Acquire up to 750 acres per year.	Acquire 25,000 acres in total.

Registry sponsored by the group Friends of the Minnesota Valley. Landowners make a verbal commitment to "protect and preserve the land to the best of their abilities, notify the Friends of any potential threats to the area, and notify the Friends of the intent to sell the property. In return, landowners are provided with educational information on stewardship techniques, incentives (books and plaques) and public recognition of their efforts.

Land Selection Criteria

Potential refuge units were selected by a set of criteria based on the site's potential to provide habitat for migratory birds, threatened and endangered species, or rare plant communities. General site locations were identified during the initial agency and public scoping for the Draft CCP. We received some feedback from the public and government agencies during review of this plan. The number and location of potential Refuge units are now identified in the Final CCP. These units were selected based on a set of resource criteria. The highest priority areas have one or all of the following characteristics:

1. Land adjacent to or linking permanently protected habitat.
2. Total size of floodplain or upland forest block created by acquisition over 250 acres.
4. Property contains an oak savanna block over 100 acres in size.
5. Existing native prairie over 50 acres in size.
6. Lands restorable to original, native prairie over 200 acres in size.
7. Areas containing threatened or endangered species, or rare or unique natural communities.
8. Areas with existing or restorable wetlands larger than 100 acres.

Figures 1-4 show locations for new units of the Minnesota Valley National Wildlife Refuge. Please note the identification of a "Conservation Boundary" adjacent to the proposed new units. These Conservation Boundary lands depict areas where the Service would like to encourage conservation measures through partnerships with others. The areas contain valuable fish and wildlife habitats. However, the Service does not foresee the availability of federal land acquisition funding within the next 15 years for these lands to be included in the National Wildlife Refuge System. However, we can contribute funding for restoration work through the Partners for Fish and Wildlife program and can assist in linking local, state, and non-profit organizations for land conservation purposes. Table 2 lists the acreage of each unit and the recommended priority level for protection. The following paragraphs briefly describe the resource values of each unit and Conservation Boundary.

Table 2: Acreage Summary and Land Protection Priority for Proposed Refuge Units

Unit	Acres	Priority
Chaska (Addition)	16	1
Rapids Lake (Addition)	836	1
Ahlswede Lake Unit	511	1
San Francisco Unit	1,514	1
Saint Lawrence Unit	632	1
Jessenland	1,911	2
Rush River	2,763	2
Kasota Prairie	2,554	1
Total	10,737	

Description of Proposed Units

Chaska Unit Addition (16 Acres)
This area is comprised of former recreational ballfields, floodplain forest, and wetlands. The protection and restoration of the disturbed areas to native habitats will provide a buffer between the Minnesota River and a floodplain marsh to the north within the Chaska Unit of the Refuge. Restoring the river banks to forest will also facilitate the stabilization of the banks which are currently eroding. Wildlife observations in the area include the only Higgins eye mussel specimen found in the Minnesota River during an extensive survey of the Minnesota River for mussel species in 1989.

Rapids Lake Unit Addition (836 Acres)
This area includes active upland agricultural fields and old floodplain agricultural fields currently regenerating to forest, a portion of a floodplain lake marsh, and bluff /ravine topography which supports remnant native dry prairie, oak savanna and associated Big Woods plant communities. Once restored, the area will support a wide variety of native species that use the upland and floodplain habitats including Cerulean Warblers and Red-shouldered Hawks. Rare wildlife and plant communities occurring in the area include bull snake, ground plum and kitten-tails. The Rapids Lake Unit of the Refuge and a State Wildlife Management Area are located adjacent to and nearby this area. The unit near Carver, Minnesota will provide and important connection between the State owned Gifford Lake State Recreation Area and the Rapids Lake Unit of the Refuge which will allow wildlife and people travel corridors and a pathway for the continued transfer of genetic material to maintain biodiversity.

Figure 1: Potential New Units of the Minnesota Valley National Wildlife Refuge

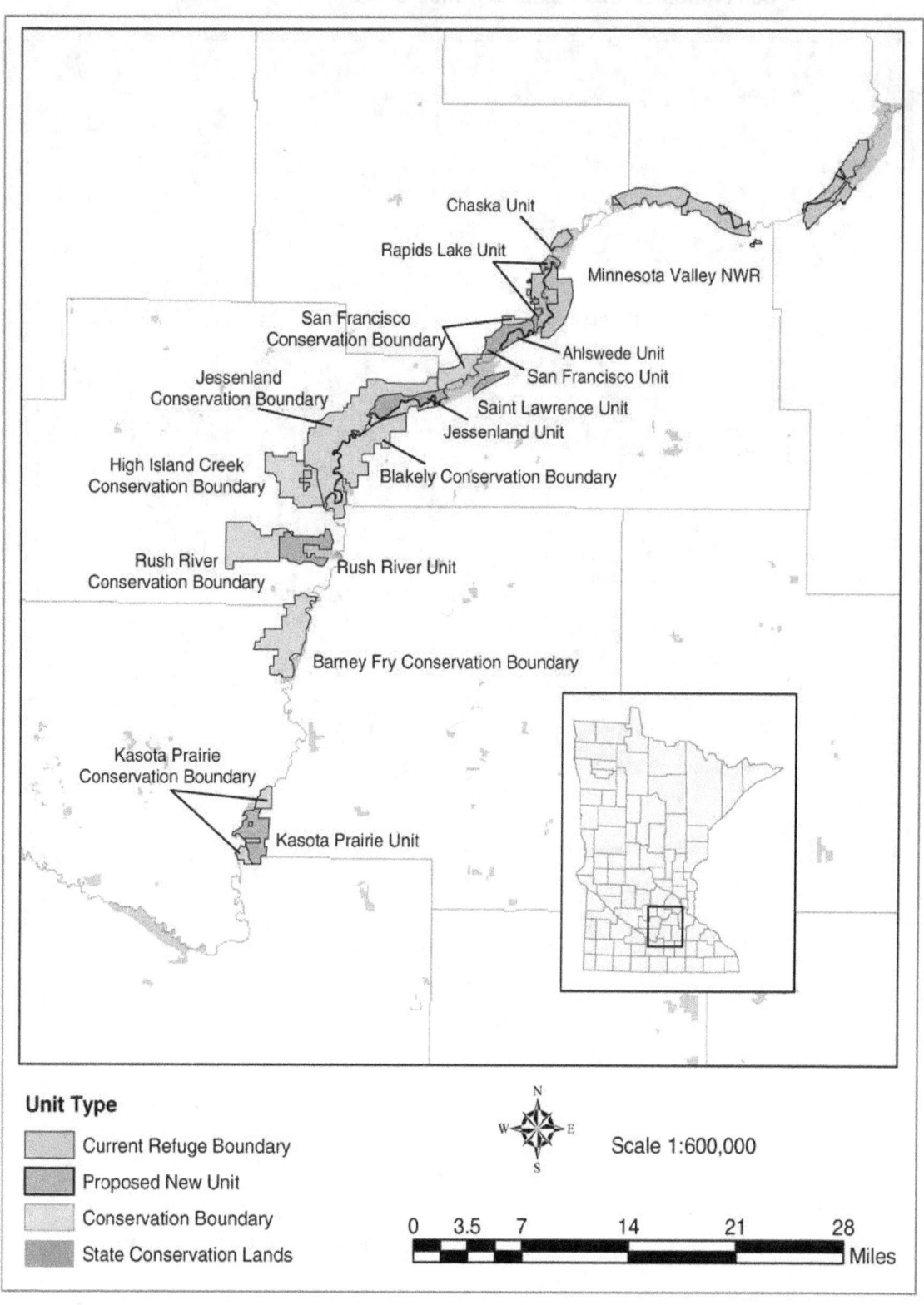

Figure 2: **Proposed Chaska and Rapids Lake Additions, Ahlwede Lake, San Francisco, and Saint Lawrence Units**

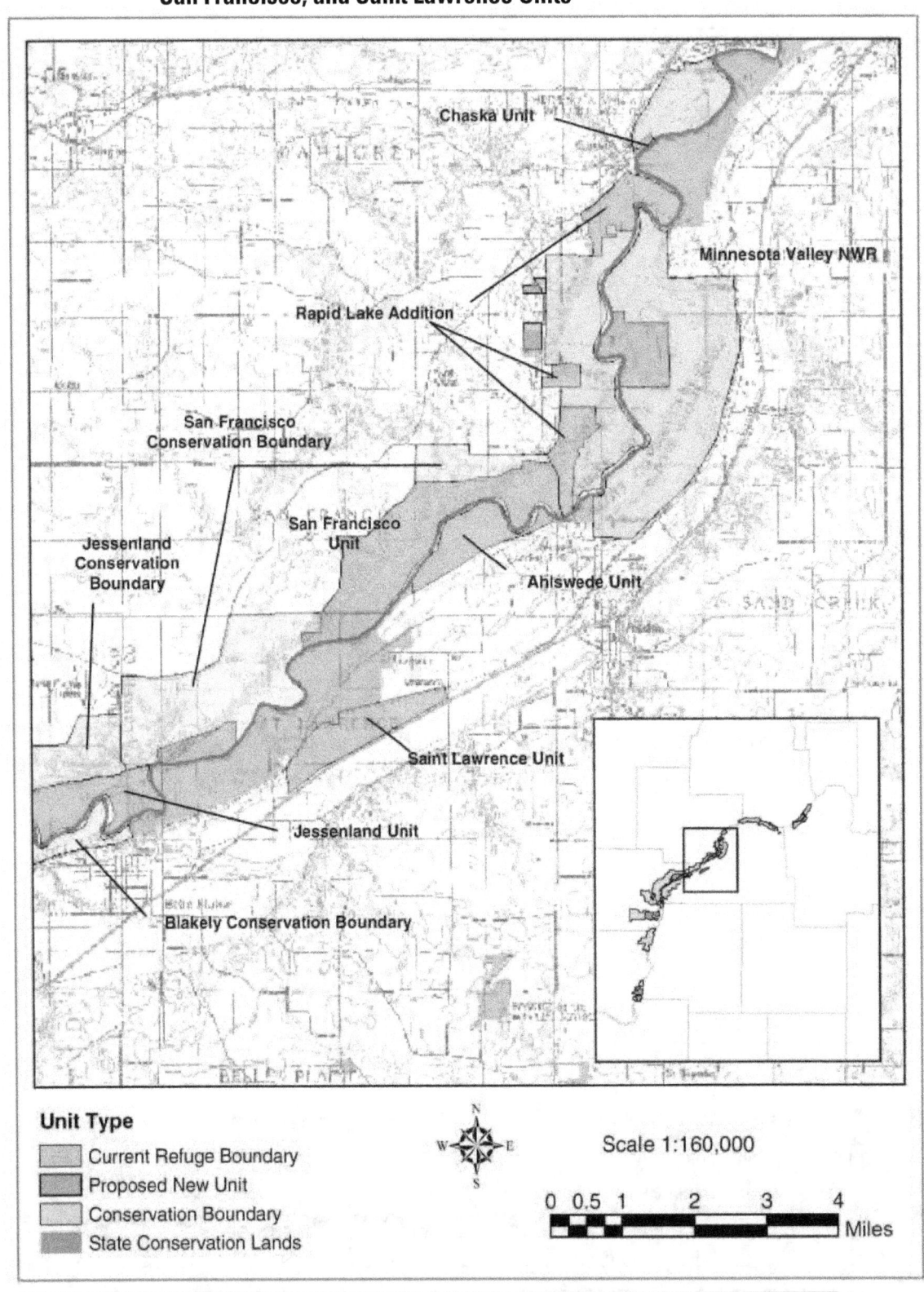

Minnesota Valley National Wildlife Refuge and Wetland Management District

Figure 3: Proposed Blakely, Jessenland, High Island Creek, and Rush River Units

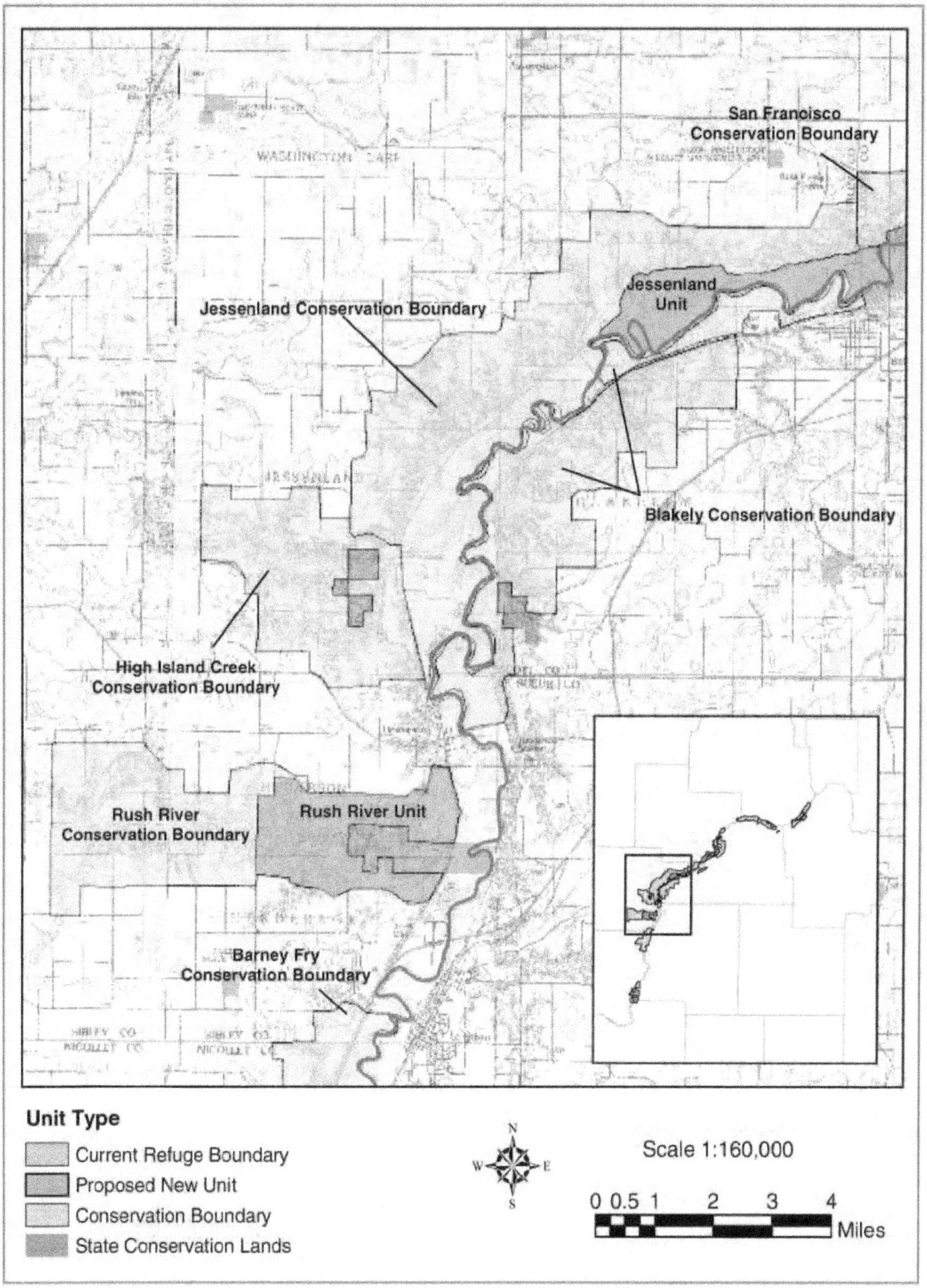
San Francisco Conservation Boundary
Jessenland Unit
Jessenland Conservation Boundary
Blakely Conservation Boundary
High Island Creek Conservation Boundary
Rush River Conservation Boundary
Rush River Unit
Barney Fry Conservation Boundary
Unit Type
Current Refuge Boundary
Proposed New Unit
Conservation Boundary
State Conservation Lands
N
W
E
S
Scale 1:160,000
0 0.5 1 2 3 4
Miles

Figure 4:   Proposed Barney Fry and Kasota Prairie Units

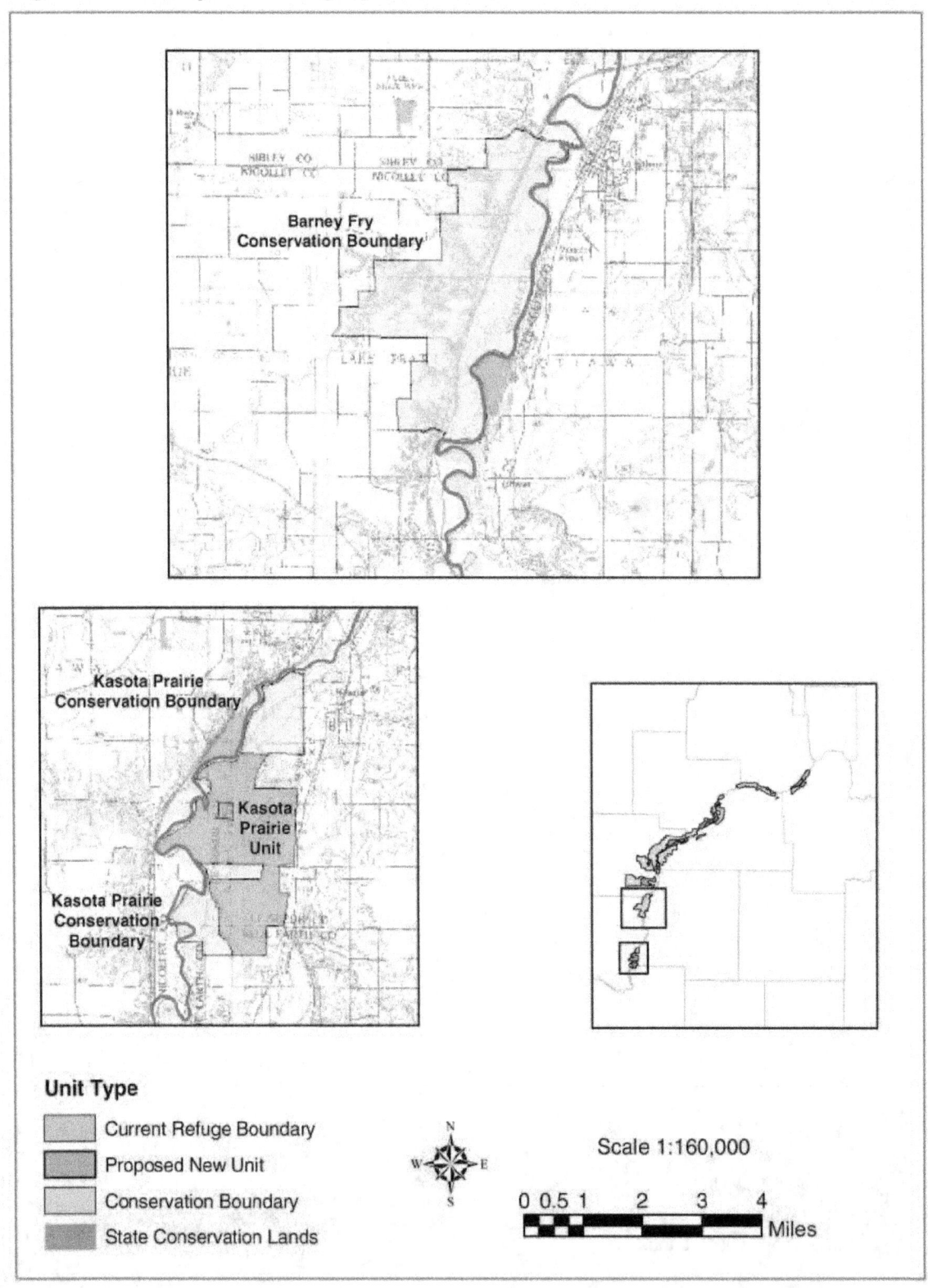

Barney Fry
Conservation Boundary

Kasota Prairie
Conservation Boundary

Kasota
Prairie
Unit

Kasota Prairie
Conservation
Boundary

Unit Type

- Current Refuge Boundary
- Proposed New Unit
- Conservation Boundary
- State Conservation Lands

Scale 1:160,000

0 0.5 1   2   3   4
Miles

Saint Lawrence Unit (632 Acres)

This site supports approximately 80 acres of agricultural land and the remainder consists of a rare wet prairie pothole community. This type of habitat is extremely rare within the prehistoric Great River Warren bed. This native prairie habitat and wetlands support a myriad of native of aquatic and terrestrial species, including waterfowl. Wildlife and plant communities observed in the area include wet prairie and gopher snake.

Ahlswede Lake Unit (511 Acres)

This floodplain area is comprised of a large lake marsh, Ahlswede Lake, old growth northern floodplain forest along a double meander in the Minnesota River and regenerating flood plain forest in former agricultural fields. Once restored to closed canopy forest the area will support a wide variety of forest interior and migratory waterfowl and wading birds. Rare wildlife observations in the area include milk snake and tiger beetle. The area provides a very important connection between the Louisville Swamp Unit within the Refuge and the Lawrence Wayside State Park. This connection will remedy the current habitat fragmentation, provide a travel corridor for people and wildlife, and facilitate the continued transfer of genetic material to sustain biodiversity.

San Francisco Unit (1,514 Acres) and Conservation Boundary

This area includes the bluffs and adjacent lands within the Lower Bevens Creek watershed, active agricultural land, former agricultural lands, floodplain wetlands and bluffs of the Minnesota River. Once disturbed areas are restored to native plant communities the area will support and wide array of migratory bird species, including raptors, waterfowl, waterbirds, shorebirds, and neotropical migrant songbirds. The area will provide excellent habitat for forest interior wildlife. Rare wildlife and plant community observations in the area include dry prairie, Kentucky coffee tree, American ginseng, kitten-tails, and breeding Cerulean Warblers. In addition, this area will make an important connection between the Rapids Lake Unit of the Refuge to the Lawrence Wayside State Park. This connection will prevent habitat fragmentation, provide travel corridor for people and wildlife and facilitate the transfer of genetic material to sustain biodiversity.

Blakely Conservation Boundary

This corridor of floodplain land consists of a mosaic of mature to old growth northern floodplain forest and early succession forests in former agricultural fields, and to a much lesser extent flood plain wetlands. Once the young forests growing in the former agricultural fields mature, the closed canopy forest will proved habitat for a variety of resident species and high quality habitat for forest interior birds such as Cerulean Warblers and Red-shouldered Hawks. Rare wildlife observed in the area include a shovelnose sturgeon. Once protected this area coupled with the protection of Jessenland unit will form a contiguous unfragmented travel corridor for wildlife and people and facilitate the transfer of genetic material to sustain biodiversity.

The upland portion consists of a series of bluff/ravine topography and associated lands intermixed with active agricultural lands. The lower reaches of two major watersheds drain a large portion of the area, Big Possum and Little Possum Creeks, respectively. Big Woods plant communities are present in the non-agricultural lands including oak and maple/basswood forests. The area adjoins the Blakely Wayside Unit of the Minnesota Valley Recreation Area on the south boundary. When agricultural lands are restored to Big woods habitats a large block of unfragmented highly diverse forested habitat will be very valuable for forest interior wildlife especially rare neo-tropical migrants that need a large expanse of forest for breeding. Rare wildlife, plant and plant communities observed in the area include smooth softshell turtle, false map turtle, kitten-tails, American ginseng, dry prairie and maple/basswood forest.

Jessenland Unit (1,911 Acres)

This corridor of floodplain land consists of a mosaic of mature to old growth northern floodplain forest and early succession forests in former agricultural fields, and to a lesser extent flood plain wetlands and lakes. Once the young forests in the former agricultural fields mature the closed canopy will provide habitat for a variety of resident species and high quality habitat for forest interior birds such as Cerulean Warblers and Red-shouldered Hawks. Rare wildlife observations in the are include a colonial bird nesting site. Once protected, this area coupled with the protection of the Blakely Conservation Area form a contiguous unfragmented travel corridor for wildlife and people and ensure the transfer of genetic material to sustain biodiversity.

Jessenland Conservation Boundary

This upland area consists of a series of bluff/ravine topography intermixed with active agricultural lands. Big Woods plant communities are present in the non-agricultural lands including oak, maple/basswood forests and lowland hardwood forests. Once the agricultural lands are restored to Big woods habitats a large block of forested habitat will be very valuable for forest interior wildlife especially rare neo-tropical migrant songbirds that need a large expanse of forest for breeding. Rare wildlife and plant communities found in the area include a pair of nesting Bald Eagles, lowland hardwood and maple/basswood forests. When coupled with the Jessenland Unit the result is and large unfragmented block of a wide variety of native plant communities.

High Island Creek Conservation Boundary

This area consists of the lower portions of two major watersheds, High Island and Buffalo Creeks, which drain large areas of land west of the Minnesota River. Because of the hilly topography the majority of the area remains in forested habitat and represents one of the two largest remaining tracts of relatively high quality Big Woods habitat in the Minnesota river valley. The remaining land is in agriculture. The area surrounds a state wildlife management area and a county park. Once the agricultural lands are restored the area will provide an extremely diverse block of Big Woods habitat supporting a wide array of resident and migratory species, especially rare forest interior birds such Cerulean Warblers and Red-shouldered Hawks. Wildlife and plant communities observed in the area include Kentucky coffee tree, yellow-fruited sedge, American Ginseng maple/basswood, and oak forest. Sedimentation to the Minnesota River is occurring via the streams that drain highly erodible agricultural lands. Restoration of native plant communities will greatly reduce erosion.

Rush River Unit (2,763 acres) and Conservation Boundary

This area is regarded as the largest and highest quality remnant of the Big Woods ecosystem. This hilly wooded area bounds the confluence of the north and south branch of the Rush River and the main stem to the Minnesota River. The river has formed a deep gorge especially in the middle and lower reaches. Agricultural lands are interspersed throughout the area but are mainly concentrated on the periphery of the unit. The lower portion of the unit encompasses the Minnesota Valley State Recreation Area. A growing number of single family houses exist within the area. The area currently provides habitat for a wide variety of native resident and migratory bird species but agricultural lands result in enough fragmentation of the forest canopy to limit the use of forest interior species. Restoring forest and savanna habitat in these agricultural fields will increase the use by forest interior species and other wildlife. Wildlife and plant communities observed in the area include breeding Cerulean Warblers, Red-shouldered Hawk, Louisiana Water Thrush, snow trillium, maple/basswood, oak and lowland hardwood forests. Soil erosion from the fields currently results in silt entering the Rush River. Restoration would greatly reduce the erosion.

Barney Fry Conservation Boundary

This area lies within the floodplain of the Minnesota River and is comprised of active and former agricultural lands interspersed with a variety of wetlands including an oxbow lake. The lower reach of Barney Fry Creek flows through the middle of the area. Once the agricultural lands are restored to mature forests the area together with the State-owned Chamberlain Woods Scientific and Natural Area (SNA), will provide an unfragmented block of upland and floodplain wildlands that will support a variety of resident and migratory wildlife, including interior forest bird species, waterfowl and waterbirds. Wildlife observations and plant communities observed in the area include Acadian Flycatcher, Cerulean Warbler, small white lady slipper and calcareous seepage fen.

The upland portion consists of a series of bluff/ravine topography intermixed with active agricultural lands. Big Woods plant communities are present in the non-agricultural lands including oak and maple/basswood forests. Once the agricultural lands are restored to Big woods habitats a large block of forested habitat will support a variety of interior forest wildlife especially rare neo-tropical migrants. Rare wildlife and plant communities found in the area include a nesting Cerulean Warblers and maple/basswood forests.

Kasota Prairie (2,554 Acres) and Conservation Boundary

This area is a rock outcrop supporting a native prairie and associated wetlands complex. Some parts of the unit are farmed (less than 10%); most of the remainder is grazed by horses and cattle. The State owns and manages an 80-acre Scientific and Natural Area (SNA) and a mining company has protected another 60-acre area. This area is one of the largest existing tallgrass prairies in the Midwest. The remaining acreage consists of wetlands and oak and floodplain forest. Rare and endangered wildlife, plants, and plant communities include jumping spider, fox snake, Loggerhead Shrike, racer, Upland Sandpiper, a pair of nesting Bald Eagles, rattlesnake master, small white lady slipper, marsh arrowgrass, and dry and mesic prairie. The area currently supports an extremely varied assortment of native plants and animals. Prescribed burning of the grasslands and controlled grazing would like lead to an even greater diversity of species. The area has a high potential for future use by endangered and rare wildlife, especially grassland birds.

IV. Environmental Consequences

The Socioeconomic Environment

The following section examines potential effects on tax revenue and the local economy that may result from the acquisition, operation and maintenance of new Refuge units.

Property Taxes

The Refuge Revenue Sharing Act of June 15, 1935, as amended, provides for annual payments to counties or the lowest unit of government that collects and distributes taxes based on acreage and value of National Wildlife Refuge lands located within the county. The funding for these payments comes from two sources: (1) net receipts from the sale of products from National Wildlife Refuge System lands (oil and gas leases, timber sales, grazing fees, etc.) and (2) annual Congressional appropriations.

Originally, counties received 25 percent of net revenues from the sale of various products or privileges from refuge lands located within the county. The result was that many counties received no payments as no revenue was generated from local refuge lands. The Refuge Revenue Sharing Act was amended in 1964 to provide for a payment of the greater of 25 percent of net receipts, $0.75 per acre or 3/4 of 1 percent of the adjusted purchase price for all purchased land. In the state of Minnesota, 3/4 of 1 percent of the appraised value always brings the greatest return to the taxing bodies (townships and counties).

The Refuge Revenue Sharing Act was again amended in 1978 by Public Law 95-469. Important changes are: (1) Congress is authorized to appropriate funds to make up any shortfall in the revenue sharing fund; (2) all lands administered solely or primarily by the FWS (not just refuges) qualify for revenue sharing; and (3) payments to units of local government can be used for any governmental purpose.

The amount of a revenue sharing payment is directly tied to the appraised market value of a property. In some cases, annual payments to local governments exceed what the local tax, based on assessed value, would have been if the land was still in private ownership. In other cases, revenue sharing payments, and supplemental Congressional appropriations, fall short of the local assessed property tax revenue.

The Local Economy

The local economy can experience some changes during the formation of a new national wildlife refuge. In general, new refuge units would likely create increased spending in the area by visitors, reduced agricultural production comparable to the Conservation Reserve Program, and increased expenditures by the Service to build and maintain refuge facilities.

New refuge units would likely be developed over the course of twenty years or more. During that time, funds would be needed for engineering and construction of facilities. Several hundred thousand dollars will be expended returning the lands to floodplain forest, native grasslands and wetlands. This money will be expended locally for items such as native grass seed, fuel and contracts with heavy equipment operators in the case of wetland restorations.

The Service estimates that federal purchases of land or conservation easements in the area could amount to more than $15 million during the next 20 years. Economists generally view land transactions as having a neutral effect in a local economy. They suggest that proceeds of a land sale generally go back into real estate. However, it is reasonable to assume that some portion of the land acquisition dollars will be used by sellers to construct new homes, purchase new vehicles, etc.

In summary, the proposed expansion of the Refuge would likely have a small *net* effect on county-level economic activity and could generate considerable social benefits. The value of natural areas, such as wildlife refuges, to people and their quality of life is difficult to measure in conventional economic terms. National Wildlife Refuges enhance the regional, state and the nation's stock of natural assets and provide significantly, but less tangible, benefits to its citizens, including clean water, natural beauty and abundant wildlife, fish and plants. Nevertheless, the Service recognizes that potential changes in the local and regional economy are important considerations.

Local Land Use including Land Acquisition, Cultural Resources, Refuge Management and Administration

This section examines potential effects on landowners and local residents that may result from the acquisition, operation and maintenance of new units of a national wildlife refuge in the Minnesota Valley.

Landowner Rights Adjacent to Refuge Lands

The Service has no more authority over private land within or adjacent to the boundaries of the refuge than another other landowner. Landowners within a project boundary retain all of the rights, privileges, and responsibilities of private land ownership. The presence of refuge lands does not afford the Service any authority to impose restrictions on any private lands. Control of access, land use practices, water management practices, hunting, fishing, and any other general use is limited to those lands in which the Service has acquired an appropriate real estate interest or rights.

Owning land adjacent to Service land does not change any of the regulations that currently apply and does not impose any new regulations on the land. Regulations pertaining to pesticides, drainage, pollution, hunting, fishing, trapping, etc., on private land are managed and enforced by other local, state or Federal agencies. The Service abides by these regulations the same as any other landowner. In addition, land managed by the Service will be posted in order to avoid trespass on private land by refuge visitors.

Service Land Acquisition Policies

Service policy is to buy land only from willing sellers. Service policy is that there would be no rights of landowners or citizens transferred without the willing participation of the individual(s) owning land or rights to the land, including appropriate just-compensation for those rights. The Service is required to make purchase offers based on fair market value; matching the price of comparable land in the same area.

It is also Service policy to seek the least amount of land ownership necessary to meet resource protection goals. Fee acquisition is only one option available to the landowner and the Service. Conservation easements, cooperative agreements and other options may meet conservation objectives in some locations.

Relocation Policies

The Uniform Relocation Assistance and Real Property Acquisition Policies Act of 1970, as amended (Uniform Act) provides for certain relocation benefits to home owners, businesses, and farm operators who, as willing sellers, are displaced as a result of Federal acquisition. The law provides for benefits to eligible owners and tenants in the following areas:

- Reimbursement of reasonable moving and related expenses;
- Replacement housing payments under certain conditions;
- Relocation assistance services to help locate replacement housing, farm, or business properties;
- Reimbursement of certain necessary and reasonable expenses incurred in selling real property to the government.

Cultural Resources

Establishment of new refuge units and subsequent land acquisition generally will have no effect on archeological resources. Traditional cultural properties and sacred sites of concern to Indian tribes and other ethnic and cultural groups receive increased protection to the extent the Service can obtain information about them. However, in some cases buildings and other structures may not receive increased attention under Service versus private ownership. The high cost of maintaining and preserving some buildings may prohibit acquisition or future use of some building sites. But overall, cultural resources receive increased protection from loss because of the several Federal laws that apply to property owned and administered by the Federal government.

Effects on Current Drainage Patterns

Wetland restorations conducted by the Service would not cause any artificial increase of the natural level, width, or flow of waters without ensuring that the impact would be limited to lands in which the Service has acquired an appropriate real estate interest from a willing seller, e.g., fee title ownership, flowage easement or cooperative agreement. Thus, all alternatives would not have any impact on existing drainage from neighboring lands. If Service activities inadvertently created a water-related problem for any private landowner (flooding, soil saturation or deleterious increases in water table height, etc.), the problem would be corrected at the Service's expense.

Refuge Administration

Any acquired lands would become part of the National Wildlife Refuge System. The annual costs for administration, operations and maintenance would be lower than establishing a new refuge. One additional maintenance facility near the Mankato area may be necessary to store equipment for use on the west end of the refuge. Development and operation costs will ultimately depend upon the amount of land purchased in fee and easement, habitat restoration requirements, and the rate of development for the Minnesota Valley State Trail.

Public Recreational Use

The Refuge Improvement Act of 1997 identifies six priority uses: hunting, fishing, wildlife observation, photography, environmental education, and interpretation as wildlife-dependent recreational activities. These uses are encouraged on refuges when they are compatible with the purposes of the refuge. Currently, we anticipate that all six priority uses will be allowed on new units of the Refuge and District where it is feasible and safe.

V. Options for Land Protection

Land protection options vary from written agreements on land management to outright purchase of the land. Land may be acquired in fee title by several methods including exchange, purchase or donation. Conservation or non-development easements can also be purchased by the Service or donated by a landowner. Each parcel of land has unique resource values and circumstances that determine the desired level of protection.

Much of the public discussion over a refuge expansion proposal centers on full acquisition of lands (fee title). However, land purchase is only one of many options for developing a wildlife refuge. Various options for habitat protection and restoration could be used in concert with fee title acquisition to achieve refuge goals.

Fee Simple Purchase: The Service could purchase land from willing sellers within the proposed refuge unit boundaries. The land would be appraised at market value and a written offer presented to a landowner. Full rights and title to purchased property would be vested with the United States as part of the National Wildlife Refuge System. Land acquisition funds are limited and allocated on a nationwide basis. Each Service Region must compete for appropriations from Congress under the Land and Water Conservation Fund and for Migratory Bird Conservation Fund (Duck Stamp) allotments. Annual land acquisition funding cannot be assured for each refuge requesting it.

Conservation Easements: Conservation easements are a popular method for land protection used by private individuals, land trusts and governments. Conservation easements involve the acquisition of specific land rights for the purpose of achieving defined habitat objectives. Easements can either prohibit or encourage certain practices. For example, wetland easements usually involve the right to drain, burn and fill a wetland. Grassland easements usually cover the right to place timing restrictions on hay mowing to benefit wildlife. Easements become part of the title to the property and are usually permanent. If a landowner sells the property, the easement continues as part of the title.

VI. Options for Habitat Restoration

Conservation Reserve Enhancement Program: The Conservation Reserve Enhancement Program (CREP), administered by the Minnesota Board of Water and Soil Resources, pays farmers for taking marginal agricultural land out of production within the Minnesota River basin watershed. The CREP combines the federal Conservation Reserve Program with the state Reinvest in Minnesota Program. The goal of this partnership is to protect and enhance up to 100,000 acres of environmentally sensitive land in the 37 county Minnesota River basin watershed. Eligible lands include frequently-flooded croplands, wetlands and prairie potholes. Landowners sign easements guaranteeing that the land will not be cropped and that they manage it under a conservation plan. Habitat restoration measures outlined in the conservation plans are often paid for by CREP. New enrollments for the program expired September 30, 2002. The program may be renewed in the future, but no plans have been announced.

Partners for Fish and Wildlife: This program is administered by the U.S. Department of the Interior, Fish and Wildlife Service and offers technical and financial assistance to private landowners to voluntarily restore wetlands, native grasslands and other fish and wildlife habitats. The Service, along with a wide variety of partners, provides assistance and cost-sharing to complete work if the landowner agrees to maintain the area for a period of 10 years or more. Partners who contribute time and funds for these efforts include local conservation organizations, universities, businesses, school groups, other government agencies and private individuals.

Wetlands Reserve Program: The Wetlands Reserve Program is administered by the U.S. Department of Agriculture, Natural Resources Conservation Service. The program focuses on providing financial incentives to landowners in exchange for wetland restoration or enhancements. Three options are available: permanent easements, 30-year easements, and restoration cost-share agreements for a minimum 10-year duration. The landowner retains title to the land and may lease it for hunting and fishing. Additional activities, such as haying, grazing or timber cutting may be permitted if the uses are fully consistent with protection and enhancement of the wetland.

Technical Assistance: Several programs exist for people who want to improve wildlife habitat on their land. Financial assistance for habitat improvements is often available on a cost-sharing basis.

Wildlife Habitat Incentives Program: Participants work with the Natural Resource Conservation Service to prepare a wildlife habitat development plan in consultation with the local conservation district. The plan describes the landowner's goals for habitat improvement and sets a schedule for implementation. Cost-share agreements under this program generally last from 5 to 10 years.

Cooperative Agreements: The U.S. Fish and Wildlife Service can offer free technical assistance to neighboring property owners through a cooperative agreement. The Service can agree to develop wildlife or land management plans, or do wildlife surveys on private lands and provide detailed information to the landowners. These cooperative agreements are formal, written documents, and usually place no legally binding restrictions on the land. No money is involved and either party may cancel the agreement with adequate notice to the other party. A cooperative agreement would not affect the tax status of the land.

Private Conservation Efforts: In recent years, conservation organizations have been effective in promoting wildlife habitat improvement on private lands. Collectively, these local, regional or national organizations are a great source of financial and technical assistance for the private landowner who wishes to improve lands for wildlife. Some of the organizations active in the Midwest include The Nature Conservancy, The Conservation Fund, Fish and Wildlife Foundation, Izaak Walton League, Audubon Society, Trust for Public Lands, Ducks Unlimited, and Pheasants Forever.

Technical assistance for sensitive habitat management is available through the Minnesota Valley Heritage Registry sponsored by the group Friends of the Minnesota Valley. Landowners make a verbal commitment to protect and preserve the land to the best of their abilities, notify the Friends of any potential threats to the area, and notify the

Friends of the intent to sell the property. In return, landowners are provided with educational information on stewardship techniques, incentives (books and plaques) and public recognition of their efforts.

In addition, local hunting, fishing, and conservation organizations often are willing to assist private landowners with wildlife habitat improvement projects. Many of these organizations have substantial financial and technical resources and are often a dedicated source of energy for wildlife habitat improvement on both private and public lands.

VII. Land Protection Priorities

Priorities for land protection measures are set into two categories (Figure 5). Priority 1 lands are the Service's highest priority for purchase and restoration with future available funding. Priority 2 lands would be the second highest priority. The preferred land protection method for all of the parcels would be the purchase of fee title or permanent conservation easements. However, all land purchases would be from willing sellers only and all conservation options amenable to landowners would be considered on a case-by-case basis.

Figure 5: Land Protection Priorities

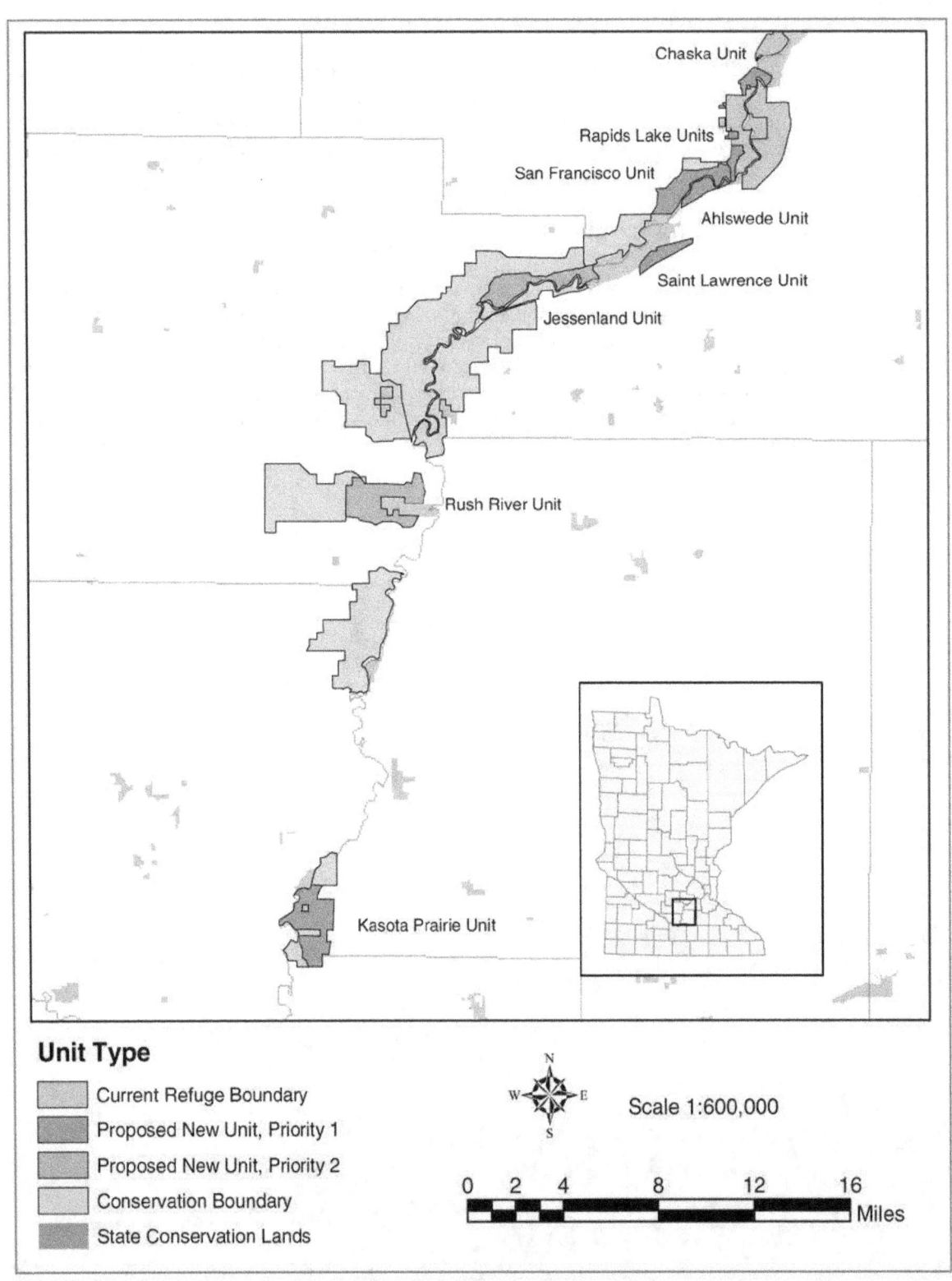

Minnesota Valley National Wildlife Refuge and Wetland Management District

Appendix J: Questions Frequently Asked About Land Acquisition

Planning a New or Expanded National Wildlife Refuge: Frequently Asked Questions

The U.S. Fish and Wildlife Service is the primary federal agency responsible for conserving the nation's migratory bird and fish species; protecting endangered plants and animals; and providing critical habitat for the diverse living resources that exist in the United 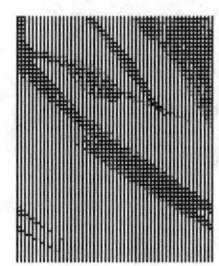 States. The National Wildlife Refuge System was established in 1903 and is a key part of achieving that mission as well as providing people with opportunities to enjoy natural environments that range from arctic tundra to coastal salt marshes, deserts and bottomland hardwood forests.

Public participation is a vital part of the Service's refuge planning process. Environmental documents such as Environmental Assessments are prepared when a new refuge is proposed or an expansion to an existing refuge is considered, and many opportunities for involvement by residents, elected officials, business representatives and local, regional and state agencies are built into the environmental documentation process.

The purpose of creating new refuges and expanding existing refuges is to preserve wildlife, plants and their habitat for the benefit of everyone. At the same time, we appreciate the concerns voiced by many communities about refuge planning and what it means to land owners, rural communities, agriculture, hunting and fishing, and local government. This list of

frequently asked questions is based on questions asked during refuge planning projects throughout Region 3 (which includes Minnesota, Wisconsin, Michigan, Ohio, Iowa, Illinois, Indiana and Missouri). These questions and answers are general in scope; you will have many opportunities to ask questions about specific refuge projects throughout the planning process.

Why locate a national wildlife refuge here?: A number of factors go into determining locations for new wildlife refuges. Generally, the Service looks at areas with significant wildlife values or the potential for restoration of wildlife values to an area. In many cases a proposal is seeking to fill a void in habitat availability for a group of species of federal interest or for a significant single species, such as an endangered species. For example, an area may provide outstanding habitat for grassland-dependant birds, which is a 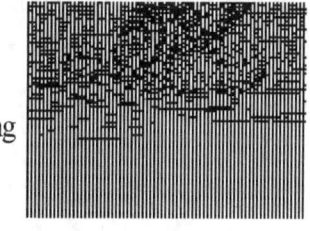 group of migratory birds that has seen consistently declining populations over the past several years. The Service may be considering a particular location because is has great potential for meeting other established objectives, such as providing environmental education opportunities.

Will my property be condemned?: Service policy is to acquire land only from willing sellers.

If I do not chose to sell my land, will my rights as a property owner be infringed as a result of the refuge designation?: No. If a refuge is established, the Service will have no more authority over private land within or adjacent to the boundaries of the refuge than any other landowner.

Is buying land the only option?: There are a number of alternatives for  achieving the natural resource goals of a proposed refuge. Resource preservation and restoration options include cooperative agreements, easements and landowner technical assistance. The Service is eager to work with landowners to find an alternative that is acceptable to them and that contributes to refuge objectives.

How will the creation of a wildlife refuge affect the area's tax base?: The Service tries to alleviate the impact of wildlife refuges on state and local taxes by reimbursing local governments for lost tax revenues. The formula that generally yields the highest return for a local unit of government is $7.50 per $1,000 of the property's fair market value. Several states have programs that also supplement payments to local school districts if the tax base declines due to the acquisition of public land.

What is the economic impact of a refuge on a community?: In many cases, refuges actually draw people into the community, generating income for tourist-oriented businesses and services. *Banking on Nature*, the Service's study of the economic benefits of refuges, found that nationally visitors contribute more than $400 million every year to local economics. The publication reports that in 1995 non-resident

funds generated at Crab Orchard National Wildlife Refuge in southern Illinois totaled $3.29 million in the Marion, Ill., region and 76 additional jobs were created. Non-resident refuge visitors spent about $1.8 million in the Horicon National Wildlife Refuge area in central Wisconsin in 1995, according to *Banking on Nature*, and 41 jobs were added in the area.

Will drainage be changed in a way that affects my property?: The Service's intent is to have no impact on drainage from neighboring lands and to follow state laws regarding drainage activities. Service staff work with adjacent landowners and drainage districts to ensure that existing drainage facilities or patterns are not negatively impacted by refuge activity.

Who is responsible for controlling noxious weeds on refuge property?: The Service's policy is to control plants listed as noxious weeds by States. This control uses non-chemical methods when possible and chemical treatments when necessary to prevent noxious weeds from spreading to adjacent private farmland.

When and how can I express my opinions about the proposal?: You can express an opinion anytime and there are a number of ways to do so. You can talk to Service personnel at one of the several public open house events that will be scheduled throughout the course of this project, or you can schedule a one-on-one meeting with Service staff to discuss the refuge proposal. If you have access to the Internet, you can address e-mail to: r3planning@fws.gov at anytime. You can obtain more information and make comments about this project and others that are under way at: http://midwest.fws.gov/planning

A refuge boundary has been established for a wildlife refuge proposal before public participation or final approval; does what I have to say about that boundary matter, or is it a done deal?: It is not a done deal, and what you have to say about the proposed boundary will be considered in the proposal evaluation process. The Service's Regional Offices are required to establish a tentative

study area before an evaluation can be initiated. These initial boundaries are flexible and, if the project is approved, the actual area proposed could be smaller or larger than the initial proposal reflects.

If the refuge is established, is the planning process the only opportunity I will have to provide input into what goes on at the refuge?: Community involvement is important to the success of a wildlife refuge. The Service encourages public participation in developing detailed management plans for the refuge. Many refuges have citizen groups that support the refuge through actively participating in refuge activities and operations.

Some people contend that the Service is destroying farmland when land is taken out of agricultural production and restored as wetlands, grasslands or other habitat; how do you respond?: Acquiring land as a national wildlife refuge protects it from development. If the nation's lawmakers someday decide it is needed for agricultural production, it will be there. The soil will actually rebuild itself when indigenous vegetative cover is restored; on the other hand, development can degrade soil and extensive commercial or dense residential development makes it very unlikely that the land will ever be restored to agricultural purposes in the future.

Is a federal refuge automatically closed to hunting, fishing and other recreational activities?: Not necessarily. The alternatives considered in refuge planning are mandated by Congress (Public Law 105-57, Oct. 9, 1997) to allow compatible wildlife-dependent recreational public uses such as hunting, fishing, wildlife observation and photography, environmental education and interpretation. Goals and objectives are identified for the refuge (with public input), and the specific public uses are determined based on their consistency with the objectives established for the refuge. A refuge that serves as production areas for a federally endangered species is likely to offer less access for people during periods when the endangered species is present than at other times of the year. In Region 3, 88 percent of the refuges offer public recreational opportunities. Those that are closed include small islands or caves where endangered species or colonial nesting birds are present.

Where does funding for land acquisition for wildlife refuges come from?: Typically, money to acquire land for national refuges comes from the Land and Water Conservation Fund or the Migratory Bird Fund, both of which were established through federal law. The Land and Water Conservation Fund primarily includes the sale of products on federal land, such as offshore oil and gas leases. The Migratory Bird Fund is derived from the sale of federal duck stamps.

Why is the federal government involved in planning wildlife refuges? Why shouldn't states manage their own refuges?: Wildlife and habitat simply do not conform to state boundaries, and neither does citizen investment in the nation's natural resources. For example, preserving migratory waterfowl habitat requires a comprehensive approach because flight patterns for particular species can extend across the entire length of the country. Conservation practices in one state would be jeopardized or even nullified by lesser efforts in another state along the flight pattern. Citizenship too extends beyond state lines, and we all have an investment in preserving this county's unique or endangered species and habitats regardless of where we live. While state departments of natural resources are responsible for managing the bulk of wildlife and habitat issues; federal involvement in refuge planning reflects this broader public interest.

How can you properly manage another refuge if you already have a maintenance backlog on existing refuges?: National wildlife refuges are not approved overnight, as this brochure suggests. If a wildlife refuge proposal is ultimately approved, the Service's policy of only buying land from willing sellers means that it may be years before there is enough contiguous land for a refuge to be viable. The Service continues to make progress on decreasing its maintenance backlog, but a great deal of habitat could be lost to development or further degradation if we did not get the ball rolling now.

Who will run the refuge if it is established?: It might be assigned its own staff and budget, however if there is an existing refuge station nearby, staff from that refuge might be assigned to run it.
How can I find out more about the National

Wildlife Refuge System?: Region 3 of the U.S. Fish and Wildlife Service would be happy to send you additional information on national refuge planning. You can request information by writing to us at: U.S. Fish and Wildlife Service, Ascertainment and Planning, 1 Federal Drive, Ft. Snelling, MN 55111; or by calling toll free 1-800-247-1247.

What happens next if a national refuge is ultimately approved? Several steps will follow the approval of a new refuge. First, funding must be obtained through congressional action and a national budget ranking process. Second, the refuge is formally established when fee title or an easement interest is acquired in a piece of land within the approved boundary. Finally, detailed management planning in the form of a Comprehensive Conservation Plan (CCP) will provide future management direction. With public input, the CCP establishes definite goals and objectives for the refuge and identifies specific strategies for achieving those goals. Specific issues, such as cleaning up a contaminated area, the presence of an endangered species or managing an overabundant deer herd, are addressed in separate, step-down plans. The CCP also identifies an implementation and monitoring plan, and progress toward the goals and strategies are reviewed on a regular basis.

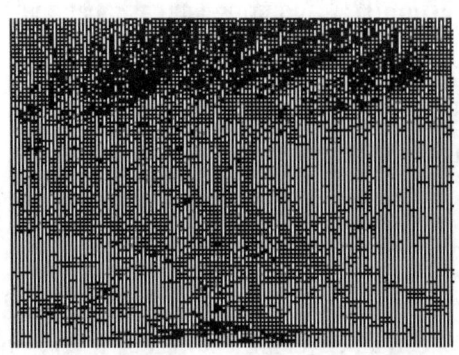

Appendix K: List of Preparers

Appendix K: List of Preparers

Richard D. Schultz, Refuge Manager, Minnesota Valley National Wildlife Refuge

Gary Muehlenhardt, Wildlife Biologist/Refuge Planner, Region 3

Tom Kerr, Refuge Operations Specialist, Minnesota Valley National Wildlife Refuge

Nick Palaia, Biological Science Technician, Minnesota Valley National Wildlife Refuge

Terry Schreiner, Refuge Operations Specialist, Minnesota Valley National Wildlife Refuge

Vicki Sherry, Wildlife Biologist, Minnesota Valley National Wildlife Refuge

Jill Torres, Environmental Education Specialist, Minnesota Valley National Wildlife Refuge

John Dobrovolny, Regional Historian, Region 3

Jane Hodgins, Technical Writer/Editor, Region 3

Jane Lardy Nelson, Editorial Assistant, Region 3

Appendix L: Refuge Mitigation Plan, Minnesota Valley National Wildlife Refuge

Appendix L: Refuge Mitigation Plan, Minnesota Valley National Wildlife Refuge

Background

The expansion of the Minneapolis-St. Paul International Airport will directly impact the Long Meadow Lake and Blackdog Units of Minnesota Valley National Wildlife Refuge. Noise sensitive public use conducted on these units, such as environmental education, wildlife interpretation and bird watching will be significantly compromised upon the construction and use of a new north-south runway. Likewise, the value of our existing Visitor Center will be compromised as increased jet noise will influence outdoors activities associated with this facility.

In response to this, the Metropolitan Airports Commission, the Federal Aviation Administration, and the U.S. Fish and Wildlife Service entered into a Memorandum of Agreement in September 1998. Through this agreement, a mitigation package, which consisted of a cash settlement of $26,090,000, will be used to offset the impacts of commercial flights over Refuge lands, programs, and activities.

On August 31, 2000, the Minnesota Valley National Wildlife Refuge Trust, Inc. was established to serve as the mitigation agent for the Metropolitan Airports Commission (MAC) and to administer the $26,090,000. The Trust was created in accordance with a Funding Agreement dated September 14, 1999, and signed by the MAC and the following five "supporting organizations" – Friends of the Minnesota Valley, Minnesota River Basin Joint Powers Board, Minnesota Department of Natural Resources, Minnesota Waterfowl Association and National Audubon Society. Each supporting organization appoints a representative to serve on the Trust's Board of Directors.

The primary purpose of the Trust, according to the Funding Agreement, is to "implement Airport Mitigation Projects, consistent with the mission and purpose of the Minnesota Valley National Wildlife Refuge as determined by the United States Fish and Wildlife Service."

Until such time as all the mitigation projects are completed or within 15 years, whichever comes first, the Trust will expend the funds in accordance with the Funding Agreement between the MAC and the five supporting organizations of the Trust, which prescribes as follows:

"Mitigation activities to be accomplished by the (Trust) include but are not limited to:

(1) acquisition of a minimum of 4,090 acres of lands within the area identified as appropriate, and making such lands available for Refuge environmental education and wildlife-dependent recreational opportunities either through donation to the United States to be administered by USFWS or its successor as part of the Refuge, or through a cooperative or other agreement for such use at no cost to the United States;

(2) construction and development of a visitor and education center on the Rapid Lakes Unit or another suitable location approved by the USFWS or its successor for the Refuge; and

(3) construction of visitor access, environmental education, and wildlife interpretive facilities at suitable locations approved by the USFWS or its successor on Refuge lands."

This document will serve as the Refuge Mitigation Plan (Plan), as called for in the Funding Agreement. The individual components of this plan were originally derived from an assessment of damages that will occur to Refuge units once the new runway becomes operational. These damages were summarized in a letter sent to FAA and MAC from Regional Director William Hartwig in May 1997. Additional suggestions were also received as input for the Refuge's Comprehensive Conservation Plan and many have been incorporated. Despite our best attempts to identify an array of appropriate mitigation projects, the Refuge and the Trust understand that it is impossible to gain a one-to-one replacement of the lost values on the Refuge lands impacted by the airport runway noise. The following list of mitigation projects, however, is our best collective attempt to compensate for the impacts that will occur to Refuge lands. As stated in the Funding Agreement, this Plan is subject to periodic review, and if deemed necessary, modification.

General Use of Mitigation Funds

The primary purpose of this Mitigation Plan is to set the general direction for the expenditure of Trust funds. In addition, it will provide long-term consistency to subsequent refuge managers and the Trust Board of Directors until such time as all components of the Plan have been completed

Land Acquisition and Habitat Restoration

Approximately 60 percent of the Trust assets, and earnings generated thereof, is intended to be spent on acquiring and restoring new lands for the Refuge within the Minnesota River Valley. Additional Refuge units will be identified and of these, no less than 4,090 additional acres will be acquired from willing sellers using these funds. It should be noted that mitigation funds cannot be used to acquire lands within the existing authorized Refuge boundary. An estimated 25 percent of funds designated for land acquisition may also be used to acquire high priority Waterfowl Production Areas (WPAs) within the watershed of the Minnesota River. Lands acquired as WPAs must have a direct linkage to the Minnesota River and serve to enhance and benefit wildlife species that inhabit the river. Where possible, however, all land acquisition funds will be leveraged with those of other programs such as WRP, CREP, and RIM to maximize the acreage made available for wildlife habitats as well as public use.

Public Use Facilities

Approximately 20 percent of the Trust assets, and earnings generated thereof, is intended to be spent on public use facilities such as an environmental education center, trails, wildlife interpretive sites, and associated support facilities. Some of these facilities will be constructed on existing Refuge lands and others will be placed on new lands acquired with mitigation funding.

Planning and Operations

Approximately 20 percent of the Trust assets, and earnings generated thereof, is intended to be spent on planning for new lands and facilities, the operation of the new environmental education facilities, construction of support facilities, and the maintenance of new Refuge lands. It is expected that these funds will be invested for the long-term. In order to maintain its future purchasing power, an estimated 5 percent per year on average may be made available for planning and operations. As of 2002, up to $250,000 of the Trust assets may be made available annually to the Service for these items. Under no circumstances, however, should funds from the Trust be used to replace or supplant the Refuge's existing operational funds.

Should the above framework and the accompanying mitigation projects prove to be unworkable or unrealistic once work is initiated, the Service, in consultation with the Trust, has the option of modifying this framework to meet changing needs.

Plan Implementation Process

Optimizing Trust Assets

The Trust and the Service together will strive to manage the pace of land acquisition and other major expenditures to optimize the use of the Trust's assets. The Trust will seek appreciation of the Trust's assets through prudent investment, closely watching project costs such as land values and, when possible, timing acquisitions to optimize returns. To the degree possible, the Service will cooperate with the Trust in meeting these objectives by spacing out the mitigation projects over the 15-year period beginning with the Trust's incorporation date (August 31, 2000).

Project Priority

The Service and the Trust will cooperate in determining priorities for the completion of mitigation projects through the preparation and submission of Refuge Mitigation Project Proposals by the Service. To the degree possible, the Service will notify the Trust at least 6 months in advance of any pending or proposed mitigation projects.

Project Approval

This Plan will be implemented through a process that depends upon significant cooperation and collaboration between the Trust and Service at all times. Consistent with the Funding Agreement, the Trust will not initiate any mitigation projects without prior approval of the Service. Similarly, the Service will not commit any Trust assets to a project or activity without the prior approval of the Trust Board of Directors. This process has already been established through the development and use of Refuge Mitigation Project Proposals.

Administration of Large and/or Complex Projects

Prior to the initiation of any large or complex mitigation projects, the Trust and the Service will enter into a cooperative agreement that will serve to articulate the respective roles and responsibilities of each party. This agreement will assign responsibilities for such items as project design, project and site management, progress reviews, insurance, bonding, and related contractual requirements.

Remaining Assets

Consistent with the Memorandum of Agreement and the subsequent Funding Agreement, any remaining assets following the successful completion of the Refuge Mitigation Plan are to be made available to the Service specifically for the benefit and use of Minnesota Valley National Wildlife Refuge. Following the completion of this Plan or 15 years from incorporation of the Trust, whichever comes first, the Service, in consultation with the Trust, will develop guidelines for the completion of any remaining mitigation projects and/or the long-term administration and use of the remaining Trust assets.

Specific Mitigation Projects

Land Acquisition

Refuge lands: As required by the Funding Agreement, a minimum of 4,090 additional Refuge acres will be acquired by the Trust for mitigation purposes. It is hoped that significantly more acreage can be acquired by the Trust, pending investment performance, ability to identify other sources of funds, the price and availability of land and other factors.

The Service has identified approximately 50,000 acres that are candidates for acquisition by the Trust, as noted on the attached maps. These lands include possible new Refuge units, plus lands that will serve to either connect existing units or lands that will serve to enhance the management of these units.

Waterfowl production areas: To fulfill its 4,090-acre minimum acreage requirement, the Trust may acquire up to 2,000 acres of fee lands to be managed as waterfowl production areas. As with Refuge lands, these units will provide high quality wildlife dependent recreational opportunities including hunting, fishing, wildlife observation, wildlife photography, plus wildlife interpretation and environmental education. Due to the nature of the Service's Small Wetlands Acquisition Program, specific waterfowl production areas have not been identified at this time. As opportunities develop, these areas will be delineated and identified on all Refuge Mitigation Project Proposals prior to their submission to the Trust.

Habitat Restoration

Contracts, materials, and equipment: Mitigation funds may also be used to restore habitats on new Refuge lands, including waterfowl production areas. Items eligible for purchase under this category include restoration contracts, seed, fertilizer, herbicide, trees, saplings, acorns, cultural resource surveys, and associated materials. To a limited degree, equipment such as tractors, drills, and associated implements are eligible for purchase, rent, or contract where Refuge staff assume direct responsibility for habitat restoration.

Visitor/Education and Support Facilities

Rapids Lake Historic Home: This component of the mitigation plan will be addressed by converting the Rapids Lake historic home into an environmental education site. Included in this project will be the relocation of the structure out of the floodplain, replacement of all utilities, and the development of office space in the upper story. Upon completion, the home will be used by school groups and others for programs and meetings. If needed, an annex to this home will be constructed to address any of the Refuge's environmental education or interpretive needs at this site.

If demand for additional environmental education facilities becomes apparent in the next 15 years, the Service, in consultation with the Trust, will assess the need to construct visitor education and support facilities at other locations. Under no circumstances, however, will new structures be built in communities where similar private or public environmental education facilities currently exist.

Interpretive Facilities

With the exception of trails and kiosks associated with the restoration of the Rapids Lake Historic Home and its use as an environmental education contact station, all of the nature trails, parking lots, and demonstration sites will be located on new Refuge lands or waterfowl production areas. The specific location of each of these facilities on these units is largely dependent upon the purchase of individual tracts. Once an adequate land base has been acquired, specific plans will be developed by the Refuge for locating parking lots, nature trails, and associated interpretive facilities.

Nature trails: No less than 5 linear miles of hiking trails or trails designated for hiking and bicycling will be constructed on new Refuge lands or waterfowl production areas or on existing Refuge lands outside the airport noise area. The primary purpose of these trails is to provide access to these lands by our visiting public.

Boardwalks and observation platforms: No less than 1,000 linear feet of accessible board walk and three observation platforms will be constructed at appropriate locations for the purpose of advancing the public's understanding of the Refuge, the Wetland Management District, and its fish and wildlife resources.

Parking lots and associated facilities: As new Refuge lands and waterfowl production areas are acquired, parking lots with appropriate kiosks, signs, and interpretive brochures will be constructed and/or developed. No less than one parking lot will be developed on each new unit.

Habitat management demonstration sites: Where appropriate, habitat management demonstrate sites will be constructed. At a minimum, one water control structure and associated facilities will be installed and used as a demonstration site.

Funding for Planning and Operations

Additional Refuge staff: Up to four additional Refuge staff may be funded using mitigation funds. These staff will initially be put on board to plan for mitigation projects. As lands are acquired and facilities are constructed, these staff will assume habitat management, environmental education, and interpretive programming responsibilities.

Volunteer/intern dormitory: As an operational support facility, intern housing capable of hosting 16 individuals will be constructed on or near the Rapids Lake Unit. Individuals using this facility will support the Refuge's expanded environmental education and wildlife interpretive programs, and help address the development and management of new Refuge lands. Both interns and volunteers will be housed in this facility.

Planning and operations: Within the mitigation fund expenditure guidelines set forth above, a limited amount of funds can be used first for costs associated with planning for mitigation projects, and upon completion, for the operations of the new facilities. Under no circumstances, however, should the mitigation fund be used to supplant existing operational funds for the Refuge.

Busing assistance for schools in need: Consistent with our plan to develop visitor/ environmental education facilities is a realization that some of our target audiences (e.g., inner city school districts) are unable to participate in Refuge programs due to unmet transportation costs. We also realize that the relative costs of transportation will increase as we conduct a larger percentage of our outdoor programs on Refuge lands upstream and away from aircraft noise. With this in mind, a portion of the Trust funds may be expended each year to assist those schools that may otherwise not have the opportunity to visit the Refuge due to transportation costs.